# Who's Who in World War II

# Who's Who
# in
# World War II

## EDITED BY JOHN KEEGAN

Oxford University Press
New York

Oxford University Press
Oxford   New York
Athens   Auckland   Bangkok   Bombay
Calcutta   Cape Town   Dar es Salaam   Delhi
Florence   Hong Kong   Istanbul   Karachi
Kuala Lumpur   Madras   Madrid   Melbourne
Mexico City   Nairobi   Paris   Singapore
Taipei   Tokyo   Toronto

and associated companies in

Berlin   Ibadan

First published 1978 by Bison Books Ltd

First published in paperback 1995 by Routledge
11 New Fetter Lane, London EC4P 4EE

First published in the United States in paperback by
Oxford University Press, Inc.,
200 Madison Avenue, New York, New York 10016

Oxford is a registered trademark of Oxford University Press

*Library of Congress Cataloguing-in-Publication Data*

Keegan, John
   Who's Who in World War II / John Keegan.
      p.     cm.
   Originally published: London : Weidenfeld & Nicolson, 1978.
      1. World War, 1939–1945—Biography—Dictionaries.     I. Title.
D736.K44   1995
940.53'03—dc20     94-43807

9 8 7 6 5 4 3 2 1

ISBN 0-19-521080-8

Typeset in Sabon by Datix International Limited
Printed and bound in Great Britain by
T.J. Press Ltd, Padstow, Cornwall

# Contents

# Introduction

World War II, unlike World War I, was truly a global conflict, fought in every one of the five continents, from the Caribbean to the South China Sea, from New Guinea to the North Cape, and by combatants from every continental region, Latin America, the Balkans, Scandinavia, the Middle East, South Asia and Africa as well as from Europe and North America. It was also, as World War I had not been, a conflict of ideologies. Its dramatis personae was therefore of a peculiar richness, including not only soldiers and statesmen of orthodox background but three dictators of world stature – Hitler, Mussolini and Stalin, demagogues like Goebbels and ideologues like Alfred Rosenberg, politicians of charismatic power, like Franklin Delano Roosevelt, prophets of national renaissance, like Charles de Gaulle, and of national liberation like Mahatma Gandhi, showmen, mountebanks, martyrs, heroes, traitors and quislings – a word we owe to the politics of World War II. This book attempts to assemble the most important among this vast cast of characters, from every country and from every sphere of responsibility – or irresponsibility – and to convey not only the salient facts about the life and career of each but also the flavor of his individuality.

*Editor's Notes*
*Cross-references*: separate entries can be found for those personages whose names appear in capital letters within another entry or a caption.

*Dates*: information regarding the birth and/or death dates for some personages is unavailable. All relevant data which have been obtained are included even if incomplete.

# A

**Adachi, Lieutenant General Hatazo, 1890–1947** Adachi was the Japanese Commander in New Guinea. In November 1942 Adachi took over as Commander of the Eighteenth Army and fought the desperate battle to hold on to New Guinea. His headquarters was at Rabaul which meant that all his supplies had to come by sea; this became a severe problem because the US had air superiority and were trying to encircle Rabaul. His Army, which was equivalent to a US Corps, was forced to retreat down the Kokoda Trail and shortly thereafter was pushed back from Buna, Salamaua and Madang. Adachi would not give up and was determined to reach Hollandia to establish a base from which he could fight the Americans and Australians. He reached Wewak but in April 1944 the US anticipated him and made an amphibious attack on Hollandia. Adachi and his men (31,000) were now cut off at Wewak and their attempt to break out was contained by General Hall's XI Corps. They faced death from disease and starvation but Adachi determined 'not to set foot on my country's soil again but to remain as a clod of earth in the Southern Seas with 100,000 officers and men.' He made another brave but pointless attempt to break out in May 1945. This time the Australian 6th Division repulsed his men and the Japanese lost 9000. When news of the Japanese capitulation reached him, he surrendered on 13 September 1945 with 13,500 men. In 1947 he was sentenced to life imprisonment for war crimes.

**Ainsworth, Rear Admiral Walden, 1886–1960** Ainsworth held numerous commands in the Pacific but he is remembered for his part in the Battles of Kula Gulf and Kolombangara. Ainsworth was in command of a task force of three cruisers and five destroyers which was escorting the invasion force to New Georgia. On 4–5 July 1943 his guns shelled Vila and Bairoko but he lost a destroyer in this action. On the night of 5–6 July Ainsworth's force was patrolling the Kula Gulf when they ran into Japanese transports on a reinforcement mission to New Georgia. The 'battle' was very confused: the US ships did not stay in formation and one cruiser, the *Helena*, was sunk. It was thought that Ainsworth had repulsed the transports but the Japanese had landed on New Georgia.

On the night of 12–13 July Ainsworth took part in his fifteenth combat mission up the Slot, the channel dividing the Solomons in two. The US had the advantage of radar but the Japanese had an anti-radar tracking device. The Japanese were also equipped with 'Long Lance' torpedoes which had greater range and higher speed than US torpedoes. Ainsworth did not know of the potential of these torpedoes and was lucky to lose only one destroyer in this action. Ainsworth continued to serve in the Pacific and supported the amphibious operation in the Marianas. He retired in 1948.

**Alexander, Field Marshal Sir Harold, 1891–1969** Alexander was one of the outstanding Commanders of the British Army, who was called in by CHURCHILL in times of trouble. In 1940 he went to

France to command the 1st Division of the British Expeditionary Force and at Dunkirk was chosen to command the last corps to remain on the beach. In January 1941 he was appointed Commander of the I Corps and sent to Burma, where he could do little against the Japanese air superiority, except withdraw troops to India.

Appointed Commander in Chief in August 1942 by Churchill he directed the great campaigns in which MONTGOMERY's 8th Army triumphed over ROMMEL at Alamein and thereafter. After the US and British troops joined forces in Tunisia. EISENHOWER was appointed Supreme Allied Commander in North Africa, and Alexander was his deputy and Commander of the 18th Army Group. By May 1943 Tunisia had been cleared and the Allies' next target was Sicily and Italy. When Eisenhower was appointed Supreme Commander Allied Expeditionary Force (SCAEF). Alexander became the Supreme Allied Commander in the Mediterranean. The Allied campaign in Italy was drawn out and handicapped by the fact that Overlord and the campaign in France had top priority. Alexander complained frequently about his lack of landing craft and other essential equipment. He received the surrender of German troops in Italy on 29 April 1945.

Alexander's success lay in his ability to achieve co-operation between soldiers of different nationalities and between the services. His easy-going manner disguised a very tough inner discipline and Churchill found it difficult to find fault with him. Although some, for example General BROOKE felt that he had allowed Montgomery too much independence, their partnership led to a welcome success, for which Alexander will always be remembered.

**Ambrosio, General Vittorio, 1879–1950** Ambrosio was Chief of Staff of the Italian Army and took part in the plot to overthrow MUSSOLINI. He was a professional soldier who held a series of staff appointments and eventually succeeded CAVALLERO as Mussolini's Chief of Staff on 30 January 1943. This was an anti-German move because Ambrosio wanted to ensure that Italy was not treated as Germany's satellite. The North African campaign was drawing to a close and there was little Ambrosio could do to restore the situation, especially since Generals von ARNIM and KESSELRING would not consult him.

Faced with an impossible military situation Ambrosio decided to convince Mussolini to withdraw from the alliance with Germany and negotiate with the Allies. Ambrosio accompanied Mussolini to conferences with HITLER at Salzburg (April 1943) and Feltre (19 July 1943) and saw that Mussolini was incapable of speaking out against Hitler. Ambrosio claimed that he had been preparing a coup for several months and he was even considered as a replacement for Mussolini. On 24 July the Fascist Grand Council passed a vote of censure on Mussolini and on 25 July the King appointed BADOGLIO as Prime Minister. Ambrosio had the regular army Piave Division stationed in Rome and had sent Mussolini's elite body-guards on maneuvers. He maintained the pretence of loyalty to Germany and sent an envoy to negotiate with the Allies. The negotiations were protracted· and the formal surrender was eventually signed in Malta on 29 September by Badoglio and Ambrosio. This had given the Germans enough time to occupy Rome and all of northern Italy. After this fiasco Ambrosio was dismissed by Badoglio because the Allies did not trust him.

**Amery, Leopold, 1873–1955** Amery was a close friend of Winston CHURCHILL and one of the group of Members of Parliament who opposed CHAMBERLAIN's policy of appeasement from the start. He had held office in 1929 but felt he could exert more influence from the back benches where he could freely express his opinion. He was a champion of rearmament and was highly critical of Chamberlain. On 7 May 1940 he had a famous outburst in a debate on the government's handling of Germany's invasion of Norway: he addressed Chamberlain using the words of Cromwell to the Long Parliament 'You have sat too long here for any good you have been doing. Depart, I say, and let us have done with you in the name of God, go!'

A few days later Winston Churchill became Prime Minister and Amery was appointed Secretary of State for India and Burma. He supervised military training in India in 1941 and in the face of the Japanese threat set up a special committee on India in February 1942 to advise Churchill. He held the appointment until the end of the war when he espoused the concept of the British Commonwealth. In the 1945 election he was another of the prominent Conservatives to lose his seat.

**Anami, General Korechika, 1887–1945** Anami was Minister of War at the time of the Japanese surrender. He had been Vice-Minister of War in 1940 in Prime Minister KONOYE's Cabinet and had led the military clique which brought TOJO to power.

After Tojo's fall, Anami was called upon to join SUZUKI's 'peace' Cabinet as War Minister. He was unable to admit to himself that Japan would lose the war and wanted to fight to the bitter end. On 11 August 1945 he issued the following instructions 'The only thing for us to do is to fight doggedly to the end in this holy war for the defense of our divine land. It is our firm belief that though it may mean chewing grass, eating dirt and sleeping in the field, a resolute fight will surely reveal a way out of a desperate situation.' He opposed the peace-seeking faction until the Emperor's pronouncement in favor of peace when he bowed down (11 August 1945). He refused to join a military coup to reverse this decision although his brother-in-law was involved. His failure to join led to the failure of the coup and shortly afterwards he committed suicide (15 August 1945).

**Anders, Lieutenant General Wladyslaw, 1892–1970** Anders was in command of the Nowogrodek Cavalry Brigade stationed in south Poland when the German blitzkrieg hit his country (1 September 1939). He was captured by the Russians and interned in Lubianka jail where the Red Army tried to recruit him. After the German invasion of the USSR he was freed and set about tracing the Poles who had been held in camps after 1939. The Soviets were unco-operative and Anders was faced by a bureaucratic wall of silence. He asked Stalin twice to help him trace officers who were missing but received no assistance. Stalin wanted the Polish Corps to fight for the USSR but would not arm them. Eventually he agreed to allow the Poles, about 60,000 men and 100,000 women and children, to leave via Persia for Palestine in 1942. The Polish 'Army' received extensive training in Palestine and was ready for combat in late 1943 and joined the British 8th Army in Italy. The Poles were noted for their courage and the Polish II Corps was involved in the close hand-to-hand fighting at Monte Cassino and eventually took the hill on 18 May 1944 after suffering very high casualties. His Corps was withdrawn for a while to build up its numbers. Soon after Anders led his Corps in the Adriatic sector, fought at Pescara and Ancona and liberated Bologna.

After the death of SIKORSKI in July 1943 the Poles looked to Anders as their national leader. Although it seemed as if the Soviets would install a puppet regime in Poland after its liberation. Anders was determined to fight until

HITLER was finally defeated and *then* to look at the political problems. After the war his army was 112,000 strong and was a considerable embarrassment to the Western Allies. There was talk of using it to garrison Germany but it was finally decided to disband it. Anders and all but seven officers and 14,000 men decided not to return to Poland. Anders was head of the Polish community in England until his death.

**Anderson, General Sir Kenneth, 1891–1959** A brigade and divisional Commander in the Dunkirk campaign, Anderson was appointed in 1942 to command the British 1st Army which was to undertake the invasion of North Africa under EISENHOWER's command. He proved less than wholly successful in the post, or at least did not satisfy CHURCHILL's and ALEXANDER's exacting standards, and from June 1943–45 held inactive commands in Britain and East Africa.

**Anderson, Sir John, 1882–1958** Anderson was a very influential figure in CHURCHILL's Cabinet and had been British Home Secretary in CHAMBERLAIN's cabinet. His name became a household word when he introduced a scheme to build special steel shelters – called the Anderson shelter – to protect 20,000,000 people in 1940. As Lord Privy Seal, he was responsible for air-raid precautions and national voluntary service. From 1940–43 Anderson was Lord President of the Council, and sat on the Manpower Committee which had to decide manpower priorities. He also sat on a committee which examined policy-making in all government departments. From 1943–45 he served as Chancellor of the Exchequer and was responsible for introducing the Pay-As-You-Earn (PAYE) system of income tax collection, which had been devised by his predecessor Sir Kingsley WOOD. He was also put in charge of Tube Alloys, the atomic bomb project. Anderson's job

essentially was to run home affairs smoothly while Churchill ran the war. He performed his job well and unobtrusively.

**Antonescu, Marshal Ion, 1882–1946** Antonescu was a stupid rather than sinister Rumanian dictator throughout the war. He was an army leader who had assumed leadership of the fascist Iron Guards. King CAROL II who was afraid of his power had him imprisoned but when faced with growing territorial demands from Germany and the USSR (he had ceded Bessarabia and northern Bukhovina to the USSR and more territory to Hungary and Bulgaria) Carol abdicated and appointed Antonescu Prime Minister. Antonescu came to power with the support of the Iron Guards on 5 September 1940 and immediately sent messages of loyalty to HILTER and MUSSOLINI. He called in German troops to protect the Ploesti oilfields which were to supply Germany with 46,000 tons of fuel per month in 1941. On 23 September 1940 he signed the Axis Pact and by this time had won Hitler's trust. In January 1941 he asked Hitler for permission to suppress the Iron Guards who had been persecuting the Jews and committing other atrocities, and Hitler readily assented. Antonescu secured his hold on Rumania by using the army to put its citizens down. Later that year Rumanian divisions joined Army Group South in the invasion of the USSR. These divisions went on to fight at Stalingrad and after their defeat Antonescu was soon thinking in terms of getting Rumania out of the German alliance. He sent his Prime Minister, Mihai Antonescu, to Mussolini to discuss the possibility of the withdrawal of Italy, Rumania and Hungary from the alliance but although Mussolini agreed with this scheme, he never took any action against Hitler. As the Red Army swept through the Ukraine there was little Antonescu could do. On

23 August 1944, King MICHAEL summoned him and after a stormy interview Antonescu was arrested and replaced by Sanatescu. He was tried for his war crimes and executed after the war.

**Antonov, General Alexei I, 1896–1962** Antonov was made the Soviet Chief of General Staff at the end of the war (February 1945). Antonov was one of a group of officers who came to the force after the Soviet Purges of 1938–39 thanks to the protection of SHAPOSHNIKOV. When Germany invaded the USSR in June 1941 Antonov was made Chief of Staff on the South and North Caucasus and Transcaucasus Fronts in quick succession. VASILIEVSKY chose him to be his representative in Moscow but because STALIN did not like him he was posted to the Voronezh Front. His distinguished services led to his appointments as Deputy Chief of Staff and Chief of Operations Department. His job was to plan military operations and liaise with front commanders. He took part in the planning of the Kursk, Belorussian and Berlin offensives. In 1944–45 he was chief spokesman on military affairs at the Moscow, Potsdam and Yalta Conferences. He co-ordinated with US and British Chiefs of Staff and at the end of the war he was involved in a brisk interchange with EISENHOWER over which army should invade Czechoslovakia. Eisenhower had to restrain PATTON from occupying the country and the Red Army liberated Prague. After the war he fell from favor and was sent to the Caucasus.

**Aosta, Duke Amadeo of, 1898–1942** Governor of Italian East Africa and Commander in Chief of the Italian Armies in Eritrea and Ethiopia. Aosta, a cousin of the King of Italy, undertook the invasion of British Somaliland in August 1940. His campaign was initially highly successful but as soon as the British were able to concentrate reinforce-

ments, the tide swung in their favor. In April they reoccupied the Ethiopian capital, Addis Ababa, and a month later Aosta himself was forced to surrender at Amba Alagi (16 May 1941). He died the following year in captivity in Kenya. He was liked and respected by friend and enemy alike as a gentleman, a patriot and a brave man.

**Appleyard, Major Geoffrey, 1916–1943** Appleyard began his career in the army as an officer in the Royal Army Service Corps in France but then joined the commandos. In late summer 1941 he was sent to explore Vichy France's coastal areas off West Africa in the 65-ton Brixham trawler *Maid Honor*. He then joined the SSRF (Small Scale Raiding Force) and undertook at least eighteen different missions in northern France and on the Channel Islands to collect details of lights, tides and German positions. He became the Commander of the SSRF but after the commando failure at Dieppe the force was transferred to North Africa and conducted reconnaissance raids on Pantelleria. On 12–13 July 1943 he was involved in a SAS (Special Air Service) parachute-dropping operation over northern Sicily and is presumed to have died when his plane disappeared.

**Arnim, Colonel General Jurgen von, 1889–1971** Arnim was the offspring of a traditional Prussian military family. He became a member of the elite German General Staff and commanded a corps in the USSR. At the end of 1942 HITLER selected him at short notice to command the Fifth Panzer Army. Arnim was not the right man because he habitually failed to co-operate with ROMMEL in the field and did not consult the Italian allies preferring to deal directly with KESSELRING and the German High Command. He took over command in early December 1942 in Tunisia and secured lines of communications with

Rommel on the Mareth Line. He was ordered to attack Sidi bou Zid and the Germans captured the Kasserine Pass but had to fall back for lack of support. Arnim then decided to go through with his own *Ochsenkopf* plan to take Béja, but as it should have been initiated earlier he failed to make any progress. In March Arnim was made Commander of Army Group Afrika but he never received enough supplies and fought a depressing retreat until he had run out of space, ammunition and equipment. The Germans had orders to fight until their last round of ammunition was fired but the spirit of defeatism that spread through the ranks led them to take their orders literally: they fired their last shots in the air. Arnim was captured on 12 May 1943 but only after he had severed communications with his units so he could not call for the surrender of all his troops. He spent the rest of the war in Prisoner of War camps.

**Arnold, General Henry 'Hap', 1886–1950** Arnold was the US general who commanded the USAAF in all theaters throughout the war. In 1936 he was appointed Assistant Chief of the Air Corps and became Chief of Air Staff in 1938. Although no funds were available he persuaded the US aviation industry to step up the production of airplanes and to prepare plant and training facilities in anticipation of the rush for new aircraft thereby insuring production capacity. Aircraft production in the USA grew from less than 6000 per annum to 262,000 during the years 1940–44. World War II saw a massive growth in the USAAF and Arnold was behind every change. He supervised training programs for pilots and by the end of the war, Air Force personnel had grown from 21,000 in 1935 to over two million in 1944.

He served on the US Joint Chiefs of Staff Committee and Combined Chiefs of Staff Committee of the Allies. He recommended strong support for the British and was opposed to the policy of American isolationism. He considered air power would prove the decisive factor in any future conflict. Arnold firmly believed in the war-winning capability of strategic bombing of specific targets and this brought him into conflict with his British counterparts who favored area bombing. This problem was resolved at the Casablanca Conference in January 1943 when it was agreed that both methods would be adopted.

He was a popular figure whose nickname 'Hap' or 'Happy' was well-deserved. He managed to develop a working relationship with the solitary Chief of Air Staff, PORTAL, which was essential to Allied success. In 1944 he was made a full General of the Army and when the USAAF was made into a separate force equal to the Army and Navy, he was its first Five-Star General.

**Attlee, Prime Minister Clement, 1883–1967** Leader of the Labour Party in parliament at the outbreak of the war, Attlee became Deputy Prime Minister to CHURCHILL on the formation of the coalition government in May 1940. The two men were temperamental as well as political opposites. Attlee being dry, unemotional and self-effacing almost to the point of disappearance. In education and background, however, they were closer than their party affiliations would have suggested. Attlee being a public school socialist who had been drawn into the Labour Party through his interest in social work in London's East End before World War I (in which he like Churchill, served as an infantry officer). Thus, although never friends they were able to find much common ground in the direction of the war and worked together without disharmony. A superb party manager, Attlee insured the complete support of the Labour minority for Churchill's policies and, with BEVIN, the co-operation of the trade unions in the untroubled production of war material. In the general election of July 1945 he was swept to the Prime Ministership by the landslide victory of his party and replaced Churchill as the British representative at the Potsdam Conference.

**Auchinleck, Field Marshal Sir Claude, 1884–1981** Auchinleck, affectionately known as 'the Auk,' was one of the most respected Commanders in the British Army. He had made his career as a soldier in the Indian Army and had been brought home to command the IV Corps in 1939. He spent some time as Commander in Chief in northern Norway and of Southern Command in 1940 but was then appointed Commander in Chief, India in 1941. In June 1941 he was then chosen by Churchill to be Commander in Chief, Middle East, replacing WAVELL. He arrived in Egypt at the point when British fortunes were at their lowest: ROMMEL had successfully defeated the British Battleaxe Operation. Auchinleck immediately set about planning a counterattack, which was codenamed Crusader, for November 1941. Crusader was a hard-fought battle and ended in a victory for the British and the relief of the besieged Tobruk. However Rommel did not give the British a chance to consolidate their victory and he counterattacked, forcing the British to make a strategic withdrawal to Gazala and Bir Hacheim. In June 1942 fighting was renewed and Rommel outstripped the British and took Tobruk on 21 June 1942. Auchinleck finally gave way to pressure from CHURCHILL and took personal command of the 8th Army in order to improve morale. Auchinleck suffered from being in conflict with Churchill, who demanded the impossible, the immediate defeat of Rommel. Although the first Battle of El-Alamein, in July 1942, was a decisive victory and a tremendous setback for Rommel and the Italian Army. Churchill decided it was time to replace Auchinleck by ALEXANDER. Churchill could not forgive Auchinleck for the fall of Tobruk and Auchinleck could not alleviate Churchill's fears about the desert campaign. Churchill's aim was to speed up the offensive. However, by removing Auchinleck at this crucial point the timetable for the second Battle of El Alamein was pushed back. Auchinleck returned to India and served as Commander in Chief of the Indian Army until 1947.

**Aung San, General U, 1915–1947** Aung San spent the war as Commander in Chief of the Burma Independence Army which later became the BNA (Burma National Army). He accepted the Japanese rule of Burma but, in fact, was waiting for the chance to fight for his country's independence. In March 1945 as the British were advancing through the Burmese jungle, Aung San and his BNA marched into the jungle ostensibly to fight the British but in fact to fight for independence. In mid-May Aung San flew to the 14th Army Headquarters at Meiktila to negotiate with SLIM who refused to recognize the claim of the anti-Fascist organization to be the provisional government of Burma. Aung San at first refused to serve on the Executive Council that ruled Burma, but when the political situation deteriorated Britain called in Aung San to be Deputy Chairman of the Council (September 1946), Aung San then negotiated with ATTLEE and they signed an agreement in January 1947 which promised the election of a Constituent Assembly and independence within a year. Aung San returned in triumph but this was short-lived since he was assassinated along with six members of his cabinet on 19 July 1947.

# B

**Bader, Group Captain Sir Douglas, 1910–1983** Bader was a British pilot who became a legend in his own time because he overcame the physical disability of having artificial legs. In December 1931 he lost both legs in a flying accident and was invalided out of the RAF. He argued his way past the RAF Volunteer Reserve Medical Board and in November 1939 was flying again. In June 1940 he was given command of Fighter Squadron 242, which was manned by Canadians. His outstanding leadership qualities were rewarded during the Battle of Britain when he was given five squadrons. However he was often in disagreement with Fighter Command Headquarters and often ignored their orders, especially over his development of the 'Big Wing' Formation, which earned him the respect of his German adversaries. In August 1941 he collided with an enemy aircraft over Béthune and was captured. He spent the rest of the war in POW (Prisoner of War) camps.

**Badoglio, Field Marshal Pietro, 1871–1956** Badoglio was an Italian Field Marshal and a veteran of Italy's colonial wars having fought in the disastrous campaign of 1896 in Ethiopia and in that of 1911–12 against Turkey in Libya. Badoglio made a considerable reputation for himself during World War I in the fighting against the Austrians on the Isonzo where he planned and executed the capture of Monte Sabotino in August 1916. He negotiated the armistice at the end of the war. He was their Chief of Staff after the war, governor of Libya 1928–33, commanded the army which annexed Ethiopia in 1935–6 and subsequently became Viceroy of Ethiopia. He was re-appointed Chief of Staff on Italy's entry into World War II but resigned on the failure of the invasion of Greece in December 1940. Long an opponent of MUSSOLINI, he was the principal instigator of the dictator's downfall in 1943 and signed the armistice with the Allies in September. He became the first Prime Minister of the anti-Fascist government.

**Bagramyan, Marshal Ivan, 1897–** At the beginning of World War II. Bagramyan served as a Soviet staff officer on the Southwest Front, as Chief of Operations Department in the Kiev Military District and also as Chief of Staff to TIMOSHENKO after BUDENNY's dismissal. He was given command of an army, the 16th Guards (later the 11th Guards), in July 1942. His army fought on the Western Front and at Kursk (July 1943) where it attacked from the north and achieved the envelopment of Orel. In November 1943 he was promoted to General and replaced YEREMENKO as Commander of First Baltic Front, which became known as the Samland Group in later operations. During the Belorussian campaign his armies unexpectedly broke through in the north and encircled Vitebsk killing 20,000 Germans and capturing 10,000. The Front Armies then crossed the Dvina, took Daugavpils and reached the coast west of Riga. Now all that was left was to complete the encirclement of German Army Group North. In January 1945 his Group occupied Memel and was then ordered to take

Königsberg. This proved a stumbling block and Bagramyan was held responsible for the failure to take it until April 1945. After the war he was appointed Commander of the Baltic Military District.

**Balbo, Italo, 1896–1940** An Italian politician, Balbo was one of the most flamboyant figures of the Fascist movement. He was a distinguished pioneer aviator, had been Minister of Aviation and in 1936 was appointed Governor of Libya. He opposed Italy's alliance with HITLER and urged MUSSOLINI not to enter the war on Hitler's side. Ironically he was killed shortly after Mussolini nevertheless did so he was accidentally shot down over Libya by his own side.

**Balck, Lieutenant General Hermann, 1893–1950** Balck was a very energetic German tank Commander, who rose to command an Army Group in France. Balck was very successful in the opening stages of the Battle of France: he managed to establish a bridgehead across the Meuse at Sedan. He commanded a regiment in the First Panzer Division of GUDERIAN's Group and for Operation Barbarossa he was promoted to command a full Panzer Division. In November 1943 he was given command of the XXXXVIII Panzer Corps and took part in the defense of Sicily. In August 1944 he was ordered back to the USSR to command the Fourth Panzer Army but arrived too late to contain KONEV's attack in the Ukraine. In September 1944 he was sent to relieve BLASKOWITZ and pursued a policy of elastic defense which held up PATTON's advance into Lorraine. He was then sent to command the Sixth Army in Hungary but he displeased HITLER and ended the war commanding a mere subgroup.

**Ba Maw, Dr U, 1893–** Ba Maw was the Prime Minister of Burma during the Japanese occupation. He had been Prime Minster under the British until 1937 but was arrested for sedition in 1940. In 1942 he was appointed national leader by the Japanese and began negotiating for Burma's independence and was forced to accept the loss of part of the Shan states. In August 1943 Burma was declared independent and Ba Maw was appointed its head of state, however this was a purely nominal title – in fact, he merely served as an adviser to the Japanese military rulers. Once the British began to overrun Burma he left for Japan and was interned by the US in Tokyo (December 1945–July 1946). He returned to Burma to face further imprisonment under the A Nu regime.

**Bao Dai, Emperor of Assam, 1913–** Bao Dai was the Emperor of Assam (a province of Indo-China) from 1925 until 1945. (Until he reached eighteen Assam was governed by a regent.) He ascended the throne in 1932 and after the Japanese invasion he acquiesced to their rule. In 1945 he was on good terms with HO CHI MINH and abdicated the throne. He was proclaimed Supreme Counselor of the Democratic Republic of Vietnam by Ho on 2 September 1945. However he soon became dissatisfied with Ho's regime and left for Hong Kong in July 1946. He returned to Vietnam the following year to rally anti-Communist forces under French rule based on Saigon but civil war was well under way.

**Baruch, Bernard, 1870–1965** Baruch was one of ROOSEVELT's economic advisers and was an extremely influential businessman. In 1941 he put forward his criticisms of the war economy and was appointed special adviser to BYRNES' Office of War Mobilization. In 1943 he produced a comprehensive report on how industry should adapt to wartime requirements. In 1946 President TRUMAN appointed him US representative to the United Nations Atomic Energy Commission and Baruch produced a plan to establish control of all atomic energy activities dangerous to the world, but it was rejected by the USSR.

**Bastico, General Ettore, 1876–1976** Bastico fought in Libya, Yugoslavia and in the Greek campaign and in recompense for his services MUSSOLINI had made him Governor of Libya. On 12 July 1941 he was made Commander in Chief of Axis troops in North Africa. ROMMEL was not under his orders but was to be responsible to him. Rommel succeeded in making Bastico's job impossible by ignoring him and eventually troops were placed directly under Rommel. In February 1942 Bastico's appointment finally lapsed and he returned to obscurity in Italy.

**Bayerlein, General Fritz, 1899–1970** Bayerlein was a Panzer Commander who fought on all the fronts during the war. In 1940 after the Polish Campaign he served under GUDERIAN in France and then commanded a combat group in the XXXIX Corps' advance on Moscow. In 1941 he was transferred to the Western Desert and became Chief of Staff to ROMMEL. He commanded the unsuccessful attack on Alam Halfa. On Rommel's departure Bayerlein took direct command of the Afrika Korps. (After the war he helped write operational histories of the Desert Campaign.) He returned to Germany and was given command of the Panzer Lehr Division until the end of the war. This Division took part in the fighting at Bastogne during the Battle of the Bulge.

**Bazna, Elyesa 'Cicero', d. 1970** Bazna was a Turkish subject of Albanian origin who became the highest paid spy in World War II. Before the war he had worked as the valet of the German Ambassador in Ankara, Jenke, RIBBEN-TROP's brother-in-law. He had transferred to the British Embassy without difficulty and served as valet to the Brit-

ish Ambassador, Knatchbull-Hugesson during the war. In October 1943 he visited the German embassy and saw the Intelligence Attaché, Moyzisch, to whom he offered secret British documents for £20,000 (US$80,000 at the time). Cicero, as he was codenamed by the Germans, had obtained a key to the embassy safe and was photographing all the papers that passed through the embassy. He supplied the Germans with many important documents including the minutes of the Teheran and Cairo Conferences and details of the planned Allied invasion of Europe. He was paid some £300,000 (US$1,200,000 in the currency of the time) in bank notes but British embassy officials became suspicious and Bazna disappeared. The information he had given the Germans was treated with suspicion by the Germans who thought it was planted, and was never presented to Hitler because Ribbentrop and KALTENBRUNNER argued as to who should present it. Bazna was traced after the war to South America where he was arrested for trying to pass counterfeit money – the Germans had given him forged bank notes. Neither side profited from this coup in espionage.

**Beaverbrook, Lord Maxwell Aitken, 1879–1964** A Canadian self-made multi-millionaire and the founder of a great press empire, Beaverbrook had played a major part in British coalition politics during World War I when he had directed the government's information services and had become a close friend and political ally of Winston CHURCHILL. On the latter's assumption of the premiership in 1940, Beaverbrook was made Minister of Aircraft Production, with the task of increasing the output of desperately needed fighters. By ruthless simplification of production methods he did succeed in keeping the numbers of replacements ahead of losses during the Battle of Britain. Subsequent investigation suggested, however, that the disruption he caused in established procedures resulted in an eventual net shortfall of aircraft by the end of 1940. Then, however, the crisis was over. He subsequently acted as Minister of Supply (1941–42) and Lord Privy Seal (1943–45), and also as administrator of the Lend-Lease scheme in America in 1942. A 'political gadfly' with an irrepressible urge to create mischief around him, Beaverbrook was valued by Churchill less for his administrative skills than for his creative unorthodoxy.

**Beck, General Ludwig, 1880–1944** A former Chief of Staff, Beck had resigned in 1938 in protest against HITLER's plans for aggressive war which he believed would bring about disaster for Germany. He then became the focus for the 'military opposition' to Hitler, which maintained a timorous existence during the early years of the war. A man of genuine moral courage, however, he gladly joined with STAUFFENBERG in the active conspiracy which culminated in the Bomb Plot of 20 July 1944, was arrested in the War Office by the opportunist FROMM, and committed suicide under his supervision that evening.

**Bedell Smith, General Walter, 1895–1961** A staff officer who had risen from the ranks, he became, at the outbreak of the war, Secretary of the US Joint Chiefs of Staff and American Secretary of the Anglo-American Combined Chiefs of Staff. In September 1942 he went to England to become Chief of Staff to EISENHOWER, with whom he remained to the war's end. Eisenhower enormously valued his services and talents which were those of the perfect soldier-diplomat. He laid the basis for the negotiation of the Italian armistice of 1943 and arranged the surrender of the German forces in the west in May 1945.

**Bell, Bishop George, 1883–1958** A leading British clergyman of progressive views, Bell, as Bishop of Chichester, attracted widespread notice and criticism during World War II for his condemnation of the policy of bombing German cities. A man of unflinching moral courage, he was not the least deterred from expressing his views despite the violent hostility they attracted. Dietrich Bonhöffer was sent by the German resistance circle to negotiate with Bell but nothing came of this.

**Beneš, President Edouard, 1884–1948** Beneš was the President of the Czech republic-in-exile during World War II. Beneš was President of Czechoslovakia at the time of the Munich Agreement (29 September 1938), which compelled the Czechs to cede fortified Sudetenland to Germany. After this defeat for the Czech republic, Beneš resigned and left for the West. In 1939 after the German occupation of Czechoslovakia, Beneš formed the Czech National Committee in Paris. In 1940 it transferred its base to London and Beneš immediately started trying to get the Allies to repudiate the Munich Agreement and get recognition for his government. He organized refugees into units which served in the British Army and RAF. He was unwilling to encourage sabotage and guerrilla warfare so long as Czechoslovakia was far from the front but he gave the order for the operation to assassinate HEYDRICH. When this was accomplished it increased his standing in the eyes of the Czechs. Beneš' government was finally recognized by Britain in July 1941 and the Munich Agreement was repudiated in August 1942. He negotiated with the USSR because he felt he had to accommodate the Communists in Czechoslovakia. Beneš signed a Pact of Friendship and Mutual Assistance with the USSR in December 1943. At the end of the war he obtained agreement to massive transfers of Czechoslovakia's Germans to Germany which made for stability in postwar Czechoslovakia. Beneš returned to Prague and was elected President of the Republic in 1946. After the Communist takeover in 1948 he resigned and died shortly afterwards.

**Ben-Gurion, David, 1886–1974** Ben-Gurion led Israel to independence in May 1948 and was its first national leader. Ben-Gurion was of Polish origin and a long-time chairman of the Jewish Agency for Palestine. In 1939 Britain brought out a White Paper which set a limit on Jewish immigration into Palestine of 75,000 and Ben-Gurion announced that the Jews would fight this. HITLER's persecution of the Jews made them more anxious to set up an independent state and in 1944 the Stern gang embarked on a program of terror. Ben-Gurion stepped up demands for a Jewish national state and unofficially favored the terrorist campaign.

**Bennett, Air Vice-Marshal Donald, 1910–1986** Bennett was an Australian-born RAF officer. In April 1942 he was given command of No 10 Squadron and while active over Norway he was shot down. He managed to escape to neutral Sweden and after a short period in jail he returned to England. In August 1942 he set up the Pathfinder Force to guide strategic bombers over Germany: this Force consisted of two types of aircraft, the finders and the illuminators. The finders found the target area and dropped flares over an area of ten miles radius. The illuminators pinpointed the target area and dropped a concentration of flares over it which gave the following Bomber Force adequate lighting for their operations. Bennett set up the Light Night Strike force of Mosquito bombers and continued to play a vital role in the strategic bombing offensive over Germany.

**Bennett, Major General Henry Gordon,**

1887–1962 Bennett was an Australian soldier who served as a Brigadier during World War I but was not on active duty between the wars. He was loud in his criticism of the regular army and especially British officers, but in 1939 he returned to the Army and was made the youngest Major General on the active list. He was given command of a Training Depot initially but in February 1941 he was made General Officer Commanding of the AIF (Australian Imperial Forces) in Malaya – his 8th Division was stationed at Johore. The Australians tried to hold the Japanese on the River Muar and scored some early success by digging deep traps in the jungle. However they were forced to retreat to Singapore where they engaged in the final battle with the Japanese on the northwest of the island. When the situation became desperate Bennett decided to escape without informing his superior, General PERCIVAL. He made his way in a junk to Batavia and returned to Australia. He was promoted to Lieutenant General in April 1942 but subsequently faced severe criticism for abandoning his forces and was never given another active command. After the war a military court of inquiry ruled that he should have remained in Singapore.

**Beria, Lavrenty, 1899–1954** Beria was head of the Soviet intelligence, NKVD during World War II. He did not have a particularly high standing within the Communist Party organization but STALIN appointed him member of the GKO and he took part in the day-to-day running of the war. Through his intelligence network he often gave Stalin more up-to-date information on activities on the Front than Front Commanders were able to. He was also in charge of partisan activities behind German lines and his units used terror tactics to make the civilian population undertake anti-German action. His NKVD men, also ran the Prisoner of War camps.

Beria was also responsible for the dissemination of propaganda.

**Bernadotte, Count Folke, 1895–1948** Bernadotte was the nephew of Gustavus V of Sweden and Vice-Chairman of the Swedish Red Cross. Using his position he was able to arrange the exchange of sick and disabled German and British prisoners at Gothenburg in October 1943 and again in September 1944. In February 1945 Bernadotte arranged for the transfer of Danish and Norwegian political prisoners and came into contact with HIMMLER. Himmler decided to approach him with terms to make a settlement with the Allies. On the night of 23–24 April 1945 Himmler proposed surrender to the Western Allies on the condition that the war against the USSR would continue. Bernadotte agreed to transmit the terms but the Allies rejected the proposal. Bernadotte returned on 27 April and told Himmler that the Allies had turned him down. He published his account of this episode in *The Curtain Falls*.

**Bernhard, Prince of the Netherlands, 1911–** Bernhard was the German-born husband of the Dutch heiress to the throne, Juliana. He had married her in 1937 and renounced his German citizenship. After the German invasion of the Netherlands in 1940 his family left for Canada but he stayed behind and joined Dutch troops fighting in Zeeland. He left for Britain and trained as a pilot in the RAF. In November 1940 Queen WILHELMINA appointed him liaison officer between British and Dutch forces and during the war he was promoted to Lieutenant General and also Rear Admiral. In August 1944 he visited Dutch troops in Normandy and in September he was appointed Commander in Chief of the Netherlands Forces of the Interior. He set up temporary headquarters in Belgium to direct partisan activities, crossed the Albert Canal on 10 September 1944 and returned to the Netherlands secretly. After the war he received national acclaim for his leadership of the partisans.

**Berzarin, Colonel General Nikolai, 1904–1945** In 1939 Berzarin led the 32nd Infantry Division at Lake Khassan against the Japanese. Throughout the rest of World War II he commanded various armies: at the Battle of Jassy-Kishiniev, in Poland and in Berlin. Berzarin was the Soviet Army Commander who led the first Soviet troops into Berlin in April 1945. He was appointed the first military commandant of Berlin after the war but died in a motorcycle crash before he could achieve anything.

**Beurling, Flight Lieutenant George, 1922–1948** Nicknamed 'Screwball,' Beurling was a Canadian-born fighter ace who had a total of 31 victories during the war. He was sent to Malta in June 1942 with 249 Squadron and became famous for superb marksmanship.

**Beveridge, Sir William, 1879–1963** Beveridge was a British economist who produced the Beveridge Report on Social Insurance and Allied Services. He was a respected figure whom CHURCHILL called into his administration to be Undersecretary of labor. When his Report came out in December 1942 it was widely acclaimed as the foundation for a future social welfare system. It provided benefits for unemployment, health, marriage, maternity, widowhood, old age and death. However Churchill and his Cabinet decided that the Report would not be implemented and only introduced plans for a national medical service, training benefits and child allowances. Beveridge had always stood above party politics but in 1944 he stood as a Liberal candidate and became an MP, but in 1945 he lost his seat in the Labour Party landslide.

**Bevin, Ernest, 1881–1951** Bevin was a British Labour Party politician who served as Minister of Labor and National Service in CHURCHILL's War cabinet. An Emergency Powers Act was passed in 1940 which gave Bevin dictatorial powers to help mobilize manpower. He suspended the 48-hour week and the right to strike. Workmen were forbidden to leave or change jobs without official approval. In 1941 he introduced a measure which conscripted into industry all men over thirty not serving in the armed forces and all women aged 20–23. By 1943 he had successfully completed his mobilization plan and thanks to his work only one hour per worker per year was lost in industrial stoppages. He began drafting plans for postwar demobilization. After the war Bevin became ATTLEE's Foreign Secretary and attended the Potsdam and United Nations Conferences. His main concern was to decolonize British possessions and 'leave behind for ever the idea of one country dominating another.'

**Biddle, Francis, 1886–1968** Biddle was ROOSEVELT's Attorney General from September 1941 until 1945. As Solicitor General from 1939–40 he had been required to administer the Alien Registration Act of June 1940 with which he did not agree. He had to supervise the internment of Japanese and German Americans but he succeeded in removing Italian Americans from the list of aliens. As Attorney General he appointed an Interdepartmental Committee on Investigations which tried to set up procedures for loyalty investigations. After the war he served as a member of the International Military Tribunal at Nuremberg and was noted for his compassion.

**Billotte, General Gaston Herve Gustave, 1875–1940** As Commander of the First Army Group in 1940, Billotte was effectively Chief of the principal front of operations, being directly subordinate to GEORGES (Commander in Chief, North East) and GAMELIN (the Supreme Commander), and having under him the best of the French Field Armies (the 1st and 7th) as well as the British Expeditionary Force. He was also said to be the only French General who knew Gamelin's mind (for what that was worth) and in whom General Lord GORT and King LEOPOLD of the Belgians had full confidence. On the German invasion of Belgium he supervised the advance to the Dyle and the subsequent withdrawals to the Escaut and the Dendre but, at the moment of his death, in a road accident, was planning a counter-attack. His death could not have come at a worse moment for the Allies. His son, Pierre, rallied to DE GAULLE and commanded a Free French armored formation in the liberation of Normandy and Paris in 1944.

**Blakeslee, Colonel Donald, 1915–** Blakeslee was a US fighter ace who joined the Royal Canadian Air Force (RCAF) and was posted to No 401 Ram Squadron in the UK in May 1941. He was a legendary figure who commanded USAAF 4th Fighter Group which was responsible for the destruction of 1016 aircraft. Blakeslee himself shot down fifteen enemy aircraft in the air and two planes on the ground.

**Blamey, General Sir Thomas, 1884–1951** Blamey was GOC of the Australian Imperial Forces during World War II. He had served as Chief of Staff to Monash during World War I but during peacetime he was Commissioner of the Victoria police. In February 1940 he was called up to take command of the AIF, Middle East mainly because he was a well-known figure. In 1941 he arrived in Greece where he took command of the Anzac Corps and he supervised the evacuations from Crete and Rhodes. He transferred to Egypt and became Deputy Commander in Chief, Middle East but in fact had little power. After Pearl Harbor he returned to Australia in March 1942 and was appointed Commander in Chief of Allied Land Forces, under General MACARTHUR's overall command. He faced a constant stream of complaints from MacArthur about the Australians' fighting ability but he did not stand up to them. In September he had to take personal command of the troops fighting on the Kokoda trail to pacify MacArthur. He supervised the recapture of Buna and retained command of Australian Land Forces in New Guinea. The Australians had to patrol Japanese troop concentrations at Wewak and in the Solomons. Under pressure from MacArthur he planned operations by Australian troops to reduce the pockets and to recapture Borneo at the end of the war.

**Blaskowitz, Colonel General Johannes von, 1883–1948** Blaskowitz was a German General who served in 1940 in France and afterwards became Commander of the Army of Occupation in Poland. He was very independent-minded and prepared two memos protesting against SS brutality and treatment of the Jews. In 1944 Blaskowitz was given command of Army Group G covering the Biscay area and the Mediterranean coast of France. After the success of Operation Dragoon he was relieved in September 1944. HITLER complained about his childish attitudes but reappointed him in March 1945 in a last minute attempt to save the Netherlands. The task was hopeless and in May 1945 he surrendered to Canadian and Dutch troops led by Prince BERNHARD. He was put on trial at Nuremberg but committed suicide before the trial.

**Bleicher, Sergeant Hugo 'Colonel Henri,' 1899–** Bleicher was a German counter-intelligence agent who disrupted many Allied underground circuits in France. He was a businessman whose

knowledge of languages brought him to the attention of the German authorities who were recruiting people to do field work in occupied countries. His first success was to dismantle the *Interallié* network and he personally arrested Major Roman Czerniawski. He also arrested Mathilde CARRÉ and persuaded her to work as a double agent after becoming her lover. His early success led to his transference to the Abwehr but because he was so earnest and zealous he never rose above the rank of sergeant.

Bleicher's most famous coup was to arrest Captain Peter CHURCHILL and Odette SANSOM. He did this by posing as a colonel in the German intelligence who wanted to defect to the Allies. London SOE (Special Operations Executive) warned Sansom not to deal with him but Bleicher caught up with them and arrested them while they were sleeping. Bleicher worked with Henri Déricourt, the double agent, and through him came to know Major Henri Frager, a Resistance organizer, whom he arrested in 1944. At the end of the war he was arrested by Dutch police in Amsterdam and was imprisoned by an Allied court after writing his memoirs.

**Blomberg, Field Marshal Werner von, 1878–1943** As War Minister in HITLER's first cabinet. Blomberg quickly abandoned the role of watchdog which President Hindenburg had intended he should play and became a devotee of Germany's new leader. In return he was promoted to become the first Field Marshal of the new regime in 1936. In February 1938, however, he was forced from office, an unwise second marriage he had just made having provided Hitler with the pretext he needed to humiliate the high command of the army, shave its self-confidence and allow him to replace its leaders with soldiers completely subservient to himself. The 'Rubber Lion' as Blomberg was known – an apt comment on the divergence between his martial appearance and fiberless character – went quietly, consigning the once fiercely independent German Army to Nazi hegemony.

**Blum, Leon, 1872–1950** An intellectual and writer. Blum became one of the leading figures of the French socialist party (SFIO), after World War I and of the Union of the Left in the 1930s. In 1936 he became Prime Minister in the Popular Front government but was forced to resign in June 1937 when the radicals deserted the coalition. An ardent patriot, he was anxious in 1939 to see the spirit of the 'Sacred Union' of parties of 1914 rekindled, but was ostracized by many on the right. He was deported to Germany after the defeat of 1940 but was Prime Minister briefly after the war. Many Frenchmen continued to hold Blum and his Popular Front responsible for France's military unpreparedness in 1940.

**Blumentritt, General Gunther, 1892–1967** Blumentritt was a staff officer who served under Field Marshals von KLUGE and von RUNDSTEDT. In Poland in 1939 and in France in 1940 he was Chief of Planning of Operations in Rundstedt's Army Group. In 1941 he was made Chief of Staff to Kluge's Fourth Army but was then transferred back to Rundstedt's staff in France. He did most of Rundstedt's planning, especially the plans to deal with an Allied invasion, and was convinced that the Allies would not land in Normandy. After D-Day Kluge replaced von Rundstedt, but Kluge was involved in anti-HITLER conspiracies and after the July Plot came under suspicion. Kluge committed suicide and although Blumentritt remained above suspicion he was replaced in September 1944. He commanded the Fifteenth Army at the Battle of the Bulge and was able to comment on Allied strategy. He felt the broad front strategy was ill-conceived and that a concentrated push in northern Germany would have won the war earlier.

**Bock, Field Marshal Fedor von, 1885–1945** Bock had risen through the ranks of the German Army to become, alongside RUNDSTEDT and LEEB, one of the three Army Group Commanders. In the Polish Campaign, Bock was in command of Army Group North which swept aside the Polish units. In the campaign in the west he commanded Army Group B which overran Belgium and Holland and broke the line of the Lower Seine in the Battle of France. Bock's next command was of Army Group Center, which advanced from Poland to Moscow in the second half of 1941. Bock hopelessly overextended his lines and his men were completely exhausted, Bock himself was suffering from stomach cramps and could not properly exercise his command. Along with Rundstedt and other senior Generals he was purged following the Soviet counter-offensive outside Moscow in December 1941. However early in 1942 REICHENAU suffered a stroke at his Headquarters and Bock was recalled to take command of Army Group South in the USSR. While in command of the German drive into the Caucasus in July 1942, he was dismissed following a dispute with Hitler.

**Boisson, General Pierre, 1894–1948** Boisson was Governor General of Equatorial Africa at the time of Operation Menace in 1940. When France fell Boisson favored continuing the struggle against Germany in France's colonies but when PÉTAIN declared that the armistice covered the colonies, Boisson decided to fall into line. His policy was to suppress Gaullist and pro-Allied Frenchmen in West Africa. CHURCHILL decided that the Allies should control the important port of Dakar and sent a task force to seize it. Although the expedition was accompanied by Free French forces Boisson refused to allow the task force to land, despite a broadcast from DE GAULLE, who never forgave him for this. In 1942 when the Allies arrived off North Africa, Boisson, who was then Governor of that province, received them with open arms because of Admiral DARLAN's appeal to allow the landings. Boisson was then made a member of the Imperial Council to assist Darlan and after the latter's assassination he was elected onto the council as a supporter of GIRAUD. However when de Gaulle became Head of the Provisional French National Committee. Boisson resigned from the governorship (June 1943). He was tried as a collaborator in December 1943 and imprisoned for the duration of the war.

**Bong, Major Richard, 1920–1945** Bong was a US pilot who achieved the greatest number of victories in the USAAF. He served in New Guinea with the 5th Air Force and in 1942 was flight leader of the 'Flying Knights' Fighter Squadron of P-38s. During his career he managed to shoot down forty planes and was awarded the Congressional Medal of Honor. He died in 1945 while testing a P-80 jet in California.

**Bonhöffer, Dietrich, 1906–1945** Bonhöffer was a German Lutheran pastor and theologian. In 1937–9 his Church College had been closed down by Nazis and he was forbidden to write or to publish. He was used by Oster, Admiral CANARIS' Deputy, to act as a courier. In May 1942 he went to Stockholm on a pass made out by the German Foreign Office and met Bishop Bell of Chichester. On 31 May 1942 he gave details of anti-Nazi conspirators and their plans but he did not realize that Bell was an unsuitable emissary. CHURCHILL would never trust Bell because of his outspoken opposition to the area bombing of Germany. In April 1943 Bonhoffer was ar-

rested and remained in prison until he was court-martialed at Flossenberg prison camp. He was sentenced to death and executed alongside Canaris.

**Borghese, Lieutenant Commander Prince Valerio, 1912–1974** Borghese was an Italian naval commander who led the Tenth Light Flotilla on numerous missions in the Mediterranean. This flotilla specialized in individualistic operations and sank 73,000 tons of Allied shipping. For his services, Borghese was awarded a gold medal by MUSSOLINI. His most successful raid was on 18 December 1941 when he sent out three chariots (human torpedoes) from his submarine the *Sciré*. They entered the port of Alexandria and crippled the HMS *Valiant* and *Queen Elizabeth*. In 1943 he was given command of an entire destroyer flotilla and land-based assault craft off Anzio but he achieved disappointing results before the Italian government decided to come to terms with the Allies.

**Boris III, King of Bulgaria, 1894–1943** Boris III was the King of Bulgaria, who eventually joined the Axis side after pressure from HITLER. Bulgaria's position initially was difficult because Boris had married an Italian princess which had made him oppose a Balkan anti-Italian pact. He was anxious to conserve Bulgarian neutrality but was too weak to stand alone. In November 1940 Boris met Hitler at Berchtesgaden and was able to leave without committing himself but eventually agreed to sign a pact with Germany. In March 1941 Boris declared war on Great Britain and six months later on the USA but refused to declare war on the USSR. On 28 August 1943 he died under mysterious circumstances shortly after an interview with Hitler. It is probable that he died of natural causes, possibly a heart attack, since no secret service claimed responsibility for his death.

**Bor-Komorowski, General Tadeusz, 1895–1966** Count Komorowski, code-named Bor, led the Polish partisans in the Warsaw Uprising of 1944. Bor-Komorowski stayed in Poland after the German invasion in 1939 and was put in charge of resistance in southern Poland. In June 1943 Rowecki, the AK (Polish Home Army) leader, was arrested and Bor took over. He immediately put into action the first stage of his anti-German strategy, *Fly*: sabotage and the collection of intelligence. This was to be followed by *Tempest*: local revolts, diversionary guerrilla tactics; and ultimately by *Rising*: a general insurrection when Germany's defeat in Poland was imminent. On 1 August 1944 he gave the order for the *Rising* in Warsaw but unfortunately he had not liaised with the Red Army and did not know that they were about to halt their offensive short of the capital city. The AK and Communists fought together in a desperate battle but never had enough supplies or ammunition to make victory possible. On the first day the Poles seized control of three-quarters of Warsaw but the Germans brought in their special anti-partisan units led by Bach-Zelewski and captured the city street by street. The USSR only began to make air drops on the city in mid-September and by then it was too late. On 2 October Bor and his forces surrendered to the Germans and obtained POW status. Some 200,000 Poles had died in the fighting and the remaining 800,000 were evicted. Bor was interned in Colditz and the Polish government-in-exile appointed him Commander in Chief of Polish Armed Forces. Bor's aristocratic manners earned him respect but he did not have the qualities necessary to lead a partisan uprising.

**Bormann, Martin, 1900–1945?** A member of the same Freikorps as GOERING and HESS in 1918, Bormann was one of the first recruits to the infant Nazi Party and rose to become its *Reich-sleiter* (national organizer). After the defection of Hess to Britain in May 1941 he succeeded him as Head of the Party Chancery and in April 1943 was named Secretary to the Führer, in which capacity he turned himself into the watchdog at the Führer's door allowing entry only to those whom he wished the Führer to see. Functionaries as powerful as Goering were later to complain that it became virtually impossible to speak to HITLER without Bormann's assent, particularly if he suspected that they had news or opinions to voice which he did not wish Hitler to hear. At the same time he had policies of his own to put forward. His strategic and diplomatic viewpoint was as intransigent as his master's, and he is believed to have been the moving spirit behind some of the Führer's most mistaken decisions. At the very end of the war, however, he adopted a foreign policy of his own which he kept secret from Hitler, of seeking accommodation with the Soviets. This change of line is not so surprising if it is recognized that Bormann and the *apparatchiks* of the Kremlin had much in common. The policy nevertheless failed to come to fruition, but was kept secret from Hitler at whose side Bormann remained to the end. He made his escape from the *Führerbunker* on 1 May 1945 but was reported to have been killed in the streets outside. His body was never found, and reports still reach the newspapers that he is alive and well in South America.

**Bose, Subhas Chandra, 1897–1945** One of the most brilliant Indians of his generation and an inflexible opponent of British rule. Bose had become President of the leading nationalist organization, the Indian National Congress by 1938. When its other leaders decided in 1939 not to take the chance the outbreak of war offered to organize nationwide opposition to British rule, he resigned the Presidency and was arrested as a dissident. He escaped from India via

Afghanistan in 1941, made his way to Germany where he recruited some Indian POWs captured in the Western Desert by the Wehrmacht, and then traveled by U-Boat and Japanese submarine to Malaya in 1943. His idea was to organize the numerous body of Indians captured in Southeast Asia into an Indian National Army to fight alongside the Japanese in an invasion of India. He got together a force of three divisions, and in 1944 they took part in the Imphal-Kohima operation but understrength, badly-equipped and badly-treated by the Japanese who in practice treated them as hirelings rather than allies, they were ineffective. Many deserted as soon as they could to the British, who sensibly were not vindictive. Recognizing the collapse of his hopes, he tried in 1945 to take refuge in India, but was killed in an aircrash on the way there. To many Indians he remains a national hero. He was certainly the most striking and perhaps the most effective of the Southeast Asian nationalists to whom the war gave the chance to fight for freedom.

**Bracken, Brendan, 1901–1958** Bracken was a British politician who was very close to CHURCHILL. In 1940–41 he served as Churchill's parliamentary private secretary and was appointed Minister of Information in July 1941, a position he held until the end of the war. He was witty and vivid and did his job efficiently. In May 1945 he became First Lord of the Admiralty and was one of the prominent Conservative Party members to lose his seat in the 1945 election.

**Bradley, General Omar, 1893–1981** A protégé of EISENHOWER, who had been in the same class as he at West Point, Bradley's career was also linked with PATTON's. Bradley first rose to prominence when he took command of the II Corps, from Patton, in North Africa. He immediately showed his mettle, when troops under his command

stormed Bizerta on 7 May 1943 and took 40,000 prisoners. The II Corps then took part in operations in Sicily landing at Gela and Scogliti. Bradley's great contribution to the Allied victory was the part played in Operation Overlord. He was chosen by Eisenhower to command the US landings on D-Day, as Commander of the US 1st Army. After the landings, Patton arrived to take command of the new 3rd Army and Bradley became his superior, as Commander of the 12th Army Group. Although Bradley had served under Patton and was susceptible to his influence, this turned out to be a workable relationship, beneficial to both men. Bradley's great moment came during the German Ardennes Offensive, when his men were completely taken by surprise, but Bradley kept his head and was able to prevent a decisive breakthrough by the Germans. After breaking through the Siegfried Line, his troops crossed the Rhine at Remagen in March 1945, and in the following month met the Soviet troops on the Elbe. Bradley was a quiet and calm man, with a sound grasp of tactics, who inspired the confidence of his superiors and also of his men.

**Brauchitsch, Field Marshal Walter von, 1881–1948** HITLER appointed Brauchitsch Commander in Chief of the German Army after he had had Fritsch dismissed on a trumped up charge of impropriety. Brauchitsch was chosen because he was a more pliable person, who was susceptible to Hitler's powers of persuasion. He was also respected in the Army and refused to join a plot to have Hitler arrested if he took action against Czechoslovakia. Brauchitsch took part in the operational direction of the Polish Campaign but his Army High Command had no access to the higher direction of the war, except through the influence Brauchitsch could exert. At the time of the planning of the campaign in the west. Brauchitsch and HALDER tried

to persuade Hitler that logistical problems made his plan impracticable but
Hitler gave Brauchitsch a severe repri-
mand and refused to accept Brauchitsch's resignation. This effort was Brauchitsch's last attempt to stand up to
Hitler. During the Barbarossa Operation
Brauchitsch suffered a heart attack and
when Zhukov opened the Soviet counterattack outside Moscow, Brauchitsch was
in no fit state to respond. He offered his
resignation to Hitler within 36 hours
and this time it was accepted. Hitler
blamed him for this setback and called
him 'a vain, cowardly wretch.' Hitler
took over Brauchitsch's duties himself
and became the first civilian to command the German Army.

**Braun, Eva, 1912–1945** Eva Braun was
HITLER's mistress from 1932 until their
suicide. Hitler had had an ascetic image
of himself built up by Nazi propaganda
and the great demand that he made of
his mistress was that she remain discreet
and self-effacing. She met Hitler shortly
after the death of his beloved niece,
when Eva was working as an assistant
to Hoffmann, Hitler's staff photogra-
pher. Hitler soon installed her in his
house but very few people knew of her
existence and it was only towards the
end of the war that she was invited to
attend receptions – and then only because her sister had married General
Fegelein, HIMMLER's representative
with Hitler. She was very jealous of
Hitler and on two known occasions,
November 1932 and May 1935, attempted to commit suicide because of
other women, but during the war she
had no reason to get jealous because
although Hitler did not see much of her
he did not have enough time to see
other women. Braun came to Berlin to
be with Hitler during his last days and
as a sign of gratitude for her devotion
and loyalty to him he married her between 0100 and 0300 on 29 April. He
said she was 'the woman who after

many years of true friendship came of
her own free will to this city, already
almost besieged, to share my fate.' They
discussed suicide for some time and died
together on 30 April 1945.

**Braun, Wernher von, 1912–1977** Braun,
a trained rocket engineer, served as Minister of Agriculture in Papen's government. At the age of 25 (1937) he was
appointed Technical Director of the
German Army's Rocket Research Center
at Peenemünde on the Baltic. Within a
year he had produced a self-propelled
rocket, the A-4 (a prototype of the V-2),
which could carry an explosive warhead
eleven miles. Experimentation continued
but major development and production
of the rockets were hindered, however,
when HITLER chose to switch his priorities from rocket research to the Luftwaffe. It was not until 1943 that the V-2
rocket was given the full go-ahead. Vari-
ations were tested which could travel
more than 200 miles to target and mass
production began in earnest. The first
V-2 rocket was fired against Britain on
8 September 1944 and in the following
few months more than 3600 were 'deployed' to the UK and the Allied bases
in the Netherlands and Belgium. Although the range of these rockets was
more than adequate, they carried too
small a warhead to yield the results
Hitler had anticipated. Braun surrendered himself, his staff and research to
the Americans in 1945. His expertise
aided the US in its development of inter-
continental ballistic missiles and in its
space program.

**Brereton, Major General Lewis Hyde,
1890–1967** Brereton was a US flying
and fighting General who fought on
most fronts in World War II. First and
foremost an aviator, in 1941 when Japan
threatened war Brereton was appointed
Commander of the US Far East Air
Force under General MACARTHUR. Unfortunately he only had a limited

number of B-17s in the Philippines and the Japanese were able to destroy most of them on the ground. He was transferred to India and became Commander of the newly established US Middle East Air Force and had to build up supplies and supervise the training of inexperienced American pilots. In October 1942 he was sent to the Desert Front in command of the US 9th Air Force and made a valuable contribution to the end of the Tunisian campaign. In October 1943 he was transferred to the UK to build up the 9th into a formidable tactical air unit. His groups attacked the German transport network prior to Operation Overlord, attacking the bridges over the Seine, the Oise and the Meuse. In August 1944 he became the first Commander of the 1st Allied Airborne Army and took part in planning operations, co-ordinating airborne and troop carrier units. This was frustrating because after he had planned an airborne operation he found that it had to be canceled because ground troops had overrun the site of the drop. The biggest operation he was involved in was Operation Market Garden at Nijmegen, Eindhoven and Arnhem. The American landings were successful but the British landings were not. Arnhem turned into a nightmare of missed opportunities for the airborne troops. The German strength near Arnhem had been seriously underestimated.

**Brooke, Field Marshal Sir Alan, 1883–1963** Brooke was sent to France in May 1940 to command the British II Corps and carried out the evacuation from Dunkirk with great skill. At the end of 1941 he was appointed Chief of General Staff, replacing General DILL, at a particularly low point in the war for the British. Brooke was ideally suited to the job because he presented Churchill with a calm and competent exterior, keeping for his Diary his fears and frustrations. He recognized CHURCHILL's virtues as a war leader but was equally conscious of his faults, namely that Churchill could not see 'a whole strategical problem at once. His gaze always settles upon some part of the canvas and the rest of the picture is lost.' He had an excellent grasp of strategy and was able to turn many of Churchill's ideas into practical military operations. He maintained good relations with the US but was a little disappointed when he was not made Supreme Commander of Overlord. His diaries *The Turn of the Tide* and *Triumph in the West* are an invaluable source on the British conduct of the war.

**Brooke-Popham, Air Chief Marshal Sir Robert, 1878–1953** Brooke-Popham retired from active service in 1939 but was recalled to unify and oversee the command of GHQ Far East. A break-down in communications led the War Office in London to believe, incorrectly, that the defenses of Malaya were more than adequate. However the truth was that although many airfields had been built there were not enough aircraft to protect them. The Army had a contingency plan which involved fore-stalling a Japanese invasion by invading Siam – Operation Matador – which had it been successful would have prevented the collapse of Malaya's defenses. Brooke-Popham was all too aware of these weaknesses and made repeated demands to invade Siam, a neutral country, in November 1941 but the order came too late – the Japanese had already landed in Siam and land forces were caught on the hop. Putting into effect Operation Matador was no longer relevant. The Cabinet in London had already decided to replace Brooke-Popham and his replacement arrived in Singapore on 23 December 1941, too late to save the situation.

**Brossolette, Pierre, 1903–1944** Brossolette was a French resistance leader, closely associated with the Gaullists. He was a journalist of libertarian socialist views who came to England in April 1942. He was trained by the Special Operations Executive (SOE) and with Jean MOULIN and Wing Commander YEO-THOMAS went on a mission to set up a *Conseil National de la Résistance* in Paris in March 1943. Their mission was to give central direction to all anti-Nazi groups and during his stay in France, Brossolette remained under constant surveillance escaping arrest on many occasions. In February 1944 he tried to return to England by boat but he was shipwrecked and picked up by Germans. He did not have any papers and it took some time for the Gestapo to recognize him and transfer him to the Avenue Foch. There he tried to escape through a lavatory window and fell to his death, probably trying to make sure he would not talk under torture.

**Browning, Lieutenant General Frederick 'Boy,' 1896–1966** Browning was a British General who pioneered the use and training of airborne troops. From his experiences of parachuting and as a glider pilot he developed ideas on the use of advance airborne troops which were opposed by the Air Ministry. However by 1941 he had converted enough people close to CHURCHILL to his way of thinking and he was transferred from the Guards with orders to form a parachutist brigade. In April 1943 Browning was made Major General of Airborne Forces after having trained three parachutist brigades and a glider-borne brigade. The Parachute Regiment eventually totaled seventeen battalions and in 1942 was given its emblem, the red beret, from which the nickname the 'Red Devils' was derived. In September 1944 Browning was finally given a chance to test his troops; they were to participate in Operation Market Garden, an advance thurst to seize a bridgehead over the Rhine. Browning was BRERETON's deputy and responsible for ground opera-

tions. Browning was in command of the I Airborne Corps which was used to take the bridge at Arnhem. However the numbers of German troops in the area had been underestimated and the 1st Airborne Division lost touch with its headquarters and did not receive sufficient supplies. They fought bravely but were forced to withdraw. Out of 10,000 men dropped into the area only 3400 returned to Allied lines. Despite the failure of this particular operation the airborne troops had demonstrated that they could achieve spectacular gains in territory, provided the planning was thorough. Browning's men received much praise and Browning was recognized as a tough Commander. Towards the end of the war he was appointed MOUNTBATTEN's Chief of Staff in the Far East.

**Bruce, Stanley, 1883–1967** Bruce was the Australian High Commissioner in London from 1933–45. His shrewd financial mind and important contacts made him a useful man for the Australians to have in the UK. He served on various British War Cabinet Committees as the Australian representative.

**Buckmaster, Colonel Maurice, 1902–1992** Buckmaster was Chief of the French Section of the Special Operations Executive (SOE). He had been manager of the French company of Ford Motors before the war. He joined up with the Army after the outbreak of the war and became Information Officer of the French Section in March 1941. In September he became its head and his task was to set up from scratch an organization which would carry out sabotage, equip and train underground resistence armies and gather intelligence. The French Section was independent of the parallel organization of the Free French Gaullists, the BCRA. SOE eventually had about 100 circuits of subversive agents in France and armed thousands of resisters who harassed German divisions. It also sent about 400 trained agents into the field of whom about 100 did not return. Buckmaster took a personal interest in all his agents but was too worried about security ever to go to France himself. He was in many ways a controversial figure: many have questioned his judgment in sending Noor INAYAT Khan and Odette SANSOM into the field in the light of their indifferent training reports.

**Buckner, General Simon Bolivar, 1886–1945** Son of a Confederate general of the Civil War, born to his father in old age, Buckner commanded the American forces in the Aleutians for most of the war. He was eventually appointed to lead the 10th Army in the assault on Okinawa, the final stepping stone for an amphibious assault on the Japanese Home Islands themselves, and rapidly established a reputation as a dynamic and intelligent leader. He was killed in action on 18 June, almost at the very end of the battle which had cost the lives of 12,000 Americans and 110,000 Japanese.

**Budenny, Marshal Semyon, 1883– 1973** During World War II Budenny was Commander in Chief of the Russian Armies in the Ukraine and Bessarabia. He survived the Purges of 1937–38 thanks to his association with STALIN and VOROSHILOV, dating back to the Civil War. He had been a Tsarist cavalry officer but had held a series of staff appointments and had little experience of command in the field. As the Germans invaded in June 1941 the Soviet High Command fused the Southern and Southwestern groups and put Budenny in command. The Russian troops faced Field Marshal von RUNDSTEDT's Army Group South and although they had numerical superiority the Germans held the advantage in that they had the mobile Panzer Divisions of Generals

GUDERIAN and KLEIST and succeeded in driving a wedge between the two Soviet Armies. They cut off the two major troop concentrations at Kiev and Uman. Budenny could not respond to the speed of the German attacks and set into motion a series of piecemeal measures which could not alter the situation. He was removed from his command on 13 September in disgrace and was transferred to the Reserve Front. He never returned to active command but remained as Commander in Chief of the various Caucasian Fronts until January 1943 when he was made Commander of the Cavalry of the Soviet Army.

**Bulganin, Political Marshal Nikolay, 1895–1975** Bulganin was a Soviet leader whose task was to ensure that the Front Commanders did their duty. He served on the GKO (State Defense Committee) and from 1941–44 served on the Western Front, the 2nd Baltic Front and the 1st Belorussian Front. He was the political member of the War Councils on these Fronts and his job was to keep an eye on Soviet Army Commanders and make sure STALIN's orders were obeyed. He also investigated the failure of the defenses of Leningrad and Stalin's charges that Marshal ZHUKOV was giving orders without Stalin's knowledge. In 1944 he became Deputy People's Commissar of Defense and the Soviet representative to the Lublin Committee in Poland.

**Burke, Captain Arleigh, 1901–** Burke was a US Navy Commander, one of the most able destroyer commanders. In July 1940 he served in the Bureau of Ordnance; however, in May 1943 he was transferred to the Solomons and given command of Destroyer Squadron 23, the 'Little Beavers.' He was involved in 22 combat engagements and the speed with which he could engage the Japanese led Vice-Admiral HALSEY to dub him '31 Knot Burke.' He later served as Chief of Staff to Vice-Admiral MITSCHER at the Battle of the Philippine Sea and of Leyte Gulf. While he was on duty aboard the *Bunker Hill* off Okinawa, the ship was severely damaged. In July 1945 he returned to Washington to be head of the Research and Development Division of the Ordnance Bureau.

**Busch, Field Marshal Ernest, 1885–1945** Busch was one of HITLER's many Field Marshals whose main talent was his subservience to his master. He was Commander of the Sixteenth Army which would have taken part in Operation Sealion had it been implemented. He was then given command of Army Group Center on the Eastern Front from October 1943 to June 1944 but was replaced by MODEL shortly before the collapse and destruction of that Army Group in the Belorussian Campaign. Busch was then appointed Commander in Chief Northwest, stationed in Norway, where he remained until he surrendered with his troops in April 1945.

**Bush, Vannevar, 1890–1974** Bush was a distinguished American scientist. As the USA approached war, Bush put forward the policy that the USA should mobilize all scientific resources and he convinced ROOSEVELT to set up the Office of Scientific Research and Development (OSRD) on 28 June 1941 with himself as Director. Through his activities in promoting scientific research. Bush became involved in co-ordinating research into the atomic bomb. Two principles formed the bases of his policy: to

delegate supervision of specific research projects to others which left him free to give overall direction, and to keep research channeled into the war effort. He had to ensure smooth relations between civilians and Army personnel, and overcame his own objections to General GROVES' appointment as Head of the Manhattan Project. He was a gifted scientist and was President of the Carnegie Institute of Washington during the war.

**Byrnes, James, 1879–1972** Byrnes was an important behind-the-scenes operator in Washington throughout the war. A Supreme court judge, he directed the Selective Service and the Lend-Lease Acts through Congress. In 1942 he was made Director of War Mobilization and put into operation various schemes to keep the cost of living low: he froze salaries to a ceiling of $25,000 and cut down on horse-racing and civilian rail travel. He was a candidate for the Vice-Presidency in 1945 but was persuaded to stand down in favour of TRUMAN. After ROOSEVELT's third electoral victory Byrnes accompanied him to the Yalta Conference.

He resigned from office before Roosevelt's death but Truman convinced him to return to become Secretary of State and he assisted in drafting the Potsdam Declaration and at the London Conference proclaimed the United Nations Charter. He was a conservative and a hard-liner who was first to reject Japan's initial *conditional* offer to surrender in August 1945.

# C

**Callaghan, Rear Admiral Daniel, 1892–1942** Callaghan was a US Admiral who served in the South Pacific. In November 1942 he was sent with a force of heavy cruisers the *San Francisco* (his flagship) and the *Portland* and light cruisers the *Helena, Juneau* and *Atlanta*. The *San Francisco* did not have radar and had to rely on information passed on by the *Helena*. The only method of communicating was the TBS (Talk Between Ships) but there was so much interference on the system that many valuable messages were lost. The *Helena*'s radar spotted a Japanese force off Savo Island but the Americans lost their chance to fire their torpedoes first. The Japanese used their spotlights and immobilized the *Atlanta* with fire power. The action became very confused and the *San Francisco* hit the *Atlanta* mistaking it for an enemy vessel. The *San Francisco* came under fire from the *Kirishima* and her bridge was hit. Callaghan died immediately.

**Campbell, Major General John 'Jock,' 1894–1942** A Royal Artillery officer famed for his bravery, Campbell was commanding the 4th Regiment, Royal Horse Artillery in the Western Desert at the outbreak of war with Italy and quickly demonstrated a flair for handling his guns in a harassing role during the retreat which the British were obliged to make before the Italian advance. As a result he proposed the idea to his superiors that mobile or, as they soon came to be called, 'Jock' columns, should be formed, composed of infantry (in trucks), tanks and artillary which would hit the enemy wherever he would be found. His most successful enterprise along these lines was his handling of the Support Group of 7th Armored Division against an Italo-German force at Sidi Rezegh, 21–22 November 1941; for his success he was awarded the Victoria Cross. He had just been appointed Commander of 7th Armored Division (the famed 'Desert Rats') when he was killed in a car accident.

**Canaris, Admiral Wilhelm, 1888–1945** The son of an industrialist, Canaris was a U-Boat Commander in World War I. At the outbreak of World War II he was Head of the Abwehr, the Intelligence Department of the German Armed Forces High Command. Although pro-German in attitude, Canaris and other Abwehr officers loathed some of the practices of the Nazi regime, which in many ways rendered the Abwehr and its organization somewhat less effective than it might otherwise have been. His love for Germany did not allow Canaris to become *actively* involved in the military resistance to HITLER but the apparatus of the Abwehr was used to help order and spread the resistance. Canaris was arrested after the July Plot and was sent to Flossenberg concentration camp. The Abwehr was dissolved, its operations now under HIMMLER's direction. Canaris was executed at Flossenberg on 9 April 1945, weeks before the camp was liberated.

**Carlson, Brigadier Evans Fordyce, 1896–1947** Carlson served in China as a military observer for the US Army and military observer for the US Army and had marched with CHU TEH's Communist 8th Route Army before the outbreak of war. There he learned guerrilla tactics and when the Americans entered the war in 1941 he began to press for a US Marines' guerrilla band in the Pacific. He obtained permission, selected his men and appointed Captain 'Jimmy' Roosevelt, the President's son, to be the executive officer of his battalion. The Raiders' first mission was to collect intelligence on the island of Makin. Although they managed to drive the Japanese off the island the operation was very disorganized and Carlson had to leave men behind because he did not have sufficient landing craft. From November–December 1942 he led a 36-day march behind the enemy lines on Guadalcanal; they lost seventeen men and pushed the Japanese further inland. Carlson then returned to the USA for medical treatment and took part in further operations on Tarawa and Saipan but by now it was realized that these guerrilla operations could only succeed if the men were working alongside front-line troops. At Saipan he sustained further injuries while trying to rescue a wounded man and these injuries eventually led to his retirement and early death.

**Carol II, King of Rumania, 1893–1957** Carol II was the Hohenzollern King of Rumania before World War II. Although of German extraction he favoured alliance with Britain and France and on 13 April 1938 he received a guarantee that Rumania's border would be defended by them. Three months later he proclaimed himself a dictator. Rumania faced increasing pressure from the USSR and Germany after the fall of Poland. Germany's invasion of France led Carol to declare himself in favor of the Axis and in June 1940 HITLER forced Carol to cede Bessarabia and northern Bukhovina to the USSR in order to keep the USSR out of the war. In August he handed over Transylvania to Hungary and in September southern Dobruja to Bulgaria. These losses were very unpopular and on 5 September 1941, in view of his considerable unpopularity, Carol abdicated in favour of his son Michael and went into exile.

**Carré, Mathilde 'The Cat,' 1910–** Carré was a double, probably triple, agent in World War II. She had worked as a nurse when war broke out and had met Major Roman Czerniawski who recruited her to the *Interallié* network. This was the first intelligence network to be set up in France and Carré picked up her information from conversations with German officers. Her messages to London usually began with the words 'The Cat reports ...' BLEICHER who had begun to break up the *Interallié* network arrested her on 17 November 1941 and threatened her with torture. He extracted from her all the names of her contacts which led to many arrests, and persuaded her to work for the Germans using an old codename 'Victoire.' Pierre de Vomécourt was one of her contacts and he began to suspect her. He confronted her and she confessed and played another double role. The situation became too difficult and she persuaded Bleicher to allow her to go to London where she said she could give him information on the inner workings of the Special Operations Executive. She went to London in February 1942 where she was interrogated about Abwehr techniques. It was decided to take her out of circulation and she was detained in Holloway Prison. After the war she was deported to France, tried, sentenced to death, and reprieved. In September 1954 she released and published her account in '*J'ai été la Chatte* . . .'

**Carton de Wiart, General Sir Adrian, 1880–1963** A winner of the Victoria Cross in World War I in which he was nine times wounded and lost a hand and an eye, Carton de Wiart was one of the most striking figures in the British Army. He is alleged to have provided the model for the flamboyant Ritchie-Hook in Evelyn Waugh's famous war novel, *Men At Arms*. He commanded the Central Norwegian Expeditionary Force in 1940, was taken prisoner in the Western Desert in 1941, was repatriated in 1943 for medical reasons and employed for the rest of the war as special representative to CHIANG Kai-shek by Winston CHURCHILL of whom he was a special favorite.

**Casey, Richard, 1890–1976** Casey was an Australian politician who served as the British government's chief adviser in the Middle East. In November 1939 he went to London as the Australian government's representative and in the following year was sent to Washington. He made such a good impression on the British that they made him Minister of State in the Middle East at Cairo. He chaired the Middle East Defense Committee which dealt with political, economic and propaganda problems and it fell to him to announce to the US and British governments that Tobruk had fallen. After the end of the campaign in North Africa Casey became involved in the Arab-Jewish question and tried to act as a mediator between French and anti-French factions in the Lebanon. In 1944 he was made Governor of Bengal.

**Catroux, General Georges, 1877–1969** Catroux was DE GAULLE's right-hand man and the Delegate General of the Free French to Syria and Lebanon from 1941–43. In October 1940 he arrived in the Middle East to build up a propaganda campaign for the Free French. The French in Syria favored the Vichy regime and were unmoved by this so when the British invaded in June 1941 they fought the Free French forces. Catroux tried to retrieve the situation and proclaimed 'I come to put an end to the mandatory regime and proclaim you free and independent.' The Free French took over the administration of Syria and Lebanon after bitter fighting but the countries only became independent after the war. From 1943–45 he acted as Commissioner for Moslem Affairs of the FCNL (French Committee of National Liberation) and Governor of Algeria. After the war he became French Ambassador to the USSR.

**Cavallero, Marshal Ugo, 1880–1943** Cavallero was the Italian Chief of General Staff who succeeded BADOGLIO after Italy's disastrous campaign in Greece. He was a man of considerable energy and drive and made every attempt to try to modernize the Italian Army. He was a great admirer of German efficiency and as such was distrusted by his colleagues who felt he was pro-German and only in power thanks to German support. He did improve Italy's conduct of the war and forced the navy to co-operate by sending supplies to Libya. However he was at the mercy of MUSSOLINI's whims and knew he would fall when the war turned against Italy. CIANO detested Cavallero and De Bono said of him 'Cavallero is optimistic. That's the only reason the Duce prefers him' so neither were displeased when Mussolini dismissed him in January 1943 after the fall of Tripoli. He was interned for a while but tried to make a comeback when Mussolini fell and found that he was not trusted by either the Fascists or their opponents. He was found dead on a garden bench in the early morning of 14 September 1943.

## Chamberlain, Prime Minister Neville,
1869–1940 Chamberlain, a member of one of the leading Conservative Party families, became Prime Minister of Great Britain in May 1937. Although his experience had been in home affairs, he made the direction of foreign policy his principal concern. The line he adopted in his dealings with dictators quickly attracted the description of 'appeasement' but the term did not at the time carry any suggestion of the disreputable; Chamberlain himself regarded it as an accurate expression of his desire to preserve peace. His opponents were later, somewhat unfairly, to accuse him of desiring to do so at any price. Though prepared in 1938 to sacrifice the national territory of Czechoslovakia – 'a far-off country of which we know little' – he regarded that capitulation as unavoidable in Britain's current state of military unreadiness, which he was simultaneously working to change, through a program of rapid rearmament. By 1939 he had accepted that Germany's territorial ambitions could no longer be tolerated by the Western powers and, with France, issued guarantees of protection to Poland. When Germany attacked Poland in September 1939 he stood by those guarantees and, if with the heaviest of hearts, brought Britain into the war against HITLER. His credibility as a war leader had been hopelessly compromised, however, by his appeasement policies and his position was further undermined by the defeat of the British Expeditionary Force to Norway in April 1940. Criticism of his leadership was publicly and widely expressed in the House of Commons in May, notably by Leo AMERY, and on 10 May he surren-

dered the premiership to Winston CHURCHILL. He remained a member of the War Cabinet but was broken by his humiliation and the failure of his honest search for peace, and died in November 1940. His reputation, though now assessed more charitably, never recovered.

## Chennault, Major General Claire Lee,
1890–1958 In 1937 Chennault had retired from the USAAF because of faulty hearing and had left for China to become an adviser on aviation and the supervisor of a training program. In November 1940 he returned to Washington to recruit pilots and was able to get 100 veteran Army, Navy and Marine corps fliers to join him and a further 100 engineers to maintain equipment. The unit, nicknamed the Flying Tigers, was operational in 1941 and in the skies over Burma destroyed nearly 300 Japanese aircraft in six months' fighting. In April 1942 he was called to active duty in the US Army and became leader of the 14th US (Voluntary) Army Air Force in China. In May 1943 at the Washington Conference Chennault came into conflict with General STILWELL, CHIANG Kai-shek's Chief of Staff, over the distribution of resources and over strategy. Chennault wanted to build up the Air Force and, having secured a larger share of material and supplies than Stilwell, launched an attempt to drive the Japanese back. This was accomplished too successfully by July 1943 and the Japanese launched a counteroffensive, Ichi-Go, to reconquer the lost territory. In July 1945 Chennault resigned in disagreement over the decision to disband the Chinese-American joint wing of the Chinese Air Force. Chennault was a rough man, who was nicknamed 'old leather-face' because of the burn marks on his face received during the days of open cockpits.

**Chernyakhovsky, General Ivan, 1906–1945** Chernyakhovsky was the youngest High Commander of the Soviet Army. He was one of the few Jews to serve in the Army and owed much to ZHUKOV's early recognition of his talents. As Commander in Chief of the 60th Army he recaptured Voronezh on January 1943 and then recaptured Kursk. He was given command of the 3rd Belorussian Front and in the Belorussian Offensive led the right pincer against Minsk and attacked the Third Panzer Army near Vitebsk. His armies then swept over Latvia and took Vilnyus (13 July 1944) and Kaunas on the east Prussian border. After a break in action he renewed the offensive against Königsberg and broke through heavy German defenses. He was killed, however, in action near Mehlsack in February 1945 when he was hit by a shell fragment in close fighting.

**Cherwell, Lord, 1886–1957** Cherwell solved the problem of aircraft spin in World War I when he applied his theory in solo flight. Born Frederick Alexander Lindemann, Lord Cherwell was a close personal friend of CHURCHILL and became known as 'The Prof' because of his training as a physicist. Taken from his professorial position at Oxford University to become a member of Churchill's War Cabinet (Paymaster-General from 1942–45), Cherwell played an influential part in the direction of the war, one of the first scientists to do so. A strong-willed man whose opinions brooked no argument, Cherwell favored strategic bombing and insisted that all RAF strategy should be directed to that end, even at the expense of other war efforts. His judgment and opinions were often faulty but were proclaimed with such vigor that they were often upheld, even if incorrect. After the war he returned to his chair at Oxford University.

**Cheshire, Group Captain Leonard, 1917–1992** Cheshire learned to fly as a member of the Volunteer Reserve Air Squadron at Oxford University where his father was Vinerian Professor of geometry. Although inexperienced in the service, on joining the Royal Air Force he quickly demonstrated that he was a leader of outstanding flair and intelligence and, as Commander of 617 (Pathfinder) Squadron, established new standards of accuracy in the marking of targets in Germany for the massed bomber fleets of the RAF to strike. He was sent to the Far East at the end of 1944 and on 9 August 1945 was present in the camera plane at the atomic bombing of Nagasaki as official British observer. After the war he left the Air Force and began to work for the relief of suffering. The Cheshire Homes for the Disabled is now one of the most important private charities in Britain.

**Chiang Kai-shek, Generalissimo, 1887–1975** Chiang Kai-shek was the leader of the Kuomintang and Head of State of nationalist China. His country was invaded by the Japanese in 1937 and Chiang moved his headquarters to Hankow and then further inland to Chungking. Although ROOSEVELT wished to aid the Chinese in their war with the Japanese, he was bound by various laws which prevented him from helping warring states unless they could pay for goods supplied. To circumvent this law, Roosevelt did not recognize that a state of war existed in China, and sent supplies to China. Chiang's main problem in fighting the Japanese was that his own control of the Chinese central government was tenuous. He had been involved in fighting the Chinese Communists prior to the Japanese invasion and his own army's loyalty was in doubt: commands were divided into war areas and the local Commanders could be bought off by the Japanese. Chiang was constantly suspicious of his own Commanders and tried unsuccessfully to direct operations from Chungking, which was too remote.

Chiang's first direct involvement in the series of wars known as World War II, was in the Japanese invasion of Burma in 1942. Chiang appointed STIL-WELL, his US Chief of Staff, as Commander of the two Chinese armies which he sent to Burma. Stilwell was treated like all Chiang's subordinates and bypassed over crucial decisions. The antagonism between Chiang and Stilwell dates from this time because Stilwell could not direct operations effectively in Burma and because Chiang felt let down over the 'volume' of US aid. Chiang decided to back CHENNAULT and accepted the latter's view that air power would win the war in China. By maintaining a constant flow of demands for aircraft and supplies, Chiang eventually received Allied agreement to an air offensive in China in 1943. However the strategy did not succeed because it provoked, as Stilwell had pointed out, a counterattack by the Japanese, who overran the US 14th Air Force's bases in east China. After this disaster the US Joint Chiefs wanted Stilwell appointed Commander of all Chinese troops because he had achieved success in his campaign in northern Burma. However Chiang askad for Stilwell's dismissal.

Chiang's main concern was political survival and his Nationalist Armies did not have the strength to fight the Japanese armies in an all-out offensive. The most they could achieve was to keep Japanese troops tied up in China away from the battlefields of the Pacific. For this purpose, Chiang received massive Lend-Lease aid from the USA, aid which did not get used in the fight against the Japanese but in the fight against the Communists. Although Chiang was recognized by the Western powers as the Head of State in China in 1945, his power was declining and soon after World War II ended, civil war in China started again.

**Chiang Kai-shek, Mme, 1898–** Chiang Kai-shek's wife was a well-educated woman who had been brought up with Western ideas. She helped to interpret the West for Chiang and was responsible for setting up the Flying School with Major General CHENNAULT in the mid-1930s. She kept up a constant barrage of requests for war materials and on WILLKIE's suggestion visited the USA in 1943 to publicize China's contribution to World War II. She attended the Cairo Conference with her husband and created an impression on all those attending, in some cases unfavorable. General BROOKE said of her, she was 'a queer character in which sex and politics seemed to predominate, both being used to achieve her ends.'

**Chifley, Joseph Ben, 1885–1951** Chifley became Australian Prime Minister on CURTIN's death in the last months of the war. During the war he had been Treasurer and had set about introducing uniform taxation laws which prevented states from levying income tax and he also implemented a scheme of national insurance. He became acting Prime Minister on 30 April 1945 and Prime Minister in July 1945 and vigorously put into effect welfare reform and the nationalization aims of the Australian Labor Party. In the last months the main problems facing Australia were the British Empire's collapse and Asian nationalism.

**Chou En-Lai, 1898–1976** Chou was converted to Communism during his years as a student in France (1920–4) and on his return worked in a clandestine role as an instructor at the Kuomintang's

Whampoa Military Academy, of which CHIANG Kai-shek was Commandant. He later went underground, was arrested and on his release journeyed to Russia, but returned for the Long March. MAO Tse-tung sent him as communist 'ambassador' to Chiang Kai-shek during the war with Japan, 1937–45, then he maintained excellent relations with the Kuomintang government and with allied representatives at its headquarters. He became Prime Minister of China after the communist victory in the Civil War.

**Chuikov, General Vasili, 1900–1982** A Red Army volunteer in 1918, he served against Kolchak and in the Russo-Polish War of 1920, attended the Frunze Academy, acted as military adviser to CHIANG Kai-shek between 1926 and 1937, served at the Ministry of War in 1941–2, and in 1942 was appointed Commander of the 62nd Army in the defense of Stalingrad. His army held the foothold on the right bank of the Volga throughout the German siege and was the mainstay of the defense. Redesignated the 8th Guards Army, it remained under his command until the end of the war and took part in the Battle of Berlin. In postwar years he commanded the occupation forces in the Russian zone and was later Deputy Minister of Defense. His account of the Battle of Stalingrad, *The Beginning of the Road*, is a masterpiece of military literature and the most interesting war memoir published by any Soviet General.

**Churchill, Peter 'Michel,' 1909–1972** Churchill was an early agent of the Special Operations Executive's French Section. He was a colorful figure who acted fearlessly. He had travelled in Western Europe before the war and in January 1942 went on his first mission. He was landed by submarine at Miramar

with money and instructions for Resistance groups to make a brief reconnaissance of the *Carte* circuit. On his return he wrote a vivid account of his mission. In August 1942 he went on a third mission to Montpellier where he was to organize and co-ordinate supplies for Resistance groups. He was joined by Odette SANSOM in November but the military importance of their work has been exaggerated. He ran into trouble because he did not treat his contacts with sufficient tact and many resisters felt he enjoyed too flamboyant a lifestyle. The Germans began to infiltrate his networks. His main network, *Spindle*, had to transfer to Annecy. Churchill returned to London in February 1943 but returned on 15 April 1943. He parachuted into a trap and was captured the next day by BLEICHER. He spent the rest of the war in concentration camps and was liberated at the end of the war.

**Churchill, Prime Minister Winston Spencer, 1874–1965** 'What is our policy? I will say it is to wage war by land, sea and air with all our might and with all the strength that God can give us ... Victory at all costs. Victory in spite of all terror, Victory however long and hard the road may be.'

In September 1939 Winston Churchill held the post of First Lord of the Admiralty (the same post he had held in World War I) in the Conservative government of Neville CHAMBERLAIN. After the disastrous Norwegian Campaign, for which the country and parliament blamed Chamberlain, Churchill succeeded Chamberlain as Prime Minister and formed a National Government and became Minister of Defense on 11 May 1940. Churchill's contributions to World War II and the Allied cause are numerous in the extreme. A strong leader, dedicated to Britain and to total victory over the Germans, he banished any thought of surrender.

The mutual friendship between Churchill and the President of the United States, ROOSEVELT, which had developed before the start of World War II, led to the sharing and trading of war supplies and personnel even before the US officially joined the war. The Lend-Lease Act of March 1941 allowed the UK to order and 'borrow' war goods on credit – ownership remained nominally in American hands. Everyday communications between Roosevelt and Churchill were carried out by telephone and by letter but the decisions on war strategy were made at a series of international conferences with or without the presence of other leaders such as STALIN or CHIANG Kai-shek. The first conference attended by Churchill and Roosevelt was at Argentia Bay in August 1941 where the Atlantic Charter was signed. The Washington Conference in December of that year established the 'Germany First' policy. The two leaders were able to weather many disagreements on strategy, which arose from the conflicting advice of their advisers. The US was naturally suspicious about Churchill's constant postponements of Overlord in favor of intervention in the Mediterranean and the Balkans. However the US agreed to the Torch landings and then the invasions of Sicily and Italy but once Overlord was under way it received top priority. Roosevelt and Churchill also did not see eye to eye over how to deal with Stalin. Churchill's anti-Communism led him to treat Stalin with great suspicion but Roosevelt felt that he understood Stalin and could reach an understanding with him over eastern Europe. History has vindicated Churchill's view and shown him to have been the wiser. Churchill's negotiations with Stalin at Yalta in February 1945 show that he realistically expected Stalin to take over eastern Europe and

so Churchill tried to retain a British interest in Yugoslavia in more than name.

Churchill, was above all a politician and his gifts as a military commander have been called into question. He made errors of judgment – often seeking the advice of inspired amateurs such as CHERWELL and WINGATE – much to the dismay of his military advisers, such as BROOKE. Churchill would sometimes lose sight of his main strategic priorities; for example, the decision to help the Greeks in April 1941 came too late to save Greece and it greatly weakened the British presence in Egypt. Churchill was obsessed with defeating ROMMEL and in consequence, he treated his Desert Commanders badly, sending WAVELL and AUCHINLECK to India.

Churchill's personality and dynamism helped him maintain successful relations with parliament and the country. He survived two votes of no confidence which were overwhelmingly defeated in parliament. He kept the morale of the country up by broadcasting to the people on significant occasions. One such memorable occasion was on 22 June 1941 after the German invasion of the USSR, when Churchill pledged British support to the Soviets. Had Churchill died on one of his many trips abroad, British morale would have been greatly damaged. However, after the war, the British people who had admired and depended on him, rejected his leadership in the General Election of July 1945. Although often viewed as an ungrateful choice, the decision to allow ATTLEE to assume leadership should not be considered as such. The people of Britain regarded Churchill as a *War* Prime Minister but thought that someone else should help with the reconstruction of a war-torn Britain. Churchill will undoubtedly remain the principal British hero of the twentieth century.

**Chu Teh, General, 1886–1976** Chu Teh was the Commander in Chief of the Chinese Communist troops in northwest China. He had been one of the military leaders of the Long March and had continued to fight CHIANG Kai-shek until 1937 when the Communists and the Kuomintang had decided to join together in fighting China's enemy, the Japanese. Chu Teh's first significant success against the Japanese was on 25 September 1937 at the battle of P'ingsinkuan when he ambushed the Japanese 5th Division. However the Communists mainly fought using guerrilla tactics as they had very little conventional, modern equipment. Chu Teh, therefore, confined himself to political planning. In July 1946 the Communist Army he had created became the People's Army and full-scale civil war broke out shortly after.

**Ciano, Count Galeazzo, 1903–1944** A career diplomat, Ciano's marriage to Edda Mussolini, daughter of the dictator, procured his rapid promotion to Foreign Minister in 1936. In that capacity he signed the 'Pact of Steel' with Germany in May 1939. He was rightly fearful, however, of the consequences for Italy of going to war, gradually fell out with his father-in-law and resigned from the Foreign Ministry in February 1943. He remained a member of the Fascist Grand Council and in that capacity voted for MUSSOLINI's removal on July 25. In August he was tricked by the Germans into putting himself in their hands, was imprisoned and executed, with Mussolini's acquiescence.

**Clark, Admiral Joseph, 1893–1971** Clark rose through the ranks to become one of the Navy Commanders of the US 7th Fleet. At the Battle of the Philippine Sea he was in command of the Task Group containing the new carriers *Hornet* and *Yorktown*. The Group was sent to Iwo Jima and Chichi Jima to shell the islands and neutralize them. After the battle Clark was critical of SPRUANCE's policy of holding back the air arm and of his failure to attack OZAWA's carriers earlier.

**Clark, General Mark, 1896–1984** Clark was EISENHOWER's Deputy during Operation Torch and hit the headlines in October 1942 when he made a secret trip to North Africa. He negotiated with Admiral DARLAN who agreed to repudiate the Vichy regime and ordered all French forces in Northwest Africa to cease their resistance. Clark, in return, placed Darlan under protective custody and recognized Darlan as the French 'Head of State' which caused an out-cry from the British. However this potentially embarrassing commital was ended when Darlan was assassinated shortly afterwards.

In January 1943 Clark was appointed Commanding General of the 5th Army and prepared for the invasion of Italy. On 9 September 1943 the invasion of western Italy began at Salerno. The troops established a bridgehead and managed to take Naples. The terrain in Italy considerably hampered Allied mobility and the 5th Army was held up at Monte Cassino. His troops took part in the Anzio Landings (January 1944) but this did not succeed in cutting off communications from Cassino to Rome. The British 8th Army reached the American positions and joined in the attempts to break through the Gustav Line. The stalemate continued for three months and Clark asked for permission to bomb the monastery at Cassino; however this did not help the Allies as the rubble was easier to defend. Finally British, American, Polish and French troops defeated the Germans at Cassino in very bitter fighting in May and on 4 June Clark's 5th Army entered Rome.

Clark's decision to go straight for Rome gave the Germans a chance to escape north and regroup. The main Allied advance on Germany was through France and resources for the Italian Front were now diverted to the Anvil/ Dragoon Landings in the south of France. The 5th Army continued its advance but was stopped short of Bologna in October. In December Clark was elevated to command the 15th Army Group in the Mediterranean under ALEXANDER who then became Supreme Allied Commander in the Mediterranean Theater. In the last months of the war Clark achieved a decisive victory and in April 1945 he received the surrender of 230,000 German and enemy troops in Italy, the Tyrol and Salzburg. After the war Clark became Commander of the US Occupation Force in Austria.

Clark had a tremendous flair for public relations and was a well-known figure but he was also a skilled and popular Commander. His nickname was Eagle in Allied High Command parlance.

**Clay, General Lucius, 1897–1977** A military engineer who had worked on dam construction in the United States before the war, Clay acted as manager of the US Army procurement program from 1942, then as a Base Commander in Normandy, then as Deputy Director of the Office of War Mobilization until April 1945 when he moved to Germany as Deputy to EISENHOWER for the military government of Germany. He quickly became convinced that the United States must work to restore civilian government in the occupied zones, and was a major architect of the postwar Federal Government.

**Cockcroft, Sir John, 1897–1967** Cock-croft was a British nuclear physicist who played an important part in directing the use of radar against aerial attack. He had become famous in 1932 when he had collaborated with Ernest Walton to produce an atom-smasher. In 1939 he was appointed Assistant Director of Research, Ministry of Supply and from 1941–44 was Chief Superintendent of Air Defense Research and Development. In 1944 he was appointed Director of the Atomic Energy Division of the National Research Council of Canada.

**Collins, Lieutenant General 'Lightnin' Joe' Lawton, 1896–1963** A leader of consequence, Collins, in December 1942, led the 25th Infantry Division in Guadalcanal, relieving the 1st Marine Division, and he cleared the island of Japanese. In January 1943 he led part of the XIV Corps in driving the Japanese off New Georgia.

In December 1943 he went to England to take command of the VII Corps and landed at Utah beach in Normandy. He drove his men hard to keep the enemy on the defensive. His energy earned him the name 'GIs General' and by exerting constant pressure his troops took Cherbourg on 24 June. His troops closed the Falaise Gap, crossed the Seine and drove north into Belgium and took Mons, Namur and Liège. Collins participated in the counterattack and capture of Houffalize during the Battle of the Bulge and crossed the Rhine at Remagen. His troops drove through Germany, enveloped the Ruhr and met the Soviet XXXVI Corps on the Elbe.

**Coningham, Air Marshal Sir Arthur, 1895–1948** Coningham was an extremely hard-working and efficient air Commander. He first saw action in World War I as a Commander of New Zealand troops, where he gained the nickname 'Maori.' He then became a flyer and during the interwar period became an expert on long-range flying. In 1939 he was in command of No 4 Group of long-range bombers, based in Yorkshire. He then spent several years in the Desert Campaign, eventually becoming Commander of the Western Desert Air Force and conducting many joint air-ground operations in conjunction with MONTGOMERY's 8th Army. He was then given command of the British and US Air Forces in Tunisia and during 1943 his forces took part in raids and operations in Pantelleria and Sicily. He later commanded the 2nd Tactical Air Force (British and Canadian), which took part in the campaign in Normandy July 1944 and other operations in northwest Europe until the end of the war.

**Cooper, Alfred Duff, 1890–1954** Cooper was a British minister who worked for Anglo-French understanding during the war. Cooper had been First Lord of the Admiralty from 1937–38 but had resigned in a disagreement over CHAMBERLAIN's Munich policy. In the back benches Cooper joined the CHURCHILL-EDEN group in their criticism of Chamberlain's government. When Churchill became Prime Minister Cooper became Minister of Information but was unpopular and uncomfortable in this post. To cite but one example, his security-tightening measures during the period were dubbed 'Cooper's Snoopers' by the press. He was appointed Chancellor of the Duchy of Lancaster and in August 1941 was sent to Singapore to examine British defense measures. After Pearl Harbor he was appointed resident Cabinet Minister in the Far East. He returned and in October 1942 became British representative on the French Committee of Liberation. He had a good relationship with the French and worked hard for a treaty of alliance between the UK and France.

**Crace, Rear Admiral Sir John, 1887–1968** Crace was a British Admiral who commanded a squadron of Australian cruisers at the Battle of Coral Sea in May 1942. He had been sent to Port Moresby to intercept the Japanese invasion force. His squadron had no air cover and was attacked by Japanese land-based aircraft but by skillful maneuvering, Crace's ships escaped. He retired shortly afterwards and became superintendant of His Majesty's Dockyards at Chatham.

**Creasy, Admiral George, 1895–1972** Creasy was a British Admiral in charge of naval planning for the Allied invasion of northwest Europe. He had held several staff posts and active commands; for example, in 1942 he had commanded the HMS *Duke of York*. He was then promoted to Chief of Staff to Allied Naval Commander in Chief, Sir Bertram RAMSAY of COSSAC, and took part in the detailed naval planning preceding D-Day

**Crerar, General Henry, 1888–1965** In July 1940 Crerar was sent by the Canadian government to London as Chief of General Staff to plan training programs for Canadian troops. He worked seven days a week to set up the programs but in November 1941 resigned his post and took a lower command in order to see action in the field. He led the I Canadian Corps in Sicily where his troops distinguished themselves at Catania. In 1943 he was recalled to Britain to take command of the 1st Canadian Army, which in fact consisted of Poles, Belgians, Dutch and British units. The army landed near the mouth of the Orne river and was employed to 'break in' to

Falaise in August 1944. The troops succeeded and then were used to assault the Channel fortresses of Le Havre, Boulogne, Calais and the mouth of the Scheldt. Crerar decided to take each in turn and by 1 October had reached his objective and taken 72,000 prisoners. After clearing the Scheldt and Antwerp his troops moved on to the offensive, southeast of Nijmegen. On 27 February 1944 the army stormed Udem and broke through the last and weakest defenses of the Siegfried Line. Crerar came under MONTGOMERY's command. He was given a free rein by Montgomery who had faith in him and wanted to please the Canadian government.

**Cripps, Sir (Richard) Stafford, 1889–1952** A nephew of Beatrice Webb and son of one of the first Labour Party peers, Cripps followed his father into Labour political life which he combined with an immensely successful legal career. Refusing to follow Ramsay Macdonald whom he served as Solicitor-General, into coalition in 1931, he became associated with Labour's left wing. Strongly pacifist in the early 1930s, he became a leading opponent of appeasement, adopted a 'Popular Front' position and was expelled from the Labour Party in 1939. The coalition government nevertheless made extensive use of his services, first in 1940 as Ambassador to Moscow where it was believed his left-wing views would give him greater influence than a career diplomat could command, then in 1942 as emissary to Indian nationalists whom he tried to win to a policy of wartime co-operation with an offer of postwar independence, and finally in November 1942 as Minister of aircraft production. Though CHURCHILL, like many others, found his coldness and self-possession deeply antipathetic, he readily recognized his

remarkable intellectual and administrative qualities.

**Crutchley, Rear Admiral Victor, 1893–1986** Crutchley was the British Admiral who succeeded CRACE in command of a cruiser squadron based at Brisbane and was second in command to Rear Admiral TURNER at the invasion of Guadalcanal in August 1942. On the night of 6 August the invasion force came under attack from Vice-Admiral MIKAWA's cruisers and was caught unprepared in the Battle of Savo Island. The Allies lost four cruisers and Crutchley was bitterly attacked by the US press for negligence. He continued to serve with US forces and patrolled the waters off New Guinea and took part in all of MACARTHUR's amphibious operations.

**Cunningham, General Alan, 1887–1983** Cunningham was the younger brother of Admiral CUNNINGHAM, who led the forces that liberated Ethiopia from Italian occupation. In December 1940 the offensive opened and Cunningham and his troops marched into Italian Somaliland and began the long march for Addis Ababa. Displaying great skills of leadership and exploiting his forces' mobility to the full, Cunningham entered the capital of Ethiopia in triumph on 6 April 1941 and a month later the Emperor, HAILE SELASSIE, returned to the throne.

In August 1941 Cunningham left for the Western Desert to take command of the new 8th Army. He had some 630 tanks at his disposal and he immediately set about preparing for AUCHINLECK's Crusader Operation, which would lead to the relief of Tobruk. However ROMMEL was prepared for the British offensive and Cunningham failed to press the attack through, concentrating more on defense. Auchinleck lost confidence in him and he was replaced on 26

November 1941 by a younger man, RITCHIE. Cunningham spent the rest of the war in administrative posts – as Commandant of the staff college at Camberley, then as General Officer Commanding, Northern Ireland until 1944 and finally in the same post in East Africa until after the end of the war.

**Cunningham, Admiral Sir Andrew, 1883–1963** An outstanding naval Commander, in 1939 Cunningham was the Acting Commander in Chief of the Mediterranean Fleet. His main task was to harass the Italian Fleet and after the fall of Greece, insure that supplies got through to Malta. He was a man of action and immediately set out to establish British naval supremacy. One important move was establish good relations with Vice-Admiral Godfroy's French squadron at Alexandria and they had a sufficiently good working relationship that Godfroy agreed to disarm his ships peacefully after the fall of France and an unpleasant incident, such as the action at Mers-el-Kebir, was avoided. Since the Italian Fleet was reluctant to leave its harbor, Cunningham decided to attack it at Taranto and sent a squadron of Swordfish to bomb Italian battleships. On 11 November 1940 the battleships *Littorio, Conte di Cavour*, and *Duilio* were put out of commission and the Italian Fleet was never to regain the initiative in the Mediterranean. Cunningham followed this up by engaging the Italians in the Battle of Cape Matapan in March 1941 where he was able to sink the heavy cruiser, *Pola*. Cunningham was then involved in the naval actions off Crete, where despite the lack of air cover, he risked his fleet to prevent German reinforcements reaching the island. The British lost Crete and Cunningham lost three cruisers and six destroyers: this coincided with a difficult situation in North Africa and the siege

of Malta. British naval power was stretched to its limits. Cunningham was then sent to Washington to attend Chiefs of Staff planning meetings and was then appointed Eisenhower's Deputy for the Torch landings. He was also naval Commander for the landings in Sicily but after the death of Admiral POUND in October 1943, he was recalled to London and was appointed First Sea Lord. He continued to advise CHURCHILL on naval strategy but his main talent had been as a fighting Admiral.

**Cunningham, Group Captain John, 1917–** 'Cats' Eyes' Cunningham was one of the most determined and famous RAF night-fighter pilots. At the time when nightfighters had no technical gadgets to aid them, Cunningham went out night after night in the first eight months of 1940 and succeeded in shooting down twelve German aircraft.

**Curtin, Prime Minister John, 1885–1945** Curtin was Prime Minister of Australia from 1941 until shortly before the end of the war. As leader of the Australian Labor Party he had opposed conscription in the early days of the war and had resisted offers to join in a National government. In 1941 he brought down the Fadden government and came to power with a majority of one. He immediately found that he had to increase conscription because Australia declared war on Japan after Pearl Harbor. From this point he set about re-orienting Australia's foreign policy and became a firm advocate of partnership with the USA. He had difficult relations with CHURCHILL and had rows over Britain's lack of naval support in the Far East. Curtin was a firm advocate of Air Force power and gave MACARTHUR his full support. In 1942 while Australia feared a Japanese invasion Curtin became his own Minister of Defense but as the threat receded he relinquished this post and took greater interest in diplomacy and the postwar situation. He was a popular figure and led the Labor Party to electoral victory in 1943. He became ill in November 1944 and died in July 1945. His Deputy, CHIFLEY, became acting Prime Minister in April 1945 and full Prime Minister in July.

# D

**Daladier, Prime Minister Edouard, 1884–1970** Daladier came to power in France as a leader of the Radical Socialists when the Popular Front began to disintegrate. He was supposed to be acceptable to all parties but after he signed the Munich Agreement in September 1938, he lost the support of the Socialists and had to rely on the right wing. After the German invasion of Poland Daladier made a broadcast on 1 October 1939 in which he spoke of France's intention to fight Germany. His government also prepared to help the Finns in October 1939. The French people lost confidence in Daladier because of his indecisiveness as witnessed by the fact that French volunteers arrived in Finland too late to be of any use. His government fell on 20 March 1940. He retained a Cabinet post as Minister of National Defense, which was a mistake. Daladier's policy as Defense Minister was conservative – he supported the out-of-date strategies of France's old Generals and felt that a change in leadership at this late stage would create too much confusion. Following the German invasion of France he tried to help resistance in North Africa but was captured and taken back to Vichy France. He was charged with leading France into war unprepared. He was interned in Buchenwald and Dachau but was freed in April 1945.

**Damaskinos, Archbishop, 1891–1949** After the Germans had been forced out of Greece, CHURCHILL and EDEN wanted to restore the monarchy in Greece. They were prevented from doing this because of intense fighting between left and right wing groups.

After an armistice with EAM (Greek National Liberation Front Communists) had been negotiated in December 1944, they persuaded the King to delay his return until after a referendum had been held on the question of the monarchy. Damaskinos was the popular and neutral figure who was made Regent in the meantime. He had earned his popularity because he was a liberal and because of his resistance to the Germans. As Regent he was in a difficult position because he could not find a stable government and in October 1945 was forced to become his own Prime Minister since he could find no suitable candidate. However he successfully supervised the plebiscite which brought back King GEORGE II and Damaskinos resigned.

**Darlan, Admiral Jean Francois, 1881–1942** In 1939 Darlan was Commander in Chief of the French Navy. When his country was defeated in the Battle of France, Darlan was faced with the problem of disposing of the Navy, the second strongest fleet in European waters. He met CHURCHILL and promised not to let the fleet fall into German hands but seemed unsure about exactly what to do with it. Eventually he accepted the office of Minister of the Navy in PÉTAIN's government and sent his Navy to North Africa. Churchill ordered the British Mediterranean Fleet to destroy the French Navy by bombardment in July 1940. The operation became known as the Mers-el-Kebir incident. In February 1941 Darlan became Vice-Premier to Pétain in the Vichy government. He tried to co-operate with HITLER to better conditions in France and to achieve more concessions and freedom for France but was all but ignored by Hitler. In spring 1942 he lost his Ministerial posts when LAVAL returned to power but was appointed Head of the French Armed Forces and High Commissioner in French North Africa. On the eve of the Torch landings General Mark CLARK arranged an armistice with Darlan who was visiting his son in Algeria. The Americans also agreed to recognize Darlan as the Head of the French government, a situation in direct opposition to the British recognition of DE GAULLE as Head of State. Fortunately Darlan was assassinated by a young French monarchist on Christmas eve 1942 before he had rendered any damage to Allied interrelationships.

**Darnand, Joseph 1897–1945** Darnand was notorious for his organization of the *Milice*, the militarized police force of the Vichy Regime. Darnand was a collaborator by conviction rather than through convenience. He was an enthusiastic supporter of Vichy's connection with the Nazis, went to Germany after the liberation of France in 1944 and took office in the puppet Sigmaringen 'French Government.' At the end of the war he was repatriated, tried and shot for treason. His persecution of opponents of Vichy and the excesses of his hated *Milice* undoubtedly justified his execution, but he regarded himself quite genuinely as a patriot.

**De Gaulle, General Charles, 1890–1970** De Gaulle had served as a subaltern in PÉTAIN's regiment during World War I and after the war had made himself a reputation as a military writer and theorist. Among his works was *The Army of the Future* and in this he predicted the nature of armored warfare and preached the need for mechanization. In 1940 his views were finally recognized and he was given command of the 4th Armored Division which was in the

process of being set up and was completely inexperienced. He was given this command on 11 May and told by GEORGES 'here is a chance to act' although it was too late. He tried to launch an attack towards Montcornet on 17 May, to stop GUDERIAN's advance on Laon and the Somme. However the attack was quickly brushed aside but he renewed his attack on 19 May and this time some of his tanks penetrated to within a mile of the German Headquarters. The Germans took the edge off this attack by an aerial bombardment and de Gaulle then received instructions to desist, since the divisions were needed elsewhere. In recognition of his success, de Gaulle was appointed Under-Secretary for War and attended the last desperate Cabinet meetings. He left for England on 17 June and on the following day made a broadcast to the French people 'Believe me! Nothing is lost for France! The same methods which have defeated us may one day bring us victory.' The war had to go on in the colonies. He declared the existence of 'Free France' and made himself head of that organization. Few people joined him at first because he was regarded as a traitor but he determined to try to annex France's colonies and continue the fight against Germany. The first attempt was to take the port of Dakar, Operation Menace, in October 1940, but this ended in disaster when the French forces under BOISSON refused to surrender and the British ships off Dakar suffered extensive damage.

De Gaulle also convinced CHURCHILL that the French in Syria were ready to desert Germany but when the joint British and Free French forces invaded in June 1941 they faced stiff opposition from the local French armed forces under the command of General DENTZ. It was only when the Vichy government began to collaborate openly with the Germans, that the French began to look to de Gaulle for leadership. Although the British gave him their full support, de Gaulle did not receive recognition from the US until after the Torch landings. Even then the US wished to promote GIRAUD as an alternative leader so de Gaulle was forced to co-operate with him until 1943 when de Gaulle forced Giraud to resign.

De Gaulle returned to France on 13 June 1944 but his moment of triumph came on 25 August, when he entered a liberated Paris to a tremendous reception by the people. A Committee of National Liberation was set up with de Gaulle as its President but the post-liberation situation was still difficult. De Gaulle was not invited to the conferences at Yalta and Potsdam and he resented the fact that France was not treated as an equal partner by the Allies. He was the most dynamic leader France had at the time but he was overly concerned with re-establishing France as a Great Power. Unfortunately his decision to reassert France's rule in Indo-China led to a very costly war, which the country could ill afford after the war.

**De Guingand, Major General Francis, 1900–1979** De Guingand was a British General and Chief Staff to MONT-GOMERY in North Africa and northwest Europe. De Guingand had a lot of experience of staff work before he began working with Montgomery and proved invaluable in the detailed negotiations with the other service Chiefs in the Desert. Montgomery used him as a representative at planning conferences. In northwest Europe de Guingand's main contribution was to smooth relations between Montgomery and EISENHOWER and it fell to him to present the plan for a quick northern thrust into Germany. He wrote his account of the war in *Operation Victory* and his verdict on Mongomery was 'when tackling a problem ... [Montgomery] cuts away all the frills and gets down to those factors that really matter. He simplifies –

this to some extent is true, but the resultant dividend is enormous.' De Guingand was a tactful diplomat and also a great admirer of American energy and power.

**De Lattre de Tassigny, General Jean 1889–1952** In 1914 cavalry officer de Lattre de Tassigny was severely wounded by a sword in a mounted duel with a German Uhlan. By 1939 he was a General and Chief of Staff of the French 5th Army and led the French 14th Division at Aisne. In 1940 after the French capitulation he remained dedicated to the Army and to the Vichy government which sent him to Tunisia. He was soon recalled because of his Allied sympathies and was awarded ten years imprisonment for protesting against the German occupation of the *zone libre* in 1942. In 1943 he escaped from Riom prison and went to the UK where he allied himself to DE GAULLE and became the Commander of the 1st French Army in North Africa. In 1944 he led the 1st French Army in the liberation of France. He signed the German surrender on behalf of France.

After the war he led French troops in Indo-China and triumphed over the Vietminh. After his death he was made a Marshal of France.

**Dempsey, General Miles, 1896–1969** Dempsey was a British General who led the 13th Infantry Brigade at Dunkirk and because of his excellent organizational ability was selected in June 1941 to form a new Armored Division. He was then appointed XIII Corps Commander in MONTGOMERY's 8th Army and quickly impressed Montgomery with his skill. Montgomery said of him he was a 'soldier who can describe foreign terrain so vividly from a map that it becomes almost a pictorial reality for his listeners.' Dempsey led his XIII Corps in many difficult landings in Italy and Sicily. He was so successful that he was promoted and given

command of the 2nd Army in the
D-Day Landings. He had a quiet, unassuming manner and kept his Corps
Commanders under control. His Army
landed at Juno and held the area between Caen and Bayeux, keeping
German armor away from the US forces
so they could break out of Normandy.
Dempsey's Army fought at Falaise and
Mortain and then dashed over northern
France to Brussels and took part in Operation Market Garden. Their advance
faltered at this point and they were
unable to reach the British paratroops
at Arnhem in time. After the German
surrender Dempsey was appointed Commander in Chief of Allied Land Forces
in Southeast Asia.

**Dentz, General Henri, 1871–1945**
Dentz was the pro-Vichy High Commissioner in Syria in June 1941. He was
the Commander in Chief of Armed
Forces in Syria and had 35,000 well-
armed men and 159 aircraft at his disposal. When Britain and the Free
French Army invaded Syria on 8 June
1941 Dentz's men fought bitterly and
Dentz held out for as long as possible.
He had insufficient air cover and the
Vichy government was reluctant to ask
for German assistance so on 10 July
Dentz signed an armistice with the British. He was arrested a few months
later when it was discovered that he
had broken the terms of the armistice
by sending Prisoners of War out of
Syria after the armistice had been
signed.

**De Valera, Eamon, 1882–1975** De
Valera had become Prime Minister of
Eire in 1937, a position he held through-
out the war. He secured neutrality for
Eire and refused to allow Britain to use
bases in Southern Ireland, a policy
which made CHURCHILL very bitter. De
Valera wanted to remove all ties with
Britain but he was also afraid that the
Germans might invade from France. He

refused to join Ulster in a defense
union.

**Devereux, Major James 1903–** Devereux
was the US Commander of Ground
Forces on Wake Island in 1941. He was
in command of 449 Marines and only
had six 5-in guns, machine guns and
twelve obsolete aircraft. On 7 December
1941 Wake Island came under attack
from 36 Japanese bombers and Devereux lost seven fighters on that day.
The following day he destroyed two
Japanese bombers. After four days of
bombing a Japanese landing party was
dispatched and Devereux held back his
fire for as long as possible. He damaged
the Force's flagship and sank two destroyers so the Japanese lost 700 men
and withdrew in confusion. On their
next attempt the Japanese made no mistake and the men of the 55th Division
landed in an area out of the range of the
batteries. They overwhelmed the Americans and Devereux and his men spent
the rest of the war in captivity on
Hokkaido.

**Devers, General Jacob, 1887–1979**
Devers was a US General appointed to
direct Operation Dragoon in August
1944. He had started his war career as
Commander of Armored Forces and
was appointed Commander of US
Forces in the UK in 1943. Since he did
not have sufficient battle experience he
was made General Maitland WILSON's
second in command in the Mediterranean Theater. The Allies argued over
tactics in this theater and the British
gave way and agreed to a landing in
southern France to link up with Overlord forces in northern France. Devers
was put in charge of the landings
which took place on 15 August 1944
and his troops only met pockets of resistance at Montélimar and Marseilles,
which they bypassed. The US troops
traveled at great speed up the Rhone
Valley and reached other Allied forces

in September. Devers was then given command of the 6th Army Group: the US 7th Army and the French 1st Army. They successfully held on to Strasbourg during the Alsace counter-offensive and swept into Germany to take Munich and Berchtesgaden.

**Dietl, Major General Eduard, 1890–1944** Dietl was the German Commander of the 3rd Mountain Division which had orders to take Narvik and the northern area in the Norwegian Campaign. His troops were an elite group of ski troops, numbering 6000. In Operation Barbarossa he commanded Army Group North. He died in 1944 and as a mark of honor HITLER delivered the funeral address in a rare public speech towards the end of the war.

**Dietrich, General Sepp, 1892–1976** One of the closest and oldest comrades of HITLER to whom he acted as bodyguard before the accession to power, Dietrich took a major part in the Blood Purge of 30 June 1934. During World War II he became a General in the Waffen SS, commanded the I SS Panzer Corps in the USSR and in December 1944 the Sixth SS Panzer Army in the Battle of the Bulge. He was given the latter command by Hitler to emphasize his mistrust of Army officers following the Bomb Plot of July. In 1946 he was sentenced by an American military court to 25 years imprisonment for the murder of American prisoners at Malmédy by soldiers of the Sixth Panzer Army and, on his release ten years later, was sentenced by a German court to eighteen months imprisonment for his part in the Blood Purge.

**Dill, Field Marshal Sir John Greer, 1881–1944** An outstanding and popular member of the British Army, Dill served as Director of Military Operations and Commandant of the Staff College before the outbreak of World War II. In 1939 he commanded I Corps in France. In October of that year he was promoted to General and in April 1940 he returned from France as Vice-CIGS (Chief of Imperial General Staff) only to succeed IRONSIDE as CIGS in May. A cautious man at all times. Dill advised restraint, a policy at odds with CHURCHILL's more-impulsive nature. Suffering from overwork and nervous strain Dill became a Field Marshal in November 1941 and was replaced as CIGS by Alan BROOK in December. He accompanied Churchill to Washington where he remained as Head of the British Joint Staff Mission. In the US he enjoyed total diplomatic and personal success and his relationship with the Americans was so favorable that they arranged for him to be buried in Arlington National Cemetery.

**Dobbie, General Sir William, 1879–1964** Dobbie was the British Governor of Malta from 1940–42 during the period when it came under the most intensive pressure from Axis forces. Dobbie was in retirement at the outbreak of World War II but in June 1940 was sent to Malta where he served as Governor and Commander in Chief of Armed Forces. He had only 5000 men and four obsolete aircraft but it was vital to hold on to Malta because it meant the Allies could weaken Axis communications between North Africa and Italy. Dobbie was a deeply religious man who regarded the struggle for Crete as a Crusade. He gave Bible readings and shared the same hardships as the civilian population, rationing food and fuel to ensure survival. After the heavy air raids of April 1942 the island of Malta was awarded the George Cross and shortly afterwards the defense Committee decided that Dobbie was worn out by the crises and on 7 May 1942 Lord GORT succeeded him. Dobbie enjoyed his retirement and in 1945 went on a lecture tour of the USA to give an account of the siege of Malta.

**Doenitz, Admiral Karl, 1891–1980** Commissioned into the German Navy as an officer in 1910 Doenitz was Flag Officer U-Boats until 30 January 1943. Convinced that the U-Boat alone could win the war for Germany, he was in fact almost proved correct: he was responsible for sinking fifteen million tons of Allied shipping. By early 1943 he had more than 200 U-Boats operating in 'wolf packs' and 181 in production. However the development of radar made the discovering and destruction of U-Boats easier and the Western Allies had closed the 'air gap' in the central Atlantic by 1943. These two facts meant that the Allies began to win the convoy battle. Doenitz was promoted to command the German Navy replacing RAEDER. Although the German Navy was now in decline, Doenitz never lost the admiration and respect of HITLER, perhaps because the Navy alone remained loyal. Leaders in the Army had proved themselves treacherous and the Reich Marshal of the Luftwaffe incompetent. Hitler chose to name Doenitz as his successor and Head of State. Doenitz assumed the leadership on 30 April 1945 and negotiated the capitulation of the German forces in the west. He was imprisoned at Flensburg until he was tried at Nuremberg where he was sentenced to ten years for war crimes.

**Donovan, William Joseph, 1883–1959** 'Wild Bill' Donovan was a US lawyer who was head of the OSS (Office of Strategic Services), the forerunner of the CIA (Central Intelligence Agency). In 1940 Donovan was the unofficial observer for the Secretary of the Navy, KNOX, in Great Britain. Knox was very pleased with his reports and he was sent on several missions by President ROOSEVELT to southeast Europe and the Middle East to observe resistance movements. On his return he was made co-ordinator of intelligence and on 13 June 1942 became director of the newly created OSS. The OSS had three branches – intelligence, operations and research – and had many influential people working for it. It was said to have employed 13,000 Americans but it also recruited agents in North Africa, Burma and Europe for its clandestine operations. On 1 October 1945 the OSS was terminated by an executive order and its functions were distributed to the Department of State and War Department. Donovan found a new post working as an aide to Judge Jackson at the Nuremberg trials.

**Doolittle, Lieutenant General James, 1896–** Doolittle, the only non-regular officer to command a major combat Air Force, began his military aviation career in 1917 in the Army Air Service of the United States. In 1922 he made the first flight across the continent of North America in less than 24 hours. Then followed a period of highly successful air racing. Working as an experimental engineer in the Air Corps Materiel Division, he played a major part in the development of aircraft instruments, making the first successful flight using these devices. He was awarded the Harmon Trophy in 1930 in recognition of this work.

Having left the Air Corps of the US Army in 1930 he returned in 1940 as a Major with the unenviable job of converting the automobile industry to aircraft production. In 1942 he led the raid on Tokyo in which squadrons of B-25s were launched from aircraft carriers and landed on airfields in China. Although the military results of this raid were of little or no consequence the strategic impact on the Japanese was awesome: the Japanese Navy had allowed the enemy to get close enough to launch an attack on the Imperial capital and therefore on the Emperor. So great was the IJN's loss of face that it sought settlement with the United States Navy in April 1942. (After Coral Sea and Midway, the Air Striking Force of the Imperial Japanese Navy never again threatened the US on equal terms.) Doolittle received the Medal of Honor for his actions in the Tokyo raid.

In 1942 Doolittle was given command of the US 12th Air Force in preparation for Operation Torch, the Allied invasion of North Africa. In 1943 he became Commander of the Northwest African Strategic Air Force, part of the Mediterranean Air Command. In 1944 Doolittle became a Lieutenant General and was created an Honorary KCB by King GEORGE VI.

In 1944 he was given command of the 8th Air Force which carried out the strategic bombing campaign against Germany and bombed the flying-bomb bases prior to D-Day. In 1945 Doolittle and his 8th Air Force sought action in the Pacific and enjoyed equal success against the Japanese.

Skillful, aggressive and versatile, Doolittle was admired by his men and colleagues.

**Doorman, Admiral Karel, 1889–1942** Doorman was a Dutch Admiral who lost his life in the Battle of Java Sea in February 1942. Doorman led a combined Striking Force of five cruisers and nine destroyers to protect the Dutch East Indies. The ships had not trained together and were manned by men of different nationalities. On 27 February 1941 Doorman sighted a Japanese force of four modernized cruisers and fourteen destroyers north of Surabaya. This force matched Doorman's; however it had the edge because it was equipped with 'long lance' torpedoes which were much faster than Western torpedoes. At first the action was inconclusive with the *Exeter*, *De Ruyter* and *Houston* all hit by gunfire. Later the *Exeter* was more seriously damaged and returned to Surabaya. Doorman decided to withdraw and also

sent his destroyers back to base. However the Japanese ships caught up with his force and sank Doorman's flagship *De Ruyter*, for the loss of all hands.

**Dorman-Smith, Major General Sir Eric 'Chink,' 1895–1969** Dorman-Smith was a British General who held command in the Desert War. He was stationed in India when the war broke out but he had himself transferred to be Commandant in the Middle East Staff College in Haifa in 1940. He was able to give tactical advice to WAVELL, AUCHINLECK and O'CONNOR on their offensives. In April–June 1942 he became temporary Director of Military Operations in Cairo and then acting Deputy Chief of General Staff to the 8th Army. His ideas inspired the fluid mobile defense at the first Battle of El Alamein. On 6 August 1942 he was dismissed with Auchinleck and never held any important Army position again. He tried to remake his career as an infantry Commander but was removed from his post and in November 1944 was removed from the active list. He was a talented military thinker whose ideas could not be used by the conventional British Army Commanders.

**Douglas, Air Marshal Sir William Sholto, 1893–1969** Douglas was Assistant Chief of Air Staff at the outbreak of the war but succeeded Dowding as Commander of RAF Fighter Command when it shifted to the offensive. His aircraft were involved in fighter battles over the Channel and northern France. In January 1943 Douglas was transferred to RAF Middle East Command and a year later became Head of Coastal Command when he planned the strategies for D-Day and also anti-submarine operations.

**Dowding, Air Chief Marshal Sir Hugh C T, 1882–1970** Dowding was a British Air Marshal who led RAF Fighter

Command during the critical period of the Battle of Britain. Dowding had spent a long and successful career, first with the Royal Flying Corps and later with the RAF, with command of squadrons in France during World War I, as Director of Training at the Air Ministry and Air Officer Commander in Chief in Transjordan and Palestine. Between 1930 and 1936 he was a member of the Air Council for Supply and Research where he vigorously supported both the development of the new monoplane aircraft types, and inventive research, especially in the field of radar.

In July 1936 he became the first Air Officer Commander in Chief of RAF Fighter Command, a force which he transformed from a single group operating in the south-east of England to a highly organized defense system covering the whole of the British Isles. Utilizing the scientific advances of the day, he developed a system of fighter control in which radio and radar communications played a fundamental role, enabling up-to-the-minute information regarding enemy activity to be passed directly from ground to air.

Dowding was a man of single-minded determination who was able to exploit all available resources, however scant, to maximum advantage. His clear appreciation of operational needs was to bring him into conflict with the British Cabinet as he fought to preserve his limited squadrons in the UK during the Battle of France, but his planning undoubtedly saved Britain during the massive Luftwaffe offensives of July, August and September 1940. He was considered to be somewhat humorless and nicknamed 'Stuffy' by his colleagues.

From November 1940 he served on a mission for the Ministry of Aircraft Production to the USA and retired in 1942.

**Dulles, Allen Welsh, 1893–1969** Dulles was the American Chief of OSS (Office of Strategic Services) in Switzerland. He was an experienced diplomat who arrived in Switzerland via Vichy France in November 1942 and soon built up a large network of resisters and informers. He achieved a famous coup at the end of the war when he was able to negotiate the surrender of German troops in Italy. Through various intermediaries, SS General WOLFF approached Dulles with an offer of surrender. However, before it could be signed there were many hitches: Wolff had to rescue his family from protective custody and send them abroad. Then STALIN objected to a separate treaty being made and Dulles had to apply considerable pressure on ROOSEVELT to get the President to agree. The instrument of surrender was finally signed on 29 April 1945 at Caserta. It came into effect on 2 May and is thought to have shortened the war.

# E

**Eaker, General Ira, 1898–1987** Eaker was a US General and the chief advocate of the strategic bombing of Germany. He led the first US bombing raid in western Europe, on marshaling yards outside Rouen on 17 August 1942. As Commander of the 8th Air Force he attended the Casablanca conference where he convinced the Combined Chiefs to allow the US bombers to continue their policy of daylight precision bombing alongside the RAF's nighttime area bombing offensive. In June 1943 he was promoted to Lieutenant General and a year after succeeded Tedder as Commander in Chief of the Mediterranean Area Command. His Air Force was based in Italy and he continued the strategic bombing offensive against Germany and the Balkans. In March 44 Eaker planned the bombing of the monastery at Monte Cassino. In August of the same year he was Air Commander in Chief of Operation Dragoon, the Allied invasion of southern France. He had 5000 aircraft whereas the Germans had only 200; his forces destroyed the German defenses and the 'Mediterranean Wall.'

**Eden, Anthony, 1897–1977** Eden was a British statesman and CHURCHILL's Foreign Secretary for most of the war. Eden was Britain's youngest Foreign Secretary from 1935–38 but resigned because he did not agree with CHAMBERLAIN's policy of appeasing HITLER. When Britain entered the war Eden was recalled to be Dominions Secretary and then Secretary of State for War (1940) but he did not serve in the Cabinet. Churchill was very close to him and eventually had him appointed to the Foreign Office where he remained until 1945. As Minister of Defense he had traveled to the fronts in France in May 1940 and on his return he inspected the coastal defenses of southern England. He decided to reorganize the local units and they became known as the Home Guard. Churchill considered Eden his successor and ISMAY said that he (Eden) 'bore a close resemblance to Churchill in methods and hours of work.' As Foreign Secretary Eden traveled extensively: to Greece (February 1941) and to Moscow (December 1941) in his first year of office. He was a man of inflexible principles and was often involved in arguments with the USSR. In December 1941 he refused to recognize the USSR's prewar frontiers but he still managed to negotiate the twenty-year Alliance Treaty which was signed in May 1942. Eden tried to dissuade Churchill from making any concessions to STALIN over eastern Europe. In September 1944 he arrived too late to stop Churchill agreeing to the MORGENTHAU Plan and there was a public outcry against this plan to dismantle all of Germany's industrial plants after the war. Eden was a very talented Foreign Minister who was able to achieve concessions from other parties in unequal negotiations by his powers of persuasion.

**Edson, Major General Merritt Austin, 1897–1955** 'Red Mike' Edson was Commander of the 1st Marine Raider Battalion which took part in special operations in the Pacific. Edson trained his

Marines in special tactics and shortly after Pearl Harbor, President ROOSEVELT set up the 1st Raider Battalion. Edson's men first saw action on Tulagi in the Solomons and took the island in August 1942. They then transferred to Guadalcanal where they defended the ridge on either side of Henderson Airfield and were so courageous that Edson was awarded the Medal of Honor for his action. His Marine Raiders worked alongside regular troops from August 1943 and participated in the operations in the Gilberts, Marshalls and Marianas. In 1944 he was appointed Chief of Staff to the Fleet Marine Force, Pacific.

**Eichelberger, Lieutenant General Robert Lawrence, 1886–1961** Given command of the US I Corps in 1942, Eichelberger directed its operations during one of the most crucial periods of the Pacific war when he helped to stem the tide of the Japanese advance on Australia through New Guinea and won the small but significant victory of Buna in January 1943. In September 1944 he was appointed to command the 8th Army and directed it in the successful invasion of the Philippines and in other operations until the end of the war.

**Eichmann, Adolf, 1906–1962** Eichmann was a German SS officer who was Head of the Gestapo's Section IV BG, the Department of Jewish Affairs. After the Wannsee Conference (January 1942) it was decided to put into effect the final solution to exterminate all Jews. On 1 July 1943 Eichmann got the final decree signed by BORMANN which deprived Jews of all rights of appeal. Eichmann introduced the convoy systems to extermination camps and had gas chambers installed because they were the most efficient means of execution. Although a member of the SS he was known to have Jewish relations and probably had a Jewish mistress when he lived in Vienna. He disappeared in 1945 and

went to South America and settled down in Buenos Aires. In 1960 he was discovered by Israeli agents and kidnapped. He was put on trial in Israel and in his defense said he was merely doing his job. He was found guilty and hanged.

**Eisenhower, General Dwight D, 1890–1969** The son of a poor family from Texas, Eisenhower paved the ground for his military success at West Point where he became a football star and was universally popular. His army career made slow progress between the wars, but he had the good fortune to attract the favorable attention of General MARSHALL, the Chief of Staff, who early in 1942 brought him to head the Operations Branch in Washington. He was then sent to lead the American staff in Britain and was shortly afterwards chosen to command the Allied landings in French North Africa (Operation Torch). In Washington, Eisenhower had been a leading exponent of the policy of opening a second front in Europe in 1942, and he naturally regarded Torch as a diversion. He nevertheless put his heart into making it the spectacular success that it became and at once demonstrated the many qualities – of imperturbability, professional skill, wise judgment, public charm and gentle conciliation – which were to make him the natural choice for Supreme Allied Commander in Europe throughout the war. He was given that title in the North African Theater in February, and during the rest of the year oversaw the final conquest of North Africa and the launching of the invasions of Sicily in July and of Italy in September. In December he was recalled to Britain to assume the Supreme Allied Command of the projected invasion of Europe with MONTGOMERY as his operational Commander. Until 1 September his role was that of strategic overlord, but on that day he assumed direct control of operations and was almost immediately confronted with a major crisis of command decision, perhaps the greatest with which he was faced during the war. The Germans were in full retreat to their own frontiers and PATTON and Montgomery, commanding the right and left flanks respectively of the Allied advance, were each clamoring for a disporportionate share of supplies strictly limited by the destruction of the French railways and the unavailability of ports beyond Normandy. Urged by each to sanction a 'narrow front' advance which each claimed would win a speedy final victory, he decided instead to pursue a 'broad front' strategy which allowed all armies to advance at a uniformly slower pace. He made to Montgomery, however, the concession of allowing him to mount a risky airborne operation (Market Garden), which Patton was later to claim robbed him of promising opportunities in Lorraine. Market Garden, conceived in a later judgment to have been aimed at capturing 'a bridge too far,' failed. Montgomery forever claimed that the failure was the result of Eisenhowever's 'broad front' strategy. This now looks unlikely. German forces were stronger on the ground near home than Montgomery would concede, and Allied supply resources, whether organized on a 'broad' or 'narrow' basis, too exiguous to have supported any sort of war-winning blow. Eisenhower appears to have realized this and to have decided that his best policy was to support both an American and a British dash to the frontier in the general interest of good inter-Allied relations even though neither General could achieve the success he expected. In that assessment he was certainly accurate for, though his subordinates seethed with frustration, the British and American publics both saw the advance to the German frontier as a triumph of Allied arms. Eisenhower certainly did not undervalue Montgomery's skill as a battlefield commander and during the crisis of the Battle of the

Bulge, judged him the right man to take over direction of the counteroffensive, even at the cost of sore feelings among American commanders. Thereafter the course of Allied strategy, both on the British and American fronts, ran smooth – during the Rhine crossing and in the advance to the Elbe and into Austria. Eisenhower ended the war as much a hero of the British people as of the American, who elected him President in 1952. Though not perhaps a great soldier in the technical sense – it is doubtful if he ever heard a shot fired in anger – he proved himself a genius in the direction of inter-Allied campaigns.

**Embry, Air Vice-Marshal Basil, 1902–1977** At the outbreak of the war Embry served in the RAF Bomber Command and in May 1940 was shot down over France. He managed to return to England after two escape attempts and joined Fighter Command to serve during the Battle of Britain. He was then sent to North Africa to improve the fighting efficiency of the squadrons there. In 1943 he became acting Air Vice-Marshal and Commander of No 2 Bomber Group. He took part in many precision bombing attacks against railways and marshaling yards prior to D-Day. He led two operations in France in mid-1944: the first against the village of Audinghen, the headquarters of the German Todt organization; the second against a Château on the Aulne which was a rest home for U-Boat crews. Another daring raid was made against Gestapo HQ in Copenhagen – Embry had to blast a door open to allow Danish resistance leaders to escape.

**Esmonde, Lieutenant Commander Eugene, 1909–1942** Esmonde was a naval airman who joined the Fleet Air Arm in 1939 and served on the HMS *Courageous* and then the *Victorious*. While serving on the *Victorious* he was involved in chasing the *Bismarck* in May

1941. He led nine Swordfish torpedo-bombers and managed to hit the *Bismarck* with a torpedo but the German ship did not sink.

Esmonde was in command of 825 Squadron of torpedo-bombers in January 1942 and volunteered to attack the three battle-cruisers *Scharnhorst, Gneisenau* and *Prinz Eugen* if they attempted to break out from Brest and return to Germany. At 1050 on 12 February word came that the *Scharnhorst, Gneisenau* and *Prinz Eugen* were making their way up the Channel and Esmonde was promised an escort of five squadrons of fighters. Only one squadron arrived in time but Esmonde set off and under heavy fire his six Swordfish attacked the German ships. All six launched their torpedoes but none found their mark. Of the eighteen men in the squadron only five survived and Esmonde was awarded a posthumous Victoria Cross for his bravery.

**Evatt, Herbert, 1894–1965** Evatt was an Australian lawyer and statesman. In 1941 he became Minister of External Affairs and worked hard to increase Australia's influence on world affairs. He traveled extensively and was the Australian representative to the British War Cabinet. At the end of the war he was a keen advocate of the United Nations because he felt Australia and smaller nations would be able to voice their opinions. He also tried to have the veto power of the great nations restricted.

# F

**Falkenhausen, General Alexander von, 1878–1966** Falkenhausen was Commander in Chief of German troops in Belgium and France. At first he conformed to Nazi policy in occupied countries and administered his territory efficiently but from mid-January 1942 Falkenhausen became involved in anti-Nazi plots. He discussed Germany's future after HITLER with HASSELL. Falkenhausen approached ROMMEL and KLUGE to get their support for the plot to assassinate Hitler and secured their lukewarm support. However, Falkenhausen could not be of any use to the plotters because he was dismissed from his post on 15 July 1944. On 20 July 1944, the day of STAUFFENBERG's attempt on Hitler, Falkenhausen tried to talk Kluge into committing himself to the plot but failed. He was arrested shortly afterwards and interned in Niederhausen in the south Tyrol along with other resisters. He was freed by the US on 4 May 1945 and although he was sentenced in 1951 to twelve years penal servitude he did not serve the full sentence because he had opposed Hitler.

**Falkenhorst, Colonel General Nikolaus von, 1885–1968** Falkenhorst was the Commander in Chief of German troops in Norway. He had been chosen in February 1940 at very short notice to prepare for the invasion of Norway. He was given a few hours to submit detailed plans of invasion which he completed with the aid of a Baedecker guide. He was then allotted no more than five divisions and by April the invasion force was ready. Falkenhorst was directly res-

ponsible to HITLER and remained in command of troops in Norway until 1944. The only military operation he took part in was a limited invasion of the USSR from Norway in 1941. He was hated by the Norwegian population because he used terror tactics to keep them under control. He was condemned to death after the war but was spared and released in 1953.

**Farouk, King of Egypt, 1920–1965** Farouk was pro-Axis throughout the war although he was bound by treaty to Great Britain. He managed to steer a middle course for most of the war. He believed that the Axis powers would give Egypt her independence and he followed a policy of being nominally pro-British but retained a pro-Nazi Cabinet. When the Axis powers were on the brink of defeat Egypt declared war on Germany and Italy in February 1945 so that she could join the United Nations.

**Fergusson, Major Bernard, 1911–1980** Fergusson was one of General WINGATE's Column Commanders in Burma. He first met Wingate in Palestine where he served as a junior intelligence officer and after various appointments in the Middle East and India, joined the Chindits expedition in 1942. The first expedition set out to damage Japanese communications in the Burmese jungle and his column destroyed a viaduct but was then stranded on a sandbank in the middle of the Schweli River. His men had to wade across the river which was nearly six feet deep and fight the strong current: 46 men were left behind or died. On the second Chindit expedition Fergusson commanded the 16th Infantry Brigade and marched overland from Assam in February 1944 to arrive near Indaw by mid-March where they sustained heavy losses. After the war Fergusson was made Director of Combined Operations.

**Fiocca, Nancy, 1916–** Fiocca was a French Resistance leader of great courage. Nancy Fiocca née Wake was an Australian journalist who had married a rich French industrialist, Henri Fiocca, and worked as an ambulance driver in the early days of the war. When the Germans arrived in Paris, she and her husband fled to Marseilles and there she came into contact with British Prisoners of War. For the next two and a half years she worked for the escape organization, Pat, run by Albert GUÉRISSE. Security in the organization was lax and she decided to leave for Toulouse and then make for Britain via Gibraltar. She was arrested in Toulouse but Guerisse secured her release by telling the police he was a friend of Laval and that Fiocca, his mistress, had committed an indiscretion. She made six further attempts to escape in 1942 and only reached Britain by sea at the end of June 1943. She was recruited by Colonel BUCKMASTER to join the Special Operations Executive to be trained as a saboteur and resistance agent. In February 1944 she was dropped over Montluçon with detailed orders for harassment operations on the Germans. At first the Maquisards in the Auvergne were suspicious of her but she convinced them that she could pick landing areas for supplies and make arrangements with London and they accepted her leadership. Her group of 7000 Maquisards was involved in a pitched battle with 22,000 Germans on 20 June 1944. She took part in several raids including one in which the Gestapo Headquarters in Montluçon was destroyed despite the presence of Germans in the town. In August Fiocca entered Vichy with her Maquisards as a national heroine.

**Fitch, Rear Admiral Aubrey, 1883–1978** Fitch was Commander of Task Force 11 at the Battle of Coral Sea. His Force was built round the *Lexington*, the heavy cruisers *Minneapolis* and *New Orleans* and five destroyers. They met FLETCHER's *Yorktown* Group on 1 May 1942 in the Coral Sea and the first carrier battle of the war began. Fitch had tactical command of the air battle on the last day, 8 May, and launched the attacks which damaged the *Shokaku* and *Zuikaku* but he kept too few fighters for his own protection and the *Lexington* was badly bombed and sank after the battle. After the battle Fitch was made Commander of land-based aircraft in the South Pacific.

**Flandin, Etienne, 1889–1958** Flandin was a French politician who was Prime Minister of France in 1934–35 and during the years leading up to the war had favored a policy of appeasement. His service in the Vichy Régime was spectacularly short – he owed his rise to LAVAL's disgrace and to his speeches about French revival. In November 1940 he became Foreign Minister and one of his first steps was to upset the German Ambassador to France by some 'throwaway' remarks. Flandin nearly succeeded Laval as Vice-Premier but PÉTAIN decided to promote Admiral DARLAN; Flandin left the government in February 1941. He had opposed helping Germany militarily and had become an embarrassment to Pétain. After the liberation he was treated roughly by DE GAULLE who hated all those who served in the Vichy administration. Flandin was tried by the French High Court but was acquitted of the crime of collaboration.

**Fleischer, General Carl, 1883–1942** Fleischer was the Commander of Norwegian troops near Narvik and inflicted the first reversal suffered by the German Army in World War II. He had been unable to save the garrison in Narvik but when the British arrived in Norway he began operations to contain the German troops in the mountains north of Narvik. Fleischer mistrusted the British and had launched his attack in terrible conditions, but when the British withdrew from central Norway he felt betrayed. However in June 1940 he accompanied the Norwegian Government into exile and left for London. Although he had no troops he was appointed Commander in Chief of the Norwegian Army abroad but was involved in frequent arguments with the British. He was posted to Ottawa, Canada as military attaché and committed suicide shortly afterwards.

**Fletcher, Vice-Admiral Frank, 1885–1973** 'Black Jack' Fletcher was the US Admiral in tactical command at the Battle of Coral Sea. Fletcher's flagship was the USS *Yorktown* and after trying to sight the Japanese forces in Coral Sea for several days, he sent out a strike force on 7 May 1942 which sank the *Shoho* and hit the *Shokaku*. The US lost the *Lexington* and the *Yorktown* was badly damaged which was a tactical defeat for them but turned into a strategic victory because it knocked the *Shokaku* out of the Battle of Midway. Fletcher was also in tactical command at Midway but his flagship was hit by three bombs early in the battle. In August 1942 Fletcher was in command of three carriers, the *Saratoga, Wasp* and *Enterprise*, off Guadalcanal: however he was so nervous about being attacked that he withdrew early to the annoyance of ground troops. Fletcher retained command of the carrier force in the Battle of the Eastern Solomons when the *Enterprise* was badly damaged but the Japanese lost the *Ryujo* and at least ninety aircraft. In 1943 Vice-Admiral Fletcher was transferred to command

the north Pacific forces and remained at this post until the end of the war.

**Forrestal, James, 1892–1949** Forrestal was ROOSEVELT's extremely vigorous Secretary of the Navy. In 1940 he had been taken on as an administrative assistant and was appointed Under-Secretary of the Navy shortly afterwards. He launched a new building program and solved the problem of establishing priorities regarding resources through a Controlled Materials Plan. In 1941 Forrestal went to London to negotiate Lend-Lease deals. In May 1944 he became acting Secretary of the Navy and set about rationalizing the service. He visited the Pacific area three times and twice visited Europe – he watched the Allied landings in the south of France. He recommended the unification of the three services into a Department of Defense in the Eberstadt Report and at the end of the war he spoke out with intense feeling against too rapid demobilization.

**Franco, General Francisco-Bahamonde, 1892–1975** Because Germany and Italy had supplied Franco with arms to help him win his Civil War, it was assumed that Franco and the Spanish Army would side with Nazi Germany when war broke out. This, however, was not the case. HITLER wasted a fair bit of time and effort trying to persuade Franco to join the Axis but Franco managed to remain neutral – his Army was tired of fighting and he could not be sure who would win the war. A skillful negotiator, Franco prompted Hitler to remark after the Hendaye meeting that he would rather visit the dentist to have teeth removed than do business with him (Franco) again. Over the years several possible alliances between Germany and Spain were considered but none actually materialized although Franco did send a division of volunteer anti-Bolsheviks to Russia (the 'Blue Division').

**Frank, Anne, 1929–1945** Anne Frank is known to millions because of the record she left of her experience of the war. In her diary she described how her family and some friends lived in an attic from July 1942, when they feared they might be sent to concentration camps because of their Jewish origins, until they were discovered by the Gestapo in August 1944. The family was hiding in rooms above Mr Frank's office which was busy during the day: thus the occupants of the attic could not make a sound during working hours. She wrote her diary in the form of letters to an imaginary friend, Kitty, and in it she described the difficulties of living as a family in the cramped conditions and falling in love with the boy, Petr, who was also trapped. After their arrest Anne and her sister Margot were sent to Belsen where they died of typhus two months before the Liberation. After the war the only survivor of the family, Anne's father, returned to the attic where he discovered her diary on the floor. Her diary has been published in many languages and the stage version has been performed around the world.

**Frank, Hans, 1900–1946** Frank was a Nazi lawyer who rose to the top administrative post in Poland. When Hitler invaded Poland part of it was annexed to Germany, part of it went to the USSR, but central Poland was put under Governor-General Frank's control. He worked in direct association with the Commanders of the German occupation forces, the head of the SS and the Security Police. He was a ruthless, emotionally unstable man and his avowed aim was to make the Poles understand that 'a master race is reigning over them.' Frank divided the country into four districts, set about stripping the country of food and supplies and undertook the liquidation of the Polish educated class. He also had the Jews rounded up and sent to the concentration camps of Auschwitz and Treblinka which were outside his jurisdiction. He tried to commit suicide on several occasions as the Red Army overran Poland and finally resigned in August 1944 at the height of the Warsaw Uprising. He was tried at Nuremberg where he said 'It was too comfortable to live on the system, to support our families in royal style, and to believe it was all right.' He was hanged on 16 October 1946.

**Frank, Karl Hermann, 1898–1946** Karl Hermann Frank was the former Deputy Leader of the Sudeten German Party who was appointed von NEURATH's Deputy and in fact ruled Bohemia and Moravia. In November 1939 he suppressed the students and put restrictions on academic freedom. When HEYDRICH became Protector of Bohemia and Moravia Frank lost some influence but as soon as news of Heydrich's assassination came through, Frank assumed power and proclaimed martial law. He arrested 3188 people and executed 1357, and a further 657 died under police investigation. He also ordered the destruction of the villages of Lidice and Lezaky. Frank effectively continued to rule Bohemia and Moravia for the rest of the war although FRICK was nominally the Protector. After the war he was sentenced to death by a Czech court.

**Fraser, Admiral Sir Bruce, 1888–1981** Fraser was Commander in Chief of the Home Fleet which engaged and sank the *Scharnhorst*. On 25 December 1943 the *Scharnhorst*, commanded by Rear Admiral Bey, was sent off on a hit-and-run attack against a convoy off Cape North. Fraser sent a squadron of cruisers to harass the *Scharnhorst*, separated her from her destroyers and forced her into a trap. The *Scharnhorst* was sunk by torpedo and only 36 of her crew survived. In 1944 Fraser was promoted to Admiral and became Commander in Chief of the Eastern Fleet and took part in some of the naval operations off Japan. On 2 September 1945 he signed the Japanese surrender documents on behalf of the UK.

**Fredendall, Major General Lloyd, 1884–** Fredendall was the US Commander of the Center Task Force of Operation Torch which landed at Oran. He had been chosen by EISENHOWER to lead the II Corps. The landing was well-planned and successfully executed on 8 November 1942. Fredendall then headed eastwards to join in the fight against the Axis forces in Tunisia. His troops were inexperienced and Fredendall was over-confident; he felt he could win an easy victory. He committed his forces to a diversionary offensive which eventually cost the Allies the Kasserine Pass. He was dismissed and replaced by General PATTON.

**Freyberg, General Sir Bernard, 1889–1963** Freyberg was the extremely competent Commander of New Zealand troops in World War II. After delaying the German invasion of Greece, Freyberg and his troops withdrew to Crete in May 1941 and there inflicted heavy casualties on General STUDENT's crack parachutists. The New Zealanders nearly reversed an inevitable victory for the Germans but in the end conceded defeat and withdrew to Egypt. Freyberg's forces then fought heroically in many operations in the Desert War – they were renowned for their ferociousness. Freyberg had to insist that his troops remain as a New Zealand Division and as the 2nd NZ Division they fought in the Crusader Operation, November 1940, where they were nearly overrun by ROMMEL's forces who re-sealed Tobruk. In fighting round Minqar Qaim in June 1942, Freyberg was wounded in the neck by a shell splinter but he recovered in time to fight in the Second Battle of El Alamein, where he led the 'Supercharge' break out. His forces pursued the Axis troops into Tunisia and fought on the Mareth Line. In November 1943 the New Zealanders moved to Italy, and were transferred from the British 8th Army to the US 5th Army of General CLARK. Freyberg was the Corps Commander leading the attacks on Monte Cassino and it was he who urged the Allies to bomb the monastery with the words 'any higher commander who refuses to authorize the bombing will have to be prepared to take the responsibility for the failure of the attack.' The bombing of Monte Cassino protracted the offensive as the Germans were able to use the rubble as defensive positions. However in May 1945 Freyberg led his troops in triumph into Trieste. After the war he was made Governor-General of New Zealand in recognition of his services to his country. CHURCHILL likened him to a salamander and he was awarded a VC for his courageous leadership.

**Frick, Wilhelm, 1877–1946** Frick was a senior civil servant and Nazi. He was Minister of the Interior in HITLER's first Cabinet and was responsible for putting into effect measures to extend the Nazi Party's control of the state. As Chief of Police he came into conflict with HIMMLER who wished to control the security forces of the regime and Frick was forced to give Himmler responsibility for law and order. Frick's influence dwindled but he retained his post until 1943 when he became Reichs Protector of Bohemia and Moravia but he had very little power and FRANK, his Deputy, was the real ruler. Frick was found guilty of crimes against humanity at Nuremberg and was executed in October 1946.

**Friedeburg, Admiral Hans von, 1895–1945** Friedeburg succeeded Admiral DOENITZ as Commander in Chief of the Navy in April 1945. Doenitz became Chancellor of the Reich in HITLER's political testament and sent Friedeburg to negotiate surrender with the Allies. Friedeburg went to MONTGOMERY's Headquarters at Lüneburg on 3 May and after some negotiation signed a surrender document covering German Armed Forces in northern Europe and Germany effective on 7 May.

**Friedman, William Frederic, 1891–1969** Famous as 'the man who broke Purple'. Friedman was born in Russia but was taken by his family to America in 1896. He began his work in military codebreaking with the American Army in 1917 and worked at Expeditionary Force Headquarters in France in 1918. He continued in government service between the wars, ably assisted by his wife Elizabeth, also a remarkably gifted cryptographer, and in 1940 succeeded in breaking the secret of the Japanese diplomatic cypher known to the Americans as Purple. The failure of the American government to forewarn their armed services of the attack on Pearl Harbor despite the access Friedman's achievement gave them to Japanese diplomatic traffic, remains one of the mysteries of World War II, though it is now regarded as less sinister than has been thought. Friedman's work on Purple was so intensive that he suffered a nervous collapse and achieved nothing of comparable importance in code-breaking during the rest of the war.

**Friessner, Field Marshal Johannes, 1892–1971** Friessner was a German Field Marshal involved in the last-ditch attempts to save the Reich. In July 1944 he had been sent to the Baltic states to try and restore the situation but after sending in a few pessimistic reports he was sent to the so-called quieter front in Rumania. Within a month of his appointment the Red Army had launched its major offensive in Rumania. He had again reported the political and military instability on the front but had not been

heeded. The Germans lost many men in the pocket at Jassy-Kishinev and Friessner barely managed to reach Hungary. He was made Commander of the new 2nd Hungarian Army which was not able to stand up to the pressure of the Red Army. He was dismissed in 1944.

**Fritsch, General Werner von, 1880–1939** Fritsch was one of the few men in power who might have stood up to HITLER in 1938. He was Commander in Chief of the German Army in 1938 and would have succeeded General BLOMBERG as Minister of War. Blomberg was in disgrace for having married a woman who was reputedly a prostitute and he was forced out of office by pressure from GOERING and HIMMLER. Fritsch, who was next in line to succeed Blomberg, was then accused of being homosexual after the Gestapo had convinced a blackmailer, Schmidt, to name him as one of his customers. Fritsch maintained an indignant silence and resigned from his post. This gave Hitler his chance to subordinate the Army High Command to his authority: sixteen high-ranking Generals were prematurely retired including von LEEB and von RUNDSTEDT: a further 44 were transferred to new commands. Although Schmidt later admitted to a court of inquiry that he had lied because of Gestapo pressure, Fritsch was never reinstated. He was given an honorary colonelcy with Artillery Regiment 12 and while he was on duty in Poland in September 1939. Fritsch was killed by a stray bullet.

**Fromm, General Friedrich, 1888–1945** His notoriety derives from his equivocal role in the 1944 Bomb Plot. A staff officer by training and career, he held throughout World War II the post of Commander of the Home Army (*Ersatzheer*) to which STAUFFENBERG was appointed as Chief of Staff in June 1943. He became aware of the conspiracy to overthrow HITLER which his new subordinate had begun to organize and appeared to lend it his support. On the morning of July 20 he allowed preliminary orders to be issued in his name for the occupation of Berlin by anti-Nazi forces. But as soon as he learned of Hitler's escape from death he voiced his 'loyalty' and was arrested by the conspirators. He then 'sought to rehabilitate himself in the eyes of the winning side' by eliminating the chief conspirators, ostensibly as part of his undying loyalty to the Führer but actually to destroy the incriminating evidence against himself. He instituted a drumhead courtmartial, condemned the conspirators to death and had them shot in the courtyard of the War Ministry. 'It is of some satisfaction,' Wheeler-Bennet concluded, 'to know that it profited him nothing.' He was arrested by the Gestapo, tortured and tried before the People's Court in February 1945 and hanged at Brandenburg Prison on March 19.

**Fuchida, Commander Mitsuo, 1902–1976** Fuchida was a veteran pilot of the China War who was selected to lead the Japanese air attack on Pearl Harbor. Fuchida coordinated all the preparations for the attack and led the first wave personally: it was unusual to have a single Flight Commander and it was a tribute to his skill and courage. Fuchida would have led the flying operations at Midway but was prevented by appendicitis and his friend, GENDA, replaced him.

**Fyfe, Sir David Maxwell, 1900–1967** Fyfe was one of the most devastating prosecutors at the war crimes trials at Nuremberg. He had been appointed British Solicitor General and began preparing cases against top German officials in 1942. At the end of the war in Europe, Fyfe was appointed Attorney General in the Caretaker Government of May 1945 but after the 1945 general election was retained by ATTLEE as Deputy Chief Prosecutor and was Britain's chief Prosecutor at Nuremberg. Fyfe cross-examined GOERING and managed to discredit one of his witnesses. In von Papen's cross-examination Fyfe was able to prove he was a weak supporter of the Nazis, incapable of standing up for himself. Fyfe won a great deal of admiration because of the lucidity and integrity with which he presented his cases: he stuck to the principle that the accused's guilt had to be proved in court.

# G

**Gale, General Sir Humphrey, 1890–1971** Gale was the British Deputy Chief of Staff and Chief Administrative Officer to EISENHOWER for Operation Overlord. He was an expert in logistics and was able to overcome the problems involved in the multi-national invasions of North Africa, Sicily and Italy. He was virtually unknown to the public but was an extremely valuable collaborator for Eisenhower.

**Galen, Archbishop Clemens von, 1878–1946** Galen was the Archbishop of Munster and one of the few Germans who openly criticized the Nazi regime. Galen's opposition to the Nazis had grown after 1934 when he began to refer to it as 'the new heathenism.' In 1941 he delivered three sermons which criticized both the Nazi administration in the occupied countries and the practice of euthanasia. News of his protest spread but the Gestapo dared not arrest such a prominent member of the Catholic Church. However many priests *were* sent to concentration camps and Church property was seized. This provoked Galen to deliver more anti-Nazi sermons but he was never arrested.

**Galland, Lieutenant General Adolf, 1912–** Galland was one of the Luftwaffe's most successful fighter aces. He held a staff post in Poland in 1939 but was then transferred to an active command in France. During the Battle of Britain he led III Gruppe of Jagdgeschwader 26 and took part in many fights over the Channel. In November 1941 he became MÖLDERS' successor as Commander of the Fighter Arm. His task was to organize the defense of Europe and to this purpose he wanted Messerschmitt to build the new 262 fighter which would be a match for the P-51 Mustangs. Galland took the side of the pilots in demanding better equipment and this frequently led him into arguments with HITLER. Hitler advocated building the new Me-210 fighter which could easily be converted for bomber use. Galland was eventually dismissed in January 1945 and was given command of an elite jet fighter squadron. He was shot down on 26 April 1945, captured and taken to England for debriefing.

**Gamelin, General Maurice Gustave, 1872–1958** A military bureaucrat rather than a soldier, Gamelin had made his name as Head of the Operations Section of the French General Headquarters during World War I. An interwar Commander in Chief, he was Commander of Land Forces in 1940, responsible for the direction of strategy and the co-ordination of the French and British forces in the defense of France. He proved unable either to give firm and clear directions to his subordinates or to react energetically to events and had to be removed from office in the first days of the German offensive of May 1940.

**Gandhi, Mohandas Karamchand, 1869–1948** The Mahatma ('great soul') had been frequently arrested for acts of civil disobedience against the British government of India before 1939. He did not, however, endorse political action against the British on the outbreak of war, but chose to work on Britain's 'sense of fair play' by arguing more and more strongly that only a free India could give Britain effective moral support in her war against the dictators. The failure of his urgings, and his dissatisfaction with Sir Stafford CRIPPS' offer of a new constitution and with the war itself led him in August 1942 to embark on a campaign of civil disobedience which led in turn to violence among his millions of followers and to his arrest. He remained in custody until May 1944.

**Geiger, General Roy, 1885–1947** Geiger was a tough Marine Commander who fought in the Pacific. He first saw action in Guadalcanal in September 1942, but was recalled to the Marine Corps Headquarters to become Director of Aviation. In November 1943 he returned to active service and led the I Marine Amphibious Corps on Bougainville. Thereafter he commanded the redesignated III Marine Amphibious Corps and led the invasion of Guam in July and August 1944. Before the invasion Geiger warned his troops 'it will be a tough and bitter fight against a wily, stubborn enemy who will doggedly defend Guam against this invasion.' He also led the III Corps at Okinawa.

**Genda, Commander Minoru, 1904–1989** Genda was a Japanese fighter commander. He was recruited by Rear Admiral ONISHI to plan a feasibility study for the attack on Pearl Harbor and with FUCHIDA prepared the attack. He served in NAGUMO's carrier fleet and gave him tactical advice on his use of air power. Genda led the first wave at Midway.

**Gensoul, Admiral Marcel, 1880–1974** With the fall of France DARLAN ordered what was left of the French Navy to assemble at Mers-el-Kebir. CHURCHILL decided that the French Fleet must not fall into the hands of the Germans

and the Royal Navy seized all French shipping in British harbors. Admiral SOMERVILLE was sent on Operation Catapult to make sure the fleet at Mers-el-Kebir would not fall into German hands. On 3 July 1940 Gensoul, who was in command of the fleet at Mers-el-Kebir, was presented with an almost impossible deadline by Somerville. He was given three alternative ways of demilitarizing his ships before 1800 hours on that day. Gensoul tried to extend the deadline by negotiation but when Somerville demanded an immediate reply, an incensed Gensoul replied that his ships would fight. At 1800 Somerville's ships opened up and the battleship *Bretagne* blew up immediately. The *Dunkerque* and *Provence* were seriously damaged but the *Strasbourg*, a seaplane carrier and five destroyers were able to escape to Toulon. Nearly 1300 Frenchmen died and the incident produced animosity between France and Britain.

**George II, King of Greece, 1889–1947** George II had acquiesced to the rule of the dictator METAXAS in the interwar period. When the Italians invaded Greece in October 1940, Metaxas swiftly mobilized the country and drove them back but he died shortly afterwards in January 1941. George II was forced to assume the Premiership himself after the suicide of his following Prime Minister, Koryzis, and he finally opted for military aid from Britain. But this came too late to stem the German invasion. George left first for Crete, and then for Cairo where his government-in-exile decided to settle. He himself preferred to live in London. In March 1943 he negotiated a Lend-Lease agreement with the USA. In July 1943 George had to broadcast his intention to hold free elections to decide whether Greece would be monarchist or republican after the war, to avoid outright civil war breaking out. In Cairo his government was in a constant state of political disagreement and some of his supporters in Athens were thought to be collaborators. Although he had CHURCHILL's backing, there was sufficient tension in Greece after it had been liberated, for Churchill to advise George not to return immediately. George was eventually convinced not to return 'unless summoned by a free and fair expression of the national will.' Archbishop DAMASKINOS was appointed Regent and, after a plebiscite, King George returned in 1946.

**George VI, King of Great Britain and Northern Ireland, 1895–1952** George was the titular head of the British Commonwealth and Empire and during World War II wanted to present himself to the public and the world as a symbol of Britain's upright resistance against the evil forces of Fascism and Nazism. In May 1940 the question was often raised about transferring the British Government and Monarch to Canada, but George and his Queen, Elizabeth, would not hear of it. They remained in Britain and spent much of their time touring the country. On 13 September 1940 a few minutes after their return to Buckingham Palace, a bomb exploded a mere eighty yards from the King and Queen but they were unharmed. After the bombing raid on Coventry the King visited the city on 16 November 1940. George made a point of having cordial relations with CHURCHILL and the Prime Minister dined at Buckingham Palace once a week. Churchill kept the King informed about the war effort. The King also maintained the morale of the Armed Forces by visits to the Navy and Army: he would have liked to have seen the men go ashore in Normandy and had to be dissuaded. The King overcame his natural shyness and stammer and became very close to the hearts of his people during the war.

**Georges, General Joseph, 1875–1951**

Georges, immediately subordinate to GAMELIN, held the position of Commander of the Northeast Front in 1940 and it was his troops which faced the German onslaught in May that year. Although he had command of GIRAUD's 7th Army, BILLOTTE's Army Group No 1, Pretelat's Army Group No 2 and the British Expeditionary Force, he was too slow in his response to the Germans and the nearest the French came to halting the Panzer advance was a last minute counterattack by DE GAULLE's 4th Armored Division. Georges gave evidence at PÉTAIN's trial after he war and said that he thought France could have fought on: 'At the very moment when we were about to stop fighting, five armies were partly imprisoned. In the groups which fought step by step over a depth of 281 miles, the trained effective strength still available were of the order of three to four hundred thousand men.'

**Ghormley, Vice-Admiral Robert Lee, 1883–1958** Ghormley was the American Naval Commander of South Pacific during the first stage of the Guadalcanal Campaign. In the summer of 1940 he served as a liaison officer in London and examined British naval tactics. In March 1942 he arrived in Auckland, New Zealand to take up his command in the South Pacific and shortly afterwards was told to organize the simultaneous seizure of Tulagi and Guadalcanal for 1 August 1942. The task facing him was formidable and he expressed his displeasure and asked for a postponement. His superiors Admirals NIMITZ and KING allowed him one week's delay and the expedition set off for a landing on 8 August. The planning of the operation was hurried and the troops did not have sufficient transports or landing craft – half their supplies had to be left behind. Intelligence reports and maps were lacking and the expedition was soon named Operation Shoestring. Ghormley made the controversial

decision which allowed Vice-Admiral
FLETCHER's aircraft carriers to withdraw shortly after the landings and this
resulted in the destruction of four cruisers in the Battle of Savo Island. Ghormley's lack of confidence in the mission
and the bad publicity the operation received led to his replacement in October
1942 by Vice-Admiral HALSEY. Ghormley returned to Washington for the rest
of the war.

**Giap, General Vo Nguyen, 1910–1975**
Giap was HO Chi Minh's Deputy, who
fought French rule in Vietnam throughout the war. Giap was bitterly anti-
French, especially after the death of his
wife in a French prison and in 1941
he returned from China to organize a
clandestine army of guerrilla fighters.
By 1945 his army was 10,000 strong and
in August it marched into Hanoi to seize
power and declare a Democratic Republic of Vietnam.

**Gibson, Wing Commander Guy, 1918–
1944** Gibson led one of the war's most
spectacular bombing attacks in World
War II. In May 1943 he was given command of the special squadron No 617
which was formed to drop Sir Barnes
WALLIS' special bouncing bomb on the
surface of dams in Germany. He had
eighteen Lancaster bombers which he
divided into three squadrons. Gibson
led No 1 Squadron on the most important mission to attack the Möhne and
Eder Dams. Gibson was the first to approach the dam on a very narrow and
difficult flight path and although he
dropped his bomb accurately, the dam
held. It was only on the fifth attempt
that the Möhne dam was breached. The
survivors of this raid proceeded home
but Gibson led the three bombers which
still had their load intact to the Eder
dam which was breached on the last
attempt. Eight bombers were lost on
this mission and Gibson was awarded a
Victoria Cross for his bravery and skill.

After a rest during which Gibson wrote
a book on his experience, he returned to
active command but was killed when
returning after a mission to the Netherlands in September 1944.

**Giffard, General Sir George, 1886–1964**
Giffard was a British Commander of
forces in West Africa. Giffard was an
expert on African affairs who was appointed Military Secretary to the Secretary of State for War. He served briefly
under WAVELL in the Middle East but
was then transferred to West Africa to
recruit, train and form West African
regiments. Once the Axis threat to West
Africa had receded Wavell asked that
Giffard be transferred to India where he
was made General Officer Commanding
Eastern Army. His main task was to
organize units for an offensive in Burma
and he faced a considerable logistical
problem. Communications in Assam
were primitive and techniques of supplying land forces by air were devised. In
August 1943 South East Asia Command
(SEAC) was set up and Giffard became
Commander in Chief of the 11th Army
Group. He was in charge of all land
forces which would be involved in the
Burmese offensive and began planning
the Arakan offensive for January 1944.
General STILWELL, under his command,
was to lead an offensive to recapture
Myitkyina but the personalities of Giffard and Stilwell clashed and the latter
refused to serve under the former.
MOUNTBATTEN, the Supreme Com-
mander of SEAC, resolved this by dis-
missing Giffard, Giffard however had to
remain at his post (throughout the
Kohima and Imphal offensives) until
General LEESE arrived in November
1944 to replace him.

**Giraud, General Henri, 1879–1949**
Giraud was in command of the 7th
Army when the German offensive in
France opened in May 1940. His Army
collapsed and was merged with Corap's

9th Army but it failed to make an impression on the German advance and Giraud and his men were taken on 19 May. He was interned in Königstein in Saxony but escaped in April 1942 to Switzerland and then Vichy France. As a popular resistance figure, Giraud was approached by the US who wanted to negotiate with him over their invasion of French North Africa. They did not realize that Giraud was out of touch with the political situation and did not have the power to stop French resistance in North Africa. Nonetheless Giraud was smuggled out of France in November 1942, a few days before the Torch landings, in the submarine *Seraph* and taken to Gibraltar. The US had negotiated a cease-fire with DARLAN and on the latter's assassination, Giraud was made High Commissioner of French North and West Africa. DE GAULLE, head of the Free French, did not wish to see Giraud rivaling him for his position as leader of the French Resistance, but the US felt de Gaulle was too controversial and they continued to promote Giraud. They codenamed him King-Pin in all their dispatches. Eventually de Gaulle and Giraud were forced by Churchill and Roosevelt at Casablanca, in January 1943, to make a temporary reconciliation and became joint Presidents of the Committee of National Liberation, which was set up in June 1943. Giraud soon found himself outmaneuvered by de Gaulle and resigned from the Committee in October. In April 1944 he also resigned from his positions in North Africa and then faded into obscurity.

**Goebbels, Dr Joseph, 1897–1945** The son of a clerk, Goebbels was an educated man with literary pretensions who joined the Nazi Party in 1924. He was soon mesmerized by HITLER's leadership and became the Gauleiter of the Berlin Nazi Party. During the Nazi struggle for power Goebbels was in charge of publicity and edited *Der Angriff* in which he attacked the Jews, the Communists and the big capitalists. With Hitler in power Goebbels became Minister of Propaganda and he controlled all aspects of communications through his Ministry – press, radio, publishing, theater and cinema. He was completely cynical and a compulsive liar: at various times he attributed his limp to World War I or to a spell in prison; however it was much more likely to have been caused by infantile paralysis. In the first years of the war Goebbels reported Hitler's successes but he always stressed that the USSR was not an easy country to conquer. After the surrender of the Sixth Army at Stalingrad, Goebbels took the step of making a speech about defeat and using a question and answer technique, pledged Germany's desire to continue fighting the war wholeheartedly. Goebbels also had to keep the nation's morale going in the face of the bombing of the cities and his constant theme was that if Germany surrendered she would be at the mercy of the USSR and her Allies. Goebbels was appointed Plenipotentiary for Total War in 1944 and he extended working hours, conscripted women, cut entertainment and education. He did not hide from the Germans the fact that things were bad but he never let them give up hope, especially through his last invention, the 'National Redoubt,' where the Nazis would fight to the last. Even the Allies believed him and feared a last stand in Bavaria. Goebbels retained Hitler's trust until the end and was nominated his successor as chancellor. He witnessed Hitler's marriage in the *Führerbunker* and was present at Hitler's suicide. Goebbels shot himself and his wife on 1 May 1945 after poisoning their six children.

**Goering, Reichsmarschall Hermann, 1893–1946** A member of the Richthofen Fighter Squadron during World War I, Goering was a flying ace who had shot down 22 planes. He was a welcome recruit to the Nazi Party in 1992 and took part in the Munich putsch in November 1933. On HITLER's accession to power he became Minister of the Interior in Prussia, organized the Gestapo and built up Germany's new Air Force. He was the only Nazi leader with upper-class pretensions: he had an estate, called Karinhall after his first wife, which he ran as a model for conservationist policies, where he entertained politicians with hunting and shooting parties. Nevile Henderson, who accompanied Goering on some of these hunts, said of him 'of all the Nazi leaders, Hermann Goering, was for me by far the most sympathetic ... I had a real personal liking for him ...'

In 1939 Goering's fortunes reached their peak when Hitler named him Reichsmarschall and his successor. However Goering was not the best choice for leadership of the Luftwaffe. He lacked concentration and was given to making extravagant claims for the Air Force which it was unable to match. During the Polish campaign in 1939, the Luftwaffe had demonstrated its power, but Goering took risks and commited all available aircraft, never keeping sufficient reserves. In May 1940 Goering convinced Hitler that the Luftwaffe could finish off the encircled British Expeditionary Force at Dunkirk. This was his biggest mistake and Hitler found difficulty in forgiving him. The Luftwaffe managed to sink a few British ships but 338,226 British and French troops were successfully evacuated, when the Wehrmacht's tanks could have easily achieved encirclement and the surrender of the mass of the BEF. Goering's next mistake of judgment was in the Battle of Britain; just as his fighters were on the point of destroying Fighter Command, he switched the attack from the airfields to London. While it dented civilian morale, the Luftwaffe lost the initiative and Hitler was forced to cancel Operation

Sealion, the invasion of Britain. Goering's next miscalculation was at Stalingrad, where he promised to supply PAULUS' Sixth Army with 500 tons of fuel and food per day. This was an impossible task to fulfill and it was the last time Hitler allowed himself to rely on Goering's judgment.

Goering withdrew from active participation in High Command decisions and turned to drugs and fantasies. He blamed his subordinates, MILCH and JESCHONNEK, for the continuing failures of the Luftwaffe, but the fatal weakness of the Luftwaffe dated from before the war when Goering neglected the possibilities of longer-range aircraft and only commissioned aircraft which could be used to aid ground operations. Living in his dream world Goering re-emerged in the final days of the war when, conscious of his position as Hitler's heir, he sent the Führer a telegram in which he suggested that he should assume power in the event of Hitler's death or capture. Hitler was furious and ordered Goering's immediate arrest. Soon after he was captured by the Americans and was put on trial at Nuremberg, where his old vigor returned. He conducted himself with great dignity assuming responsibility for all crimes. However, a showman to the end, he cheated the hangman by poisoning himself on the eve of his execution.

**Golikov, Colonel General Filipp, 1900–** Golikov was an able staff officer whose importance in the Red Army increased throughout the war. He first came into prominence after the Russo-Finnish War when he was appointed General MERETSKOV's Deputy Chief of General Staff. He then became Head of GRU, military intelligence, and had information from SORGE and others of preparations for a German invasion of the USSR. He did not take these seriously because he thought Germany would have to deal with Great Britain first, and consequently did not present these reports to STALIN. When the invasion began in June 1941 Golikov was sent on a mission to Washington and London to negotiate aid for the USSR. On his return he was made Commander of the 10th Army and took part in the counterattacks outside Moscow in December 1941. He was then given command of the Bryansk Front which he held throughout Field Marshal TIMOSHENKO's disastrous Kharkov Offensive. When Golikov informed Stalin that he could not hold up the German advance he was dismissed but was reinstated in time for the great counteroffensive to save Stalingrad. Golikov was now in command of the Voronezh Front and led the offensive to the Donets. In 1943 he became Deputy People's Commissar of Defense and was given administrative duties until the end of the war. A man of great political skill, he rose to power after the war as an associate of KHRUSHCHEV.

**Golovanov, Air Chief Marshal Alexander, 1903–** Golovanov was the Soviet Commander of the Long Range Air Force which was set up in April 1942. In many ways an elite force, it had considerable autonomy to develop its own methods and resources. Golovanov was the GKO's (State Defense Committee) specialist on aviation and it fell on him to plan the major air offensives to complement the land campaigns; for example, in Belorussia in June 1944. His long-range bomber force was also employed in the bombing and destruction of Königsberg, when ground troops failed to take it after months of siege.

**Gördeler, Karl, 1884–1945** Gördeler was one of the leaders of an anti-HITLER faction in Germany. He was a former Mayor of Leipzig and had resigned his post as Reich Commissioner of Prices in 1935 as a protest against the Nazi regime. He took a cover job as a representative for the firm Bosch and traveled around Germany recruiting sympathizers and plotting against Hitler. He was an idealist who took a romantic view of conspiracy, but did not have the forceful personality needed to lead a resistance movement. He was more concerned with the political intrigue of conspiracy and was a member of the Cabinet which would take power on Hitler's death. Gördeler was hopelessly indiscreet and was under surveillance by the Gestapo. After the failure of the July Plot in 1944 of Count von STAUFFENBERG Gordeler was one of the first to be arrested. He was sentenced to death but was able to put off his execution by writing endless memoranda presenting an excess of information which confused his captors. His luck ran out in February 1945 and he was hanged in Prinz Albrechtstrasse Prison.

**Gort, Field Marshal John, 1886–1946** Highly decorated in World War I, Lord Gort served the military between the wars as Director of Military Training India (1932) and Commandant of the Staff College at Camberley (1936–37). In 1937 HORE-BELISHA, Minister of War, promoted Gort to be Chief of Imperial General Staff (CIGS). In 1939 he became Commander in Chief of the British Expeditionary Force (BEF) and went to France. Although unimaginative and overly concerned with trivial matters of organization, Gort's guidance of the BEF in the Battle of France showed a great deal of foresight. In spite of instructions to remain in position, Gort chose the right moment to withdraw allowing the Army to be evacuated from Dunkirk with no time to spare. Gort was removed from the field after Dunkirk and became first, Governor of Gibraltar and then, Governor General and Commander in Chief in Malta (1942). He conducted the defense of Malta with vigor and resolution. He finished the war as High Commissioner in Palestine.

**Gott, Lieutenant General William 'Strafer,' 1897–1942** Gott was a Corps Commander of the British 8th Army in the Desert War. He was a highly competent commander whom CHURCHILL chose to replace AUCHINLECK as Commander of the Army in August 1942. Days after his appointment Gott was killed while flying back from Cairo and MONTGOMERY was appointed in his place.

**Govorov, Marshal Leonid, 1897–1955** Govorov was the architect of the liberation of Leningrad. An artillery specialist, Govorov had served on the Western Front in the summer of 1941. He experienced the devastation of the German onslaught and emerged to become a tough Commander. He was given command of the 5th Army outside Moscow and took part in the great counterattack of December 1941 which saved the Soviet capital. He was then made Commander of the Leningrad Front and wore down the German troops besieging Leningrad in a protracted offensive lasting over a year. He broke the blockade of Leningrad by hacking a corridor from Lake Ladoga through to Schlüsselburg and shortly afterwards was promoted to Marshal (1944). His Leningrad Front swept over the Baltic states and then, alongside General CHERNYAKHOVSKY's Front, isolated the remnants of German Army Group North in East Prussia after taking Riga. Govorov was one of the lucky Generals who survived the purges and went on to make a great contribution to the Soviet victory.

**Grechko, General Andrey, 1903–1976** Grechko served his apprenticeship for high command during World War II. He was given command of various Armies who were fighting to defend the Transcaucasus and was eventually made Deputy Commander of the 1st Ukrainian Front. He commanded the Armies that liberated Kiev and then Lvov and finally took part in the liberation of Czechoslovakia.

**Grew, Joseph, 1880–1965** Grew was a personal friend of President ROOSEVELT who served as Ambassador in Japan from 1932–41. He was an expert on Japanese affairs and realized that the Japanese Cabinet was not in control of the wilder elements of the Army. He worked hard to avoid war in the Far East but in September 1940 he sent the 'Green Light' telegram which stated that 'a show of force together with a determination to employ it if need be' could 'alone contribute effectively' to maintaining the *status quo* in the Pacific. Cordell HULL followed Grew's advice and this led to the placing of an oil embargo on Japan and eventually to war. Grew was arrested after Pearl Harbor and returned to the USA in the summer of 1942 when he was exchanged for Japanese diplomats. He then served as an adviser on Japanese affairs in the State Department.

**Griswold, Major General Oscar, 1886–1954** Griswold was Commander of the US XIV Corps which fought in Guadalcanal, New Georgia and the Philippines. The XIV Corps took over on Guadalcanal after the toughest fighting was over and its task was to mop up the last resistance. In New Georgia its task was more one of containing Japanese troops; however in January 1945 the XIV Corps was in the front-line, fighting the Japanese in the reconquest of Luzon. Griswold was a cautious Commander who advanced slowly so that his flanks would remain secure. His Corps was involved in bitter fighting at Clark Field and at Manila, where Japanese naval troops fought a suicidal last stand to save the capital which lasted a month. Griswold's men proceeded to the area east of Manila where members of the Japanese Shimbu group were holding out in caves. This was costly in casualties and the Corps was relieved on 14 March 1945 and sent south to clear the rest of Luzon.

**Groves, General Leslie, 1898–1970** Groves was the US General appointed to supervise the Manhattan Project: the building of the atomic bomb. Groves was a West Point engineer with no competence in atomic physics and after BUSH's first interview with him, Bush exclaimed 'We're in the soup.' However Groves proved an extremely competent director who dealt with all the bureaucratic problems arising from the scientific research. He arranged the purchasing of uranium and selected the site for the bomb-making project at Los Alamos. He was convinced the bomb would win the war; his scientific colleagues however had misgivings. Groves strenuously urged its use to end the war.

**Guderian, Colonel General Heinz, 1888–1953** Guderian was the architect of Germany's Panzer victories in France in May 1940, and in the USSR in June 1941. In 1937 he published a widely acclaimed textbook, *Achtung! Panzer!* in which he advocated his ideas about high-speed warfare. Most of the other officers in the German Army High Command were skeptical about his ideas; nonetheless he was selected to command XIX Panzer Corps, the vanguard of KLEIST's Panzer Army. He gave a perfect demonstration of his theory, breaking through at Sedan, crossing the Meuse, and traveling so fast that the German High felt it had to put a brake on him. Guderian led the Second Panzer Army in the invasion of the USSR, which accomplished the encirclement of the Soviet Armies in Klev and Uman. Guderian's Army was then assigned to advance on Moscow and approached from the south. Guderian, however, did not see eye to eye with his superior KLUGE, whom he persistently ignored and disobeyed. In December he was dis-

missed by HITLER in the purge of the eastern Generals for disobeying his orders and making a timely withdrawal. In February 1943 he was recalled to build up the morale of the Panzer Corps and given the honorary title of Inspector General of the Armored troops. He made reforms and reorganized the Panzer Army but what gains he had achieved were squandered at the great tank battle at Kursk in July 1943. On the day after STAUFFENBERG's Bomb Plot Guderian replaced ZEITZLER as Chief of General Staff but Hitler ignored his advice. Guderian applied pressure on Hitler to withdraw forces to a defensive line round Germany but Hitler would not countenance any withdrawal. On 21 March 1945 Guderian was finally dismissed. Hitler had never fully recognized Guderian's great gifts as a military Commander and theorist.

**Guérisse, Albert, 'Pat O'Leary,' 1911–1989** Guérisse was a Belgian doctor and an undercover agent who ran an escape route in southern France. Guérisse had been a medical officer in the Belgian Army but had come to Britain after Dunkirk. He assumed the identity of Pat O'Leary, a French Canadian, and joined the Royal Navy. While on an operation which the *Fidelity* conducted for the Special Operations Executive in the south of France, he was left behind by accident and arrested. He escaped and made contact with an escape organization run by the Scotsman, Ian Garrow, which had been set up to evacuate British troops left in France after Dunkirk. When its leader was arrested, Guérisse took over and built up the organization.

helped about 600 members of Allied ɔrces to escape in one year without ᴇceiving much help from London; it ᴠas only in July 1942 that Guérisse got M19 wireless operator. His organiza-ᴏn was not very security-conscious and all the leaders knew each other so by the end of 1942 many of them were on the run. In March 1943 Guérisse was betrayed by a double agent and arrested at Toulouse. He was tortured and imprisoned and spent the war in Dachau. On 29 April 1945 he was liberated and received a George Cross in recognition of his services.

# H

Haakon VII, 1872–1957 Haakon was a former Prince of Denmark who became the ruler of Norway after the country's independence in 1905. When the Germans invaded Norway, Haakon only just escaped capture in Oslo in April 1940 and along with his cabinet ministers fled for the north. He remained in Norway until the British withdrew and left in June 1940. With the Norwegian Government at his side he led the Norwegian Resistance from London and was recognized by the Allies as the legitimate government. Haakon made radio broadcasts to Norway to encourage his people to resist and up to 50,000 left to join his forces abroad. Morale in Norway was maintained by the production of illegal pamphlets and journals which tried to give the people an alternative version of events. In late 1944 Norwegians helped the Russians by invading German positions in northern Norway from Finland. In June 1945 Haakon returned to a liberated country which had remained staunchly anti-Nazi throughout the war.

Hacha, President Emil, 1872–1945 After the Munich Agreement President BENEŠ of Czechoslovakia resigned and in November 1938 Hacha was elected President. He was an international jurist with little political experience but the Czech people hoped that he would be able to deal with HITLER. He was given emergency powers by the National Assembly and uneasy relations with Germany lingered for several months. In March 1939 Hacha was summoned by Hitler to Germany and there broke down under pressure from the Führer and GOERING.

The Wehrmacht occupied Bohemia and Moravia on 15 March 1939 and von NEURATH was appointed Reich Protector of the provinces. The Protector had administrative control of the country but Hacha was retained as a puppet: he was powerless. After the war he was charged with high treason but died in prison before he could be tried.

Haile Selassie, Emperor of Abyssinia, 1891–1976 Haile Selassie was crowned King of Ethiopia in November 1930. In 1935 the Italians invaded Ethiopia and successfully drove Haile Selassie into exile in Britain in 1936. In 1940 he returned to Anglo-Egyptian Sudan to lead a refugee army and by January 1941 he once again had a foothold on Ethiopian soil. Together with Generals CUNNINGHAM and Platt who attacked from the southeast and the north, he was able to claim the whole country by the end of 1941. By January 1942 he had attained independence from Britain and in 1945 overcame British resistance both to his joining the United Nations as a full charter member and to his signing the peace agreement ending World War II as a national leader. A dynamic and modern-thinking man, Haile Selassie encouraged and welcomed his country into the vagaries of the twentieth century.

Halder, General Franz, 1884–1971 During World War I Halder was a member of the staff of the Crown Prince of Bavaria where he left his mark as an outstanding officer. In 1938 BECK resigned as Chief of General Staff and Halder was appointed to replace him.

Halder was *not* an admirer of HITLER and lent his support to various conspiracies to have him arrested, none of which materialized. Halder planned and led the invasions of Poland and of France. He warned Hitler against pursuing his Western offensive in 1939 but Hitler went ahead in May 1940, in spite of Halder's advice. Halder helped to plan the invasion of England and the attack on Russia in 1941. In December 1941 BRAUCHITSCH resigned and Hitler took over as Commander in Chief of the German Armed Forces. Halder continued as Chief of General Staff but was finally replaced by ZEITZLER in September 1942. He was arrested after the 1944 Bomb Plot against Hitler and was interned at Dachau. He was freed in 1945 and gave important evidence at Nuremberg.

**Halifax, Earl of (Edward Wood), 1881–1959** Halifax was the British Foreign Secretary from 1938 to 1940 in CHAMBERLAIN's government. In total agreement with Chamberlain's policy of appeasement, Halifax was nominated as Chamberlain's successor in 1940. However, he was unable to get CHURCHILL's support and was forced to step down but remained as Foreign Secretary until the end of 1940 when he was replaced by EDEN. (He remained a member of the War Cabinet until 1945.) In 1941 Halifax was appointed Ambassador to the United States of America, a position in which he excelled himself. Admired by the Americans, his integrity and diplomacy won him a large circle of friends which included ROOSEVELT and HULL.

**Halsey, Vice-Admiral William 'Bull,' 1882–1959** Halsey played a leading part in defeating the Japanese in the Pacific War. He was a leading exponent of naval air strategy, well-known for his flamboyance and quick temper. As Commander of Task Force 16, the carriers *Hornet* and *Enterprise*, he had arrived

at his Hawaiian base in April 1942 and had immediately set off to launch Lieutenant General DOOLITTLE's raid on Tokyo. He could have made a valuable contribution to the Battle of Midway but he was hospitalized because of a nervous skin disease. However he was soon fit and was called in by Admiral NIMITZ to break the stalemate in the Solomons campaign. Halsey was immediately involved in the Battle of Santa Cruz Island in October 1942 when the Japanese outmaneuvered the US. The Japanese anticipated all the American tactics and succeeded in sinking the *Hornet*. Halsey realized that the assignment to get the Guadalcanal campaign moving was a tough one. However the next major encounter between Japanese and American naval forces was the Naval Battle of Guadalcanal on 12–13 November 1942. In this case the US emerged successfully having sunk two Japanese battleships, two destroyers and six transport ships for the loss of two cruisers and four destroyers. Halsey realized that although the US had the advantage of radar they could not exploit it to the full because of the superior nightfighting skills of the Japanese. Together with Vice-Admiral KINKAID he drew up guidelines for nightfighting tactics which contributed to later successes in halting Japanese efforts to supply their troops in the Solomons.

Halsey realized that the step by step strategy in the Solomons would lead to increased resistance and so he suggested leap-frogging over concentrations of Japanese troops and on his suggestion Kolombangara was bypassed. However his forces were still used in 1943 for assaults on the Russell Islands, two islands of the Trobriand group and then Bougainville. Nimitz then decided to transfer him to the leapfrogging campaign in the Central Pacific and he became Commander of the 3rd Fleet. Halsey and SPRUANCE alternately took command of the Central Pacific Fleet (which was alternately called the 3rd or the 5th Fleet). Spruance held the command at the Battle of the Philippine Sea and Halsey at the Battle of Leyte Gulf. In October 1944 Halsey's fleet was off the coast of Leyte guarding the San Bernardino Strait. He was determined to get a crack at destroying the Japanese carrier fleet and waited for a sighting. When he was given the position of Vice-Admiral OZAWA's carrier fleet, Halsey went steaming off north with all his 64 ships leaving the San Bernardino Strait unprotected. This was the Japanese plan: they were short of naval aviators and aircraft and so the carrier force's only value was as a decoy. Admiral KURITA's battleships passed the San Bernardino Strait and but for the spirited fighting of elements of Vice-Admiral Kinkaid's 7th Fleet, they might have inflicted greater damage than the loss of one carrier and three destroyers. Halsey's pursuit of the carriers was highly successful and he either sank or damaged what remained of Japan's carrier fleet.

Halsey proved himself a brilliant director of naval aviation, liable to take unnecessary risks in contrast with Spruance who tended to be overcautious.

**Harmon, Major General Millard, 1888–1945** Harmon was an American Army officer who commanded land and air forces in the Pacific during the war. Before the war he had acted as military and air adviser to the HARRIMAN mission in England. From July 1941 to January 1942 he was Commander of the 2nd Air Force and then in June 1942 he was given command of US non-naval forces in the South Pacific. His troops took part in the fierce fighting on Guadalcanal and Harmon was made Vice-Admiral HALSEY's Deputy. He directed air offensives and in July 1944 was made Commander of USAAF for the whole of the Pacific Ocean area. He introduced the tactic of flying bombers at a low altitude so that they could improve their accuracy in hitting targets. He was lost and presumed dead in 1945 when his plane disappeared on a routine flight.

**Harriman, William Averell, 1891–1986** Harriman was a distinguished businessman turned diplomat, who served as US Ambassador in Moscow from 1943–46. He first arrived in London in March 1941 to negotiate Lend-Lease arrangements. He was given the rank of ambassador and accompanied Lord BEAVERBROOK on an Allied mission to Moscow in September 1941. The Germans had just invaded the USSR and Harriman had to reassure STALIN that the USA would send supplies and aid. In 1942 Harriman served on various Joint Allied Commissions in London including the Combined Production and Resources Board. In October 1943 he became Ambassador to Moscow and his main duty was to keep ROOSEVELT informed of Soviet attitudes. Harriman seems to have impressed Stalin, who had frequent meetings with him. Harriman became particularly concerned with the Polish problem, fearing that the Soviets would impose a Communist government on the country. In August 1944 he tried to get Soviet permission for US planes to use Soviet airfields to supply the Warsaw Uprising; however MOLOTOV and Stalin adamantly refused this request. At the Yalta Conference Harriman conducted private negotiations with Molotov to settle the question of Russian participation in the war in the Far East and is considered to have obtained the best possible solution. He was also made a member of the three-power committee to organize a new provisional government in Poland. With Sir A. Clark Kerr, Harriman tried very hard to increase the percentage of non-Communists in the new Government but Molotov did not give much ground. The USA and Great Britain had to concede that Soviet influence in Poland would be excessive and Harriman also warned that the USSR would wish to achieve the same results in other East European countries.

Harriman was a skilled negotiator, but faced with Russian intransigence there was little he could achieve.

**Harris, Air Chief Marshal Sir Arthur, 1892–1984** The Commander of No 5 Bomber Group at the outbreak of war, Harris became disillusioned with the effects of precision bombing and, when appointed Head of Bomber Command in February 1942, began to both advocate and institute 'area' bombing. This technique required the assembly of very large bomber fleets, up to a thousand or more, and the drenching of whole areas with high explosives and incendiaries. The aim was to use statistical probability rather than selectivity to destroy military targets and at the same time to make a direct assault on German civilian morale. The effectiveness of 'Bomber' Harris' methods has never been satisfactorily established though their morality has been much questioned.

**Hart, Admiral Thomas, 1877–1971** In 1939 Hart was appointed Commander of the US Asiatic Fleet which was stationed off the Philippines and consisted of two cruisers and a few destroyers, submarines and motor torpedo boats. At the time of the invasion of the Philippines by the Japanese, Hart's relations with General MACARTHUR, the Commander of Land Forces in the Philippines, were very strained. Hart's naval forces could do little to protect the Philippines and were withdrawn. Hart was appointed Naval Commander of ABDA (Australian - British - Dutch - American Command) in January 1942 but he only held the post for a month. He directed a couple of actions off the Dutch East Indies but retired from service shortly before the Battle of Java Sea. Hart returned to Washington but was soon recalled from retirement because of his experience to serve on the Naval Board, which he did until the end of the war.

**Hassell, Baron Ulrich von, 1881–1944** Hassell was a German diplomat who served as Ambassador to Italy until 1938 when he was suddenly retired and not given a further posting. In enforced retirement Hassell frequented resistance circles and members, such as GÖRDELER, BECK and the Kreisau circle. In February 1940 he made a personal initiative to negotiate peace terms with Great Britain via a mutual acquaintance of Lord HALIFAX but this faltered when none of the German Generals would give him the slightest encouragement. After this attempt Hassell increasingly put pressure on the younger members of his acquaintance to try to assassinate HITLER. Hassell was powerless himself to do anything but plan for Germany after a coup. He was an aristocrat who was a father figure to resisters. In 1942 he was warned by the Senior State Secretary in the Foreign Ministry that he was being watched by the Gestapo and he had to be careful about his behavior. He was not directly involved in the planning of the July Plot of 1944 but he was clearly implicated in it and shortly after the discovery of secret resistance documents in a safe at Zossen containing papers of Gördeler, CANARIS, Oster and Hassell, all four were arrested. Hassell was put on exhibition and his execution was public: he was hanged on a loop of piano wire.

**Heinrici, Colonel General Gotthard, 1889–** Heinrici was a German General who built up a reputation as a brilliant defensive fighter. After Field Marshal von KLUGE was promoted to command Army Group Center, Heinrici became Commander of the Fourth Army which held a line from Orsha to Rogachev. Between October and December 1943 the Russians mounted several offensives against this line but did not break through. Heinrici achieved this by concentrating his forces at Orsha and also by bringing in, daily, a fresh battalion to man the sector under greatest pressure. He only had ten depleted divisions but by putting three and a half of them at Orsha and by moving them round, battalion by battalion, so they all experienced front-line fighting, Heinrici was able to withstand forces six times greater than his own. However HITLER's orders not to retreat did not make this easy. Heinrici was then transferred to Slovakia in 1944 and fought a retreating battle in command of the First Panzer Army. In March 1945 General GUDERIAN prevailed on Hitler to replace HIMMLER with Heinrici as Commander of Army Group Vistula but it was too late. Heinrici could do little more than delay the obvious. He was captured by the Russians who jailed him until 1955.

**Henderson, Sir Nevile, 1882–1942** Henderson was the British Ambassador to Berlin from 1937 until the outbreak of the war and was a leading supporter of CHAMBERLAIN's appeasement policy. Henderson was blind to the excesses of the Nazi regime and said in 1938 that HITLER would not dare to make war 'if we really showed our teeth.' Henderson had a good relationship with GOERING with whom he went hunting. Henderson persistently ignored Foreign Office instructions to express his own opinions: for example he condemned Schuschnigg's behavior during the Austrian *Anschluss* and later played down the help Britain would give Poland. After the *Anschluss* Lord Halifax criticized his behavior. Eventually on 3 September 1939 Henderson handed RIBBENTROP Britain's ultimatum at 0900 giving the Germans two hours to withdraw from Poland. Britain was at war. Henderson was very disappointed and wrote an account of his experiences in *Failure of a Mission*. During the war Henderson founded a British War Refugees Fund. He also offered to return to Belgrade as Ambassador but this was turned down. He died shortly afterwards.

**Herrmann, Major Hajo, 1913–** Herrmann was the German bomber Commander who masterminded the use of the Messerschmitt Bf-109G as a free-ranging night-fighter. The Germans were having little success in shooting down Allied bombers with flak and Herrmann suggested to Field Marshal MILCH that daytime fighters could be used to shoot down the bombers over their target areas because flares, fire and spotlights could give enough light to pick out the bombers. This method was first tried out in July 1943 over the Ruhr and fifteen fighters shot down ten bombers. These 'Wild Boar' tactics were very successful and Herrmann was given 150 planes, better radar and infra-red detectors. These units were nearly shot down over Berlin in August 1943 by their own flak but they continued to wear down the Allied bombing offensive over Berlin with enough success to cause HARRIS to abandon it by the end of 1943.

**Hess, Rudolf, 1896–1987** A close friend of HITLER dating from the 1920s, Hess was figuratively second in line to the Führer and his Deputy in the Nazi Party. In May 1941 Hess took it upon himself to act as a peace emmissary and left Germany, alone, in a Messerschmitt 110 and crash-landed in Scotland. He intended to locate the Duke of Hamilton, whom he had met in more peaceful times, and make him persuade CHURCHILL to surrender before Britain was annihilated. Hess was astonished to find himself treated as a POW. Interned in England until after the war he was tried at Nuremberg, sentenced to life imprisonment and incarcerated at Spandau Prison in Berlin.

**Hewitt, Rear Admiral Kent, 1887–1972** Hewitt was the US expert on amphibious landings. His first major operation was the North African landings in November 1942 when he sailed from Hampton Roads in Virginia in command of 102 ships. He had to put the 24,500 strong all-American force under Major General PATTON ashore in three separate landings. As the Western Naval Task Force approached the North African coast the weather was very stormy and the forecast was not favorable but Hewitt decided to take a chance and fortunately was rewarded with a calm sea on 8 November. Hewitt was then given command of the US 8th Fleet off the North African coast and his next major operation was the landing on Sicily in July 1943. Hewitt was in command of the Western Naval Task Force and had 580 vessels under his command. Although there was an unpleasant swell on the day of the landing, the troops achieved surprise and met little opposition on the beaches. In September Hewitt commanded the US landings in southern Italy near Salerno, which nearly turned to disaster; although the Allied forces had foregone shore bombardment in order to achieve surprise, the Germans were prepared to resist them. Hewitt was then chosen to command the last major amphibious landing in Europe: the Anvil landings in southern France.

**Heydrich, Obergruppenführer Reinhard, 1904–1942** By birth and training, Heydrich belonged to the 'other side' of HITLER's Germany, the officer class which the Nazis both envied and disliked. But, cashiered from the Navy for trifling with the affections of a superior officer's daughter, he transferred his loyalties firmly to the new force in German life, joined the SS and was quickly chosen by HIMMLER as his deputy. He became head of the Reich Main Security Office, the central agency for internal counter-espionage and repression, arranged the Gleiwitz incident on the Polish border, which provided Hitler with his pretext for war in September 1939, and, after the invasion of the USSR, took charge of the operations of the extermination squads (*Einsatzgruppen*) which murdered the Jews of the occupied eastern territories in hundreds of thousands. It was his hand which drafted the protocol for the 'Final Solution of the Jewish Problem,' endorsed by the Wannsee Conference in January 1942 and led to the systematic murder of European Jews in the extermination camps of the east in 1942–4. He was then appointed Reich Protector (governor) of Bohemia-Moravia (occupied Czechoslovakia) and was assassinated in Prague by a team of Czech agents, specially parachuted into the country for the operation, in June 1942. By way of reprisal, the Germans destroyed the Czech village of Lidice and murdered its adult population. Heydrich stood out from the majority of the Nazi leadership by reason of his remarkable self-assurance, intense ability and apparently total inhumanity, a combination of qualities possessed otherwise only by Hitler himself, whom Heydrich, it is suspected, intended eventually to succeed. He frightened all who knew him, even Himmler.

**Himmler, Reichsführer-SS Heinrich, 1900–1945** After HITLER, Himmler is probably the most notorious of the leaders of the Third Reich. In the popular imagination he is indeed generally held responsible for the execution of all the terror and repression which the Reich visited on its victims. Popular belief is, in this instance, not very far from the truth. By diligent and unrelenting pursuit of power, Himmler had made himself by the last year of the war not only Head of the SS, and so Chief of the criminal and political police, of the concentration camp system and of a private army, the Waffen SS, but also

Minister of the Interior, Commander of the Replacement Army and an Army Group Commander on the Eastern Front. He was second in power to Hitler himself and widely regarded as his obvious successor, even though title to the succession was held by Goering. Himmler had begun his ascent to power early. The son of a Bavarian school-master, he had just missed war service in 1918 but joined a right-wing *Freikorps* in the Bavarian civil war which followed the armistice. He made a natural transition to the infant Nazi party and was with Hitler at the Munich putsch. He became head of the *Schützstaffel* (SS), originally a party strong-arm squad, in 1929, and quickly turned it into an efficient, disciplined rival to the SA, the party's Brownshirt militia. A decisive incident in his rise was the ruthlessness with which he and his SS subordinates liquidated the leadership of the SA, which Hitler had judged had grown overmighty, in the Blood Purge of June 30, 1934. His usefulness to Hitler was further confirmed by his provision of evidence against BLOMBERG and FRITSCH in the crisis of 1938, when the two generals were removed from the Ministry of War and the Army High Command, thus preparing the way for Hitler to subordinate the army to his direct control. On the outbreak of war he became responsible for the administration of the party's racial (anti-Semitic) policy, and, holding fanatical personal views on the subject, applied all his remarkable powers of organization to the extermination of the Jews of Poland and later of occupied Russia. In 1943 he succeeded FRICK as Minister of the Interior, thus consolidating in his hands all the judicial, police and other sanctionary powers of the German state. The attempt against Hitler's life by the military conspirators in the following year yet further increased his power, as Hitler looked to the Waffen SS to provide generals and soldiers of stronger loyalty. In January 1945 he was even appointed

to command Army Group Vistula, in the hope that he might by his devotion to the Führer stem the Soviet advance where the army generals had failed. In the last resort, however, he became impressed by his own position, suggested to Hitler, on the latter's incarceration in the Reich Chancellery, that power be passed to him and was instantly demoted by radio signal. True to his old loyalty, he at once obeyed the order. He was captured by the British after the war while disguised as a private soldier but, as soon as his identity was discovered, took poison and committed suicide. His character has continued to baffle students of the Third Reich. Despite his direct and freely admitted responsibility for monstrous cruelties, he was a retiring, even timid personality, kind to subordinates and animals, and apparently more interested in the rites and ideology of Nazism – runes, Nordic myths and Aryan genealogy – than in the pursuit of ultimate power. His loyalty to Adolf Hitler was certainly the mainspring of his actions, and he collapsed when accused of having violated the bond of trust.

**Hirohito, Emperor of Japan, 1901–1987**
Hirohito, the Imperial Son of Heaven of Great Japan, was held by many Westerners to have been responsible for the war in the Far East. He was a shy and ineffectual-looking man who was more interested in the study of marine biology than in politics and war. The Emperor's position in the constitution was not powerful: he presided over all cabinet meetings but, according to tradition, he never joined in discussions and merely gave his assent to decisions. He was not associated with any political party or group of men and his ministers would have never asked him his opinion on anything because that would have been embarrassing. The Japanese people loved their Emperor and he was respected as a deity: once the war had

begun they felt they were fighting the war for him and would gladly die for him.

Hirohito could see that TOJO's policy would lead to war and he tried to exert some pressure on Tojo to be more cautious. However when war broke out it was in his name and all proclamations and orders were issued in his name. Tojo, YAMAMOTO, and the other leading figures kept Hirohito informed of the events of the war but he chose to remain in the background. However as the war dragged on and the Homeland was in danger of being invaded, the Emperor, acting on the Marquis KIDO's advice, decided to speak out. On Hirohito's initiative Prince HONOYE was asked to go on a peace mission to the USSR. Hirohito saw the situation become even more critical: he witnessed the bombing of Tokyo and the dropping of the two atomic bombs created a profound impression on him. On 9 August 1945 the Cabinet was deadlocked in the discussion on whether to accept the Potsdam Declaration: the main stumbling block was fear over the Emperor's status after the war. Hirohito was on good terms with his Prime Minister, SUZUKI, and he decided that he was willing to risk his position to facilitate peace negotiations. For the first time Hirohito expressed his views when Suzuki appealed to him and he said 'I cannot but swallow my tears and sanction the proposal to accept the Allied Proclamation on the basis outlined by the Foreign Minister [TOGO].' On 14 August the decision to surrender was finally taken and again Hirohito made an emotional speech about the inevitability of peace. The Emperor also made a recorded speech giving the reasons for the surrender which was broadcasted the next day. It was the first time in history that the Emperor had addressed his people directly, and he used the words of his predecessor, the Emperor Meiji, that Japan had to 'accept the unacceptable,

endure the unendurable.' After the war Hirohito remained on the throne because MACARTHUR realized that to remove him would create bitter anti-American feelings and make it difficult to control Japan. However MacArthur was determined to destroy the Emperor's divinity and in January 1946 Hirohito made a declaration of non-divinity.

**Hitler, Führer Adolf, 1889–1945**
Whether or not Hitler is regarded as the author of World War II, its character and course can only be understood in terms of his own extraordinary personality and over-powering will. He himself had served as a junior soldier on the western front in World War I, and his experience of the trenches was as formative an influence upon his outlook as his indulged but unsuccessful youth and his years of adult vagrancy in pre-war Vienna. He believed that he and his generation of Germans – though he was German only by adoption, having been born a subject of Franz Josef – had been betrayed by their country's peacemakers and that it was their task to reverse the betrayal. In the aftermath of war he was drawn into extreme right-wing politics in Bavaria, joined and then took over one of the many small nationalist parties, the National Socialists. Hitler's party and some allied groups attempted a coup d'etat in Munich in November 1924. Its crushing by the police and army convinced him that he must henceforward gain power through constitutional means, which he eventually succeeded in doing at the election of January 1933. Within eighteen months he had persuaded parliament to vote him dictatorial powers and had inherited the Presidency. He had already fostered Germany's economic recovery by advanced fiscal policies and he next began the work of rearmament. By 1936 he judged himself strong, and the Western Powers weak, enough to risk reoccupying the

demilitarized Rhineland and in 1938 he embarked on outright measures of territorial aggrandizement: first the annexation of Austria, then of the Czech Sudetenland, then in 1939 of the rump of Czechoslovakia itself. His policies had by 1939, however, driven the Western Powers themselves to rearm and to guarantee the integrity of his next probable victim, Poland. When he attacked her on 1 September, France and Britain declared war. His generals viewed the outcome with anxiety, despite his last-minute diplomatic triumph in neutralizing Soviet Russia, but he proved their fears groundless by the speed of his victory in Poland. In the following spring his armies achieved effortless victories in France, Belgium and Holland. Strategic logic, as he saw it, next dictated that he should attack the USSR, lest STALIN eventually attack him, and in June 1941 he launched his armies on Moscow, Leningrad and the Ukraine. By the winter they were seriously overextended and, despite the taking of vast numbers of prisoners, still locked in combat with the Red Army. In the summer of 1942 they resumed their progress, but were checked and defeated at Stalingrad that winter. Hitler's strategy, always vulnerable at its narrow industrial and economic base, now lost its impetus and he was forced to fight defensively. He nevertheless succeeded in retaining absolute mastery over his own subordinates, in part by an apparatus of terror and repression, in part by a clever division of responsibilities. He left the generals to run the war in the USSR, but retained control of all other theaters in his own headquarters. Thus no one man had sufficient knowledge to argue with him whether or not the war was being lost. From the middle of 1943, when he lost his armored reserve in the USSR, in the Battle of Kursk, it was undeniably being lost. He nevertheless continued to wage a tenacious defense, believing that the development of miracle weapons and the appearance of rifts in the alliance of his enemies, whom he believed ideologically incompatible, would eventually bring Germany victory. After the army officers' attempt on his life in July, 1944, he directed the war more or less alone, and with sufficient acumen still to achieve a humiliating defeat of the Americans in the Ardennes Offensive (Battle of the Bulge) in December, 1944. By April, with the enemy's armies on German soil in both east and west it was clear even to him that he was beaten. Refusing the chance to escape from Berlin, he remained in his command bunker to the end, committing suicide only when his rearguards were actually locked in combat with the Soviets on the surface above. He had fought, as promised until 'five-past-midnight.'

**Ho Chi Minh, 1890–1969** Ho Chi Minh was the leader of the Vietnamese resistance to Japanese rule during the war. He had been associated with the Chinese Communist movement in Canton and had set up in China the Communist-dominated Viet Minh, which was to fight for Vietnamese independence. However CHIANG Kai-shek had him interned in jail from 1942–43 and it was only on the insistence of the OSS (Office of Strategic Services) that he was released to fight in Vietnam. He turned to the US in Kunming to help his movement and received arms and supplies from the Americans but instead of pursuing an out and out offensive against the Japanese, the Viet Minh remained in the highlands of Tonkin building a network of support and waiting for the defeat of the Japanese. In August 1945 his forces were strong enough to march into Hanoi and set up the Provisional Government of the Democratic Republic of Vietnam.

**Hodges, General Courtney Hicks, 1887–1966** An expert in infantry warfare, Hodges was Chief of Intelligence in 1941–42 but was commissioned to lead the X Army Corps late in 1942. Promoted to Lieutenant General of the 3rd Army in 1943, he soon was appointed by EISENHOWER to be Deputy to BRADLEY, Commander of the US 1st Army, which was preparing for the invasion of Europe. When in 1944 the Normandy forces were joined together into the 12th Army Group under Bradley, Hodges took over full command of the US 1st Army. He breached the Siegfried Line, captured Aachen and helped in winning the Battle of the Bulge by holding the northern half of the American line. His Army captured the bridge at Remagen and helped to encircle the Ruhr. When Germany fell he led his troops to the Pacific where they helped to capture Okinawa. Although not one of the most famous American commanders, Hodges was perhaps one of the best.

**Holland, Vice-Admiral Lancelot, 1887–1941** Holland was, appointed Commander of HMS *Hood* on 8 May 1941. He led the battlecruiser, the world's largest warship, in an attempt to intercept the *Bismarck* and *Prinz Eugen* on 24 May. They were sighted in the Denmark Strait and made contact at 0052. The ships opened fire and the Germans concentrated their fire on the *Hood* and although she managed to retaliate, a salvo from the *Prinz Eugen* started a fire. At 0600 the *Hood* blew up and sank. Holland was lost with his crew of 1400: only three survived.

**Homma, General Masaharu, 1888–1946** Homma was the Japanese General who led the invasion of the Philippines. Homma was an intelligence officer who was selected to lead the operation to take Luzon despite his lack of battle experience. He landed in northern Luzon a few days after Pearl Harbor and found that the Filipino troops melted away when faced by his seasoned veterans from the war in China. He had orders to take Manila first and hesitated

over whether to block off the US and Filipino withdrawal to the Bataan Peninsula or march into Manila knowing that General MACARTHUR had already left the city. Homma decided to take the capital and wasted valuable time. He then underestimated the numbers in Bataan and left only nine battalions to complete the capture of Luzon: his best division, the 48th, was withdrawn to take part in the invasion of the Dutch East Indies. His forces launched their first offensive against Mount Rosa in Bataan on 9 January 1942 and after a month of fierce fighting the offensive was halted. Homma was relieved of his command for incompetence and replaced by General YAMASHITA although Homma remained as a figurehead. In April 1942 70,000 US and Filipino troops surrendered but the Japanese Army had not prepared for a surrender on this scale and took the most expedient course: they marched the troops sixty miles to a railway line and then shipped them to Camp O'Donnell. En route the Japanese treated their prisoners badly: giving them no food or drink for five days, shooting stragglers and inflicting other hardships. This was the infamous Bataan Death March in which about 16,000 US and Filipino troops died and for which Homma was held responsible. In September 1945 Homma was arrested in Tokyo. He was tried in Manila and executed by firing squad in April 1946.

**Honda, Lieutenant General Masaki, 1889–1964** Honda was the Commander of the Japanese Thirty-third Army in Burma and one of the most able Army Commanders of the Burma Campaign. Honda's Army fought in the long battle of retreat following the failure of the Kohima and Imphal offensives in 1944. He had orders to hold a line from Lashio to Mandalay in January 1945 but his troops fought as far north as Mogaung and Myitkyina and held up the combined US and Chinese troops trying to open the Burma Road. In mid-February 1945 General SLIM's 14th Army made a brilliant maneuver which threatened to cut off Honda's forces and take Meiktila. The Japanese Commander Kimura put Honda in charge of operations outside Meiktila and Honda nearly cut off the British troops who had broken through to the city. The British had superior resources and Honda was forced to fight a long and bitter retreat through southern Burma.

**Hopkins, Harry, 1890–1946** Hopkins was a close friend and adviser of President ROOSEVELT. He had served as Secretary of Commerce and played a leading part in the direction and strategy of the war as Chairman of the Munitions Assignment Board and as a member of the Pacific War Council, the War Production Board and the War Resources Board. He was also Roosevelt's special adviser to the Allied leaders: in January 1941 he had talks with CHURCHILL to set the Lend-Lease arrangements in motion; in July of the same year he visited STALIN to discuss the USSR's needs. He visited London twice in 1942 and also attended all the major Allied conferences that took place. During these conferences he often acted as Roosevelt's spokesman and was called in to deal with tricky questions. At the Casablanca Conference he tried to mediate between Generals DE GAULLE and GIRAUD. At Yalta and Teheran he was particularly concerned with the future of Europe after the war. Hopkins's last important mission was after Roosevelt's death when President TRUMAN asked him to go as his special envoy to Moscow for talks with Stalin. Hopkins's poor health caused him much pain throughout the war but even on this last mission he overcame his suffering to get an agreement on the future government of Poland. He died shortly after the war.

**Höpner, General Erich, 1886–1944** One

of the Wehrmacht's tank experts and Panzer leaders, Höpner led the Fourth Panzer Group into the USSR in June 1941. As part of Army Group North, he headed first towards Leningrad but was then deployed to Moscow where his tanks penetrated enemy lines and almost reached Moscow, breaking through past Mozhaysk. He contracted dysentry in December 1941 when the Soviet counterattacks began. He was dismissed by HITLER in the purge of the eastern Generals and he was held responsible for the failure to take Moscow. Höpner was involved in STAUFFENBERG's July Plot of 1944 to kill Hitler and was at the War Office in Bendlerstrasse to direct a military takeover of power. When the news broke that Hitler was alive, he was arrested that evening by FROMM. He chose to go on trial and was hanged on 8 August.

**Hor-Belisha, Sir Leslie, 1894–1957** Hore-Belisha was the British Secretary of State for War from 1937–40. He was the only Jewish member of the Cabinet and was very outspoken in his views. As Secretary of State for War his brief was to modernize the Army but he ran into problems with his Chiefs of Imperial General Staff: GORT and later IRONSIDE. He criticized the slow speed of rearmament and was one of the ministers who agreed that Sir John Simon should tell CHAMBERLAIN to declare war at once on 2 September 1939. His outspokenness led to his fall in January 1940, but from the back-benches Hore-Belisha spoke out against CHURCHILL's conduct of the war. During the Vote of Confidence debate in June 1942, Hore-Belisha made a detailed attack on the War Cabinet's conduct of the war saying 'The army must have more mobility and more armor' but in the vote Hore-Belisha supported Churchill.

**Horrocks, General Sir Brian, 1895–1985** Field Marshal MONTGOMERY felt that Horrocks was one of the best Corps Commanders available for World War II and appointed him to command XIII Corps in the Battles of Alam Halfa and Alamein in the Western Desert. He accompanied Montgomery to Europe where he commanded XXX Corps in the Battle of Normandy, the advance to Brussels, Operation Market Garden to take Arnhem and the drive into Germany. An outstanding Commander, Horrocks led his Corps and Armies with drive and ability.

**Horthy, Admiral Miklos, 1868–1946** A former Admiral in the Austro-Hungarian Navy, Horthy served as Regent of Hungary from 1920–44. During World War II his main preoccupation was to keep Hungary's contribution to the war to a minimum. At first he decided to join the Axis because he would never fight on the side of the USSR, but on the other hand he was reluctant to condemn Great Britain and the USA. In August 1941 he sent an army into Yugoslavia and also one to the USSR. However in May 1943 Horthy refused to send in reinforcements. In March 1944 he tried to persuade HITLER to allow Hungarian troops to return but Hitler refused and threatened to occupy the country. Horthy continued trying to decrease the Hungarian contribution to the war by stopping the persecution of Jews but Hitler brought him to heel again with threats. In August 1944 Rumania collapsed and Horthy began negotiations with the Allies, and in October he announced Hungary's withdrawal from the war. Hitler immediately dispatched SKOR-ZENY, who kidnapped Horthy's son and took the citadel in Budapest. Horthy gave in, abdicated and was taken to Germany where he remained until the US freed him in May 1945. Horthy was a greater Hungarian nationalist – and caught between the two power blocks Germany and the USSR

had the misfortune to join the losing side, leaving Hungary to a Communist coup.

**Horton, Admiral Sir Max, 1883–1951** An expert in the field of submarine warfare, Horton was given command of the Reserve Fleet from 1937 to 1939. At the beginning of World War II he was in command of the difficult and dangerous Northern Patrol and in January 1940 became Flag Officer Submarines. In 1942 he was appointed Commander in Chief of the Western Approaches which meant that he was responsible for seeing that the convoys carrying supplies to and from North Africa could cross the Atlantic safely. Confronted with 400 German U-Boats, this was to prove a difficult task. Fortunately the 'air gap' in the mid-Atlantic was closed and more escorts were made available. By May 1943 the shrewd and competent Horton was able to turn the Battle of the Atlantic into the Allies' favor.

**Hoth, General Herrmann, 1885–1971** In June 1941 Hoth led the Third Panzer Army in the invasion of the USSR. His Group was to penetrate along the River Niemen to Kaunas and Vilna and link up with Genera GUDERIAN's Panzer Group at Minsk. In the first few weeks of the war Hoth and Guderian sealed off the pocket at Bialystok which led to the surrender of about 290,000 Russians. Hoth's forces regrouped east of Vyazma and continued the advance on Moscow but his Panzers were fighting in severe cold and in difficult terrain. However they reached the Moscow-Volga canal and were only twelve miles from Moscow when they faced the Soviet counterattack and were pushed back. The other Panzer Commanders, Guderian and HÖPNER, were dismissed but Hoth retained his command and led the Fourth Panzer Army in the advance on Stalingrad. When it became clear that General PAULUS' Army was trapped in Stalingrad Hoth led the valiant attempt to break through and relieve them. He only just failed. At Kursk Hoth led the Fourth Panzer Army in the southern pincer but he had insufficient artillery to achieve a breakthrough. HITLER finally lost confidence in him after the fall of Kiev in November 1943 and he was dismissed. A less volatile and colorful figure than Guderian, Hoth was a thoroughly competent tank Commander.

**Hoxha, General Enver, 1908–1985** In April 1939 MUSSOLINI's troops invaded Albania and King Zog and his government fled. Hoxha, an Albanian resistance leader had been trained in Moscow and set about organizing guerrilla bands to fight the Italian threat. In November 1941 he officially founded the Communist Party and in September 1942 he summoned a meeting of other groups which joined together in the LNC (National Liberation Movement). Although this was a broadly based popular movement, it stimulated the opposition of the more conservative elements in the country who formed the *Balli Kombetar* or National Front. The two sides were hostile to each other and fighting between them broke out after the Germans had occupied the country after the fall of Mussolini. Although the Special Operations Executive sent arms to both sides, they favored Hoxha's Army which had about 13,000 men and could count on the support of 60,000. By the time the Germans left Albania Hoxha was strong enough to proclaim a Provisional Government in October 1944 and a few months later set up his government in Tirana, capital of Albania. Hoxha was a very efficient political leader who was more concerned with seizing power than with driving the Germans out of Albania.

**Hull, Cordell, 1871–1955** Hull was ROOSEVELT's Secretary of State from

1933–44. He was a confirmed internationalist and played a large part in founding the United Nations. Before the USA declared war on Japan, Hull was involved in protracted negotiations with the Japanese (which began in July 1941) over the situation in the Far East. He had the advantage of having all Japanese messages from Tokyo to Washington decoded and this meant that he could see that the Japanese were preparing for war. In September 1941 Hull persuaded the President not to meet Prime Minister KONOYE because he felt that there would have to be a diplomatic agreement to prepare the ground. The final stage of negotiations opened on 22 November 1941 when the US and Japanese considered draft proposals for an interim agreement which outlined a timetable for Japanese withdrawal from Indo-China and eventually from China. This could have saved the day but the Chinese did not like the proposal, fearing that they were being abandoned by the US. After consultations with the President, Hull submitted a final demand that Japan withdraw from all of mainland Asia. This was unacceptable to the Japanese and they handed Hull the Declaration of War two hours after Pearl Harbor had begun (7 December 1941).

During the war Roosevelt conducted much of US foreign affairs himself through his special envoys, HOPKINS and HARRIMAN. Hull had no more than weekly meetings with the President. However he had his own concerns and pursued a policy of trying to win over the Vichy Regime in France which led to the DARLAN Agreement. US relations with the Free French movement of DE GAULLE were soured by this and Hull refused to recognize de Gaulle's Committee until August 1943. He suffered from ill-health but was able to lead the US delegation to the Foreign Ministers' Conference at Moscow in 1943 which solved many postwar problems.

Hull also did much work for the Dumbarton Oaks Conference in which the workings of the proposed United Nations were discussed. He retired shortly afterwards because of ill-health.

**Hurley, Major General Patrick, 1883–1963** ROOSEVELT appointed Hurley as US Minister to New Zealand in 1942 and also used him as a personal envoy to the battlefronts in the USSR and Middle East sending back reports on the situation. He was then sent as a trouble-shooter to China in August 1943 to deal with the military and supply problems. He was soon appointed Ambassador as the situation in China became more difficult and General STILWELL was dismissed. Hurley tried to mediate between CHIANG Kai-shek and the Communists. He visited MAO Tsetung's Headquarters and almost won his confidence but Chiang was unwilling to come to any agreements with the Communists and Hurley's mission failed.

**Husseini, Amin el (Grand Mufti of Jerusalem), 1893–1974** Husseini was an active opponent of the formation of a Jewish state in Palestine and fomented the Arab revolt of 1936 in Palestine. In October 1939 the Mufti visited Iraq which, under Nuri el-Said, was pro-British. Pressure from the Mufti and support from within Iraq from Arab freedom fighters helped to bring down the pro-British government replacing it with the pro-German government of RASHID Ali (1 April 1941). The new government was short-lived; the successful British invasion of Iraq, 2 May 1941, forced Husseini into exile in Germany. He spent the rest of the war working for the Axis and introduced units of Moslems into the ranks of the German Army. In 1945 he was placed under house arrest in France but escaped to Cairo in May 1946.

**Hyakutake, Lieutenant General Haruyoshi, 1888–1947** Hyakutake was the Commander of the Japanese Seventeenth Army which fought in Guadalcanal in 1942. In early August 1942 it became clear that the US troops on Guadalcanal were planning on staying on the island and Hyakutake was given orders to re-capture the island. He had some 50,000 men under his command but they were scattered in the Solomons, Philippines, New Guinea, Manchuria, Guam and Java so he decided to send the 2nd Division under General Ichiki. Ichiki launched an attack on the airstrip on Guadalcanal, Henderson Field, but lost most of his 900 men on 21 August. Hyakutake decided to send a stronger force, about 4000 men, under General Kawaguchi, but again they were massacred at the Battle of Bloody Ridge on 12–13 September 1942. Hyakutake put off plans to take Port Moresby and decided to take over operations on Guadalcanal himself. He had 30,000 men landed on the island and on 23 October launched a complicated operation which again failed. His troops did not attack as planned and their communications were bad. He continued to plan the destruction of Henderson Field but after the Navy failed to knock it out in the Naval Battle of Guadalcanal (12–13 November) his troops' morale slumped. His men were disease-ridden and starving but continued to fight the Americans despite the lack of air support. On 31 December 1942 the Japanese High Command decided to order Hyakutake to withdraw but he only learned of this two weeks later. His men were withdrawn in secret over the next week.

# I

**Ibn Saud, Abd-ul Aziz, King of Saudi Arabia, 1880–1953** King Ibn Saud was the founder of Saudi Arabia and its King from 1932–53. During the war American interest in the country increased because of its rich oil deposits. Germany and Japan had both tried to convince Ibn Saud to sell them oil but he decided to stick to his policy of neutrality and friendship with Great Britain. (In fact the British government paid him a subsidy in 1940, 1941 and 1942 to compensate him for his loss of revenue from the pilgrimages to Mecca.) The US oil companies felt British influence was too strong and in 1943 President ROOSEVELT announced that Saudi Arabia was eligible for Lend-Lease aid. The Americans sold the Saudis arms and sent a military mission to train soldiers. In 1945 after the Yalta Conference, Roosevelt and CHURCHILL visited Saudi Arabia and were most impressed by their talks with Ibn Saud.

**Ickes, Harold, 1874–1952** Ickes was President ROOSEVELT's Secretary of the Interior and had responsibility for protecting national resources: coal mines, fuel, fisheries etc. In July 1943 he was appointed Director of the Petroleum Reserves Corporation and set about safeguarding US oil supplies by acquiring the rights to oilfields outside the USA, especially in the Middle East.

**Ilyushin, Sergei, 1894–1977** Ilyushin was a brilliant aeronautical engineer who designed one of the Soviet Air Force's most successful airplanes: the Il-2 Shturmovik. However the Il-2 he designed was never fast enough so it was improved and became the Il-10 which saw service in the last months of the war. Ilyushin also designed the main Soviet long-range bombers, the DB-3 and the Il-4. Ilyushin was awarded the STALIN Prize in 1942, 1943 and 1946.

**Inayat Khan, Noor, 'Madeleine,' 1914–1944** Noor Inayat Khan received a posthumous George Cross for her work as a wireless operator in Paris in 1943. She was the daughter of an Indian mystic and an American who was born in the Kremlin and brought up in Britain and France. When war broke out she was evacuated to Britain where she was recruited by the Special Operations Executive and trained as a wireless operator. She was a far-from-ideal agent because she was very striking and spoke both French and English with a foreign accent. She was shy and gentle and her training officers did not consider her suitable for active service; nonetheless, Colonel BUCKMASTER decided to send her to France even before she had completed her training. On 16 June 1943 she landed by Lysander aircraft and made contract with the *Cinéma* network in Paris. Unfortunately at the time of her arrival, Gestapo agents were rounding up members of the network and they obtained her full description and her codename 'Madeleine.' She had several narrow escapes but refused to return to England when the opportunity arose until a replacement had arrived. In mid-October 1943 she was betrayed by a woman for $2000. Her codebooks and a record of all the messages she had sent were captured with her but a German attempt to use her to communicate false information to London failed. She was taken to Pforzheim Prison and kept in chains until she was transferred to Dachau where she was shot on 13 September 1944.

**Inonu, President Ismet, 1884–1974** Inonu was the ruler of Turkey throughout the war and maintained a strict policy of neutrality. From 1942–44 the entry of Turkey into the war on the Allied side was a question that was constantly raised at the Allied conferences. After the Casablanca Conference CHURCHILL met Inonu at Adana on 30/31 January 1943 and proposed aid to Turkey if she would allow the Allies to use air bases to attack Rhodes, but nothing came of these talks. After the Moscow Conference EDEN visited Turkey to apply more pressure to get Turkey to enter the war but this was refused. After Teheran ROOSEVELT and Churchill again tried to persuade Inonu to enter the war and again met with little success. In 1944 Inonu finally made some concessions to the Allies and cut down the export of chrome to Germany and then in August broke off diplomatic relations with Germany. In February 1945 Turkey declared war on Germany at last but her motive was to secure a place at the founding conference of the United Nations and Turkey did not begin and military operations at that late date. Inonu's policy of neutrality was best for Turkey.

**Ironside, Field Marshal Sir Edmund, 1880–1959** A soldier of the old school, Ironside was an intelligence officer in the Boer War (1899–1902) and Commander of the Allied Forces in north Russia in 1918–19. In addition he was fluent in seven languages. In 1939 HORE-BELISHA found that he could not work well with GORT, his Chief of Imperial General Staff (CIGS), and replaced

him with Ironside who at that time was Inspector General of Overseas Forces. Gort became Head of the British Expeditionary Force, a position that Ironside had always wanted. In May 1940 Ironside was replaced as CIGS by DILL and assumed the post of Commander in Chief Home Forces. It has been stated that Ironside was the model for John Buchan's fictional hero, Richard Hannay, in *The 39 Steps*, a distinct possibility on examination of his adventurous life.

**Ismay, General Sir Hastings, 1887–1965** During World War I General Ismay sought but never found action in a major theater but did serve in Somaliland. In 1939 he became Head of the Secretariat of the Committee of Imperial Defense and when CHURCHILL became Prime Minister and Minister of Defense in May 1940, Ismay became his Chief of Staff. In this post the diplomatic and politic Ismay served as the interpreter and communicator of information between Churchill and the people who ran the machinery of war. Terse, tactless questions and answers were intercepted, rephrased and transmitted so that no one was offended. Ismay became the accepted channel of communication between Churchill and his Chiefs of Staff and Generals. He liaised with the Americans on behalf of Churchill and attended several conferences including the Foreign Secretaries Conference in Moscow. Admired by everyone, he was once toasted by Admiral KING 'Pug Ismay, whose contribution to our victory could never be properly rewarded.'

**Iwabuchi, Admiral Sanji, 1893–1945** Iwabuchi was a Japanese Commander who led a suicidal attempt to keep US troops from taking Manila, YAMASHITA, the General in command of Japanese troops in the Philippines, had ordered a general withdrawal from Manila and a last stand was to be fought in the north. Iwabuchi and his 15,000 naval forces did not come under Yamashita's control and they determined to fight to the end for the city. Iwabuchi's men demolished sections of the city and held it street by street. It took the US 37th Division over a month to clear the resistance in which none of the Japanese survived and approximately 100,000 Filipino civilians died.

# J

**Jeschonnek, General Hans, 1899–1943** Jeschonnek served as the German Chief of Air Staff from 1939–43. He was a World War I flying ace who had been picked by GOERING to help build up the Luftwaffe. He was very hard-working and anxious to prove the value of air power. The rivalry between the Luftwaffe and the German Army led to a serious mistake in May 1940: HITLER gave the Luftwaffe a free hand to clear the Dunkirk pocket and thus gave the British Expeditionary Force a chance to escape. Goering and Jeschonnek were the architects of this fiasco. Jeschonnek had his own feud with MILCH and on the whole was more successful in obtaining Hitler's ear but as German fortunes declined so the pressure on Jeschonneck and his Air Force to counter the bombing offensive increased. Jeschonnek was not used to planning defensive operations and too often his fighters arrived too late to intercept a bombing mission over the Reich. Goering lost confidence in him and very rarely consulted him. Finally the situation became intolerable: Jeschonnek gave orders for the Berlin air defenses to fire on 200 German fighters who had mistakenly assembled there during a catastrophic raid on the Peenemunde Rocket Station. Jeschonnek shot himself on the next day.

**Jodl, General Alfried, 1890–1946** Jodl originally was a Bavarian artillery officer. In 1938 he became Head of the Operations Section of OKW (*Oberkommando der Wehrmacht*), the organization which replaced the War Ministry and the High Command. In 1939 he became Chief of Staff to KEITEL, Chief of OKW. In this position Jodl directed all the Nazi campaigns except the Russian campaign as Keitel was a somewhat weak and ineffectual leader leaving all policy decisions to the dynamic and talented Jodl. Jodl attended the twice-daily conferences over which HITLER presided and turned Hitler's strategy into concrete tactical operations. In 1944 Jodl was promoted to Colonel General. On 7 May 1945 only one week after Hitler's suicide, Jodl signed the surrender of the German Army at Rheims. He was tried at Nuremberg for war crimes and pleaded 'soldier's obedience' as his defense for his actions but he was convicted and hanged.

**Johnson, Group Captain James, 1916–** 'Johnnie' Johnson was the RAF official top fighter pilot with a score of 38 planes shot down during the war. He flew in the Battle of Britain, the Dieppe Raid and during the D-Day build up. In the last year of the war he flew with a Canadian fighter-bomber formation.

**Jongh, Andrée de, 1916–** Andrée de Jongh was a Belgian school-master's daughter who helped set up an escape route for Prisoners of War (POWs) known as the Comet Line. She organized a chain of contacts from Brussels via Paris to Bilbao and Gibraltar. In August 1941 she turned up at the British consulate in Bilbao with a British soldier and two Belgians and thereafter provided a regular supply of escapees. She was first interrogated by the Gestapo in 1941 who put a price on her father's head. He was captured and executed the year after. In May 1942 de Jongh moved the headquarters of her organization to Paris and continued to help POWs but in the spring of 1943 she was arrested on the Spanish frontier. She was sent to Fresnes Prison in Paris and then to a concentration camp in Germany but the Gestapo never realized the important role she had played in running the Comet Line. Twenty-three of those who helped to run the line were executed but de Jongh survived and went on to work with lepers in Addis Ababa after the war.

**Joubert de la Ferté, Air Chief Marshal Sir Philip, 1897–1965** Joubert de la Ferté was a senior RAF Commander with a somewhat acrimonious temperament. In 1939 he was on duty in India and was recalled to become Assistant Chief of Air Staff and adviser both on the use of radar and on co-operation with the Royal Navy. He was promoted to become Head of Coastal Command, a force which had been neglected in favour of Bomber and Fighter Command. Joubert tried to increase its reconnaissance capabilities although he often had to divert his planes to Bomber Command duties over Germany. His outspokenness did not please the politicians he had to deal with and in the fall of 1943 Joubert was posted to Southeast Asia Command to be Deputy Chief of Staff for Information and Civil Affairs.

**Joyce, William 'Lord Haw-Haw,' 1906–1946** Possessing a style and personality totally different from his Pacific equivalent TOKYO ROSE, William Joyce (Lord Haw-Haw) subjected the British population to propaganda that was a curious mixture of fact and fiction with a preponderance of the latter. Amusing but vicious, Joyce did all that was possible to undermine the confidence of the

Allies beginning each broadcast with, 'This is Jairmany calling,' a parody of his public-school accent. His mother was English and his father Irish. He was born in Brooklyn in New York City and moved to England in 1921. At the outbreak of war he and his wife went to Germany where he offered his services to the Nazis. Just after the end of the war he was arrested at Flensburg by the British and was taken to London to be tried at the Old Bailey for high treason. His only defense was that he was an American citizen and therefore not legally able to perform acts of treason against Britain. The prosecution however stated that for the first nine months of the war he had a British passport and therefore did owe allegiance to the crown. He was found guilty and sentenced to death. All appeals were turned down and he was executed in 1946.

**Juin, Marshal Alphonse Pierre, 1888–1967** Juin graduated from St Cyr Military Academy at the top of his class, a class which also claimed Charles DE GAULLE as a member. In 1940 while leading a Division of the French 1st Army, Juin was captured but was released at the special request of PÉTAIN. He was offered the position of Minister of War in the Vichy government but turned it down accepting instead the position of Commander in Chief in North Africa replacing WEYGAND. Disillusioned with the Vichy government he enthusiastically joined the Allies in November 1942 and distinguished himself in North Africa against ROMMEL and in Italy against KESSELRING who held Juin in high esteem as a military commander. In 1944 he became Chief of Staff of the French National Defense Committee. He helped to liberate France and was posthumously appointed Marshal of France by de Gaulle.

# K

**Kaltenbrunner, Ernst, 1902–1946** An initiator and perpetrator of many of the Nazi atrocities, Kaltenbrunner was Head of the Austrian SS (*Sicherheitsdienst*) before the *Anschluss*. In 1943 he was appointed to replace the assassinated HEYDRICH as Head of the Reich Main Security Office. He was responsible for the Gestapo, the Security Service, the extermination squads and the concentration camps. A favorite of HITLER, he sanctioned the brutal inhumanities of the Nazi regime, murdering POWs, Jews, enemies and rivals indiscriminantly. It was said that although HIMMLER was technically his superior Himmler himself was afraid of the malicious and malevolent Austrian. Refusing to recognize even his own signature at Nuremberg he was the third of ten Nazis hanged on 16 October 1946.

**Katukov, General Mikhail, 1900–** Katukov was a Tank Commander in the Red Army. He commanded various tank armies near Moscow (in 1941), on the Voronezh Front (in 1942–43) and in Belorussia and the Ukraine in 1944. He is remembered for having held up GUDERIAN's Panzer Group south of Tula in October 1941.

**Keitel, Field Marshal Wilhelm, 1882–1946** Keitel was brought in by HITLER to be head of the unified defense staff to replace the War Ministry and the Army Command, the *Oberkommando der Wehrmacht*, in 1938. He was selected for his lack of personality and lack of intellectual ability. He carried out Hitler's orders without question and was known as *Lakaitel* (*Lakai* means lackey). He was involved in most strategic decisions but only to the extent of giving Hitler advice, and then only when it was sought. JODL, his deputy, took on most of the real work of the OKW. Keitel was arrested after the war and although his defense was that he was obeying orders, he was found guilty of war crimes at Nuremberg and hanged.

**Kennedy, Joseph, 1888–1969** Kennedy was US Ambassador to Great Britain from 1937–41 and he was a firm believer in US isolationism. He did not understand CHAMBERLAIN's policy of appeasement and felt that Britain could not possibly fight a war against Germany. He told ROOSEVELT that he expected Germany to win the war. In November 1940 he resigned and returned to the USA where he became a supporter of the Lend-Lease program.

**Kenney, General George, 1889–1977** Kenney was MacArthur's Air Commander for the operations in New Guinea and the Solomons. When he arrived to take up his appointment as Commander in Chief of the US Far East Air Force in the southwest Pacific, he found the situation was confused. US-Australian rivalry led him to separate the USAAF and RAAF, and he made the administrative side more efficient. For the New Guinea campaign he developed the use of air transport for troops in the jungle. He took part in the massive invasion of the Philippines and for the operations in Corregidor started to use napalm bombs. He was a man of tremendous energy and ambition and attended the Japanese surrender ceremony in Tokyo Bay on 2 September 1945.

**Kesselring, Field Marshal Albrecht, 1885–1960** Kesselring is considered one of the half dozen most talented Generals of World War II. Like HALDER and JODL he was by origin a Bavarian artillery officer but had transferred in 1933 to the embryo Luftwaffe. He commanded air fleets in the campaigns over Poland and Belgium in 1939 and 1940, and during the Battle of Britain commanded the Luftflotte II which was stationed in northeast France and the Low Countries. His air fleet was on the verge of knocking out Fighter Command when GOERING decided that the bombing offensive be diverted to London. Kesselring launched two daylight raids on London but aircraft losses were excessive and their failure led to the indefinite postponement of Operation Sealion.

In 1941 Kesselring was sent to Italy and made Commander in Chief South. sharing with ROMMEL the direction of the North African campaign. In Rome where his head-quarters was situated, Kesselring often lost touch with events on the Front but his constant theme was the need for more aircraft in the Mediterranean which would have been decisive. The lack of air cover speeded up the withdrawal from North Africa as it became impossible to keep the troops adequately supplied. However once fighting shifted to Sicily and Italy Kesselring came into his own and conducted a brilliant defense of the peninsula. Without adequate reserves in Italy he held up the Allies in Sicily by gradually moving his line back into the northeast corner of the isle, thus giving the Allies no room to maneuver. In Italy his persistent defense of the Gustav or Winter Line gave rise to frustration in the Allied camp and even after their eventual break-through he was able to halt General ALEXANDER's forces south of the Po.

In March 1945 Hitler transferred him to the west to replace RUNDSTEDT as Commander in Chief but the Front there was beyond holding. He eventually negotiated surrender with the Americans but he remained loyal to HITLER until he had news of his death. Imprisoned in Italy after the war he was tried for war crimes. His death sentence was commuted to life imprisonment. He was released in 1952 due to ill health.

**Keyes, Lieutenant Colonel Geoffrey, 1917–1941** Keyes was awarded a posthumous Victoria Cross for his courageous attempt to assassinate ROMMEL. Keyes was a member of LAYCOCK's Commando groups who participated in various missions in Syria and Crete. He was then selected to go on a dangerous mission to attack Rommel's headquarters. On 17 November he and his group were landed by submarine near Appolonia and they attacked their target. Many were killed but Rommel no longer used the building. Keyes was killed during this mission.

**Khrushchev, Nikita, 1894–1973** During the war Khrushchev served as a Political Commissar on various fronts and his duty was to keep an eye on the military and make sure they obeyed STALIN's orders. As Marshal BUDENNY's Political Commissar on the Southwest Front in June 1941 he witnessed the failure of the massed Red Armies to subdue the Germans. Khrushchev had strict orders not to allow valuable industrial installations to fall into the hands of the Germans and dismantled as much equipment as possible and sent it east. He also blew up the Dniepr Dam and effectively disrupted all industrial activity in the Ukraine. He saw the fall of both Budenny and TIMOSHENKO for incompetence but their replacement, YEREMENKO, finally managed to reverse the trend of German victories. Khrushchev built up a good relationship with Yeremenko which continued after the war. In 1944 Khrushchev served on the 1st Ukrainian Front and undertook purges in the Ukraine so he could build a solid power base for the future political struggles.

**Kido, Marquis Koicho, 1886–1977** Kido was the Japanese Lord Privy Seal and the Emperor HIROHITO's closest adviser during the war. Early in 1944 he decided that Japan could not win the war and he began to talk to senior politicians about peace. After the fall of TOJO in July 1944 and the fall of KOISO in April 1945, Kido was behind the appointment of the peace-seeking SUZUKI as Premier. Kido's main concern was that the peace would not mean an end to the Emperor's position and power. Towards the end when it was clear that the Emperor's position was not guaranteed, Kido still pressed Suzuki into getting agreement on that clause in the surrender terms. Kido was a friend of ANAMI but in the last days of the war these two were completely opposed. After the war Kido was tried by a military tribunal and sentenced to life imprisonment.

**Kimmel, Admiral Husband, 1882–1968** Kimmel had been unexpectedly appointed Commander in Chief of the US Pacific Fleet on 1 February 1941. Although he had received a warning from Washington that war was approaching, the only action he took was to send his carriers on maneuvers. He had not been properly briefed on the seriousness of the situation and expected the Japanese to attack the Philippines first. He did not liaise with General Short, the Army Commander at Pearl Harbor, who controlled land-based aircraft and had radar. By the time the message that Japan was about to declare war arrived from Washington, Pearl Harbor had been under attack for several hours.

Kimmel was held responsible and was removed from his command on 17 December 1941. The subsequent investigation censured Kimmel and he applied for retirement and took no further part in the war.

**King, Admiral Ernest, 1878–1956** King was one of the giants of US strategic planning. When the USA entered the war, King was appointed Commander in Chief of Naval Forces and then in March 1942 took over the duties of Chief of Naval Operations, making him the most important figure in the US Navy. He was a member of the US Joint Chiefs of Staff Committee and also of the Combined Chiefs of Staff Committee with the British and never failed to expound his point of view. His constant theme was that the US Navy could win the war in the Pacific if it were given a greater share of resources. This often brought him into conflict with the British; he only received MARSHALL's support if the British were dragging their feet over operations in Europe.

As Chief of Naval Operations King was behind NIMITZ and helped to make the fleet train system work. This system helped to keep carriers and battle cruisers at sea without needing to return to base for repairs or servicing. King stayed in Washington throughout the war leaving operational command to his subordinates, but he is remembered as the architect of the victory in the Pacific.

**King, Prime Minister William MacKenzie, 1874–1950** King was the Liberal Party Prime Minister of Canada throughout the war. King was elected in 1940 with a huge majority. He soon decided to win over the Canadians to war gradually and in this he was successful. By April 1942, he initiated and passed a measure to allow conscription. King liked to play the intermediary between President ROOSEVELT and Prime Minister CHURCHILL and he was the host at two conferences in Quebec in August 1943 and in September 1944. Towards the end of 1944 he faced a crisis because of the rising number of Canadian casualties but he resolved this by getting his Defense Minister to resign.

**Kinkaid, Admiral Thomas, 1888–1972** Kinkaid made his reputation as an aggressive naval commander off the shores of Guadalcanal. In November 1942 he was in command of Task Force 16, the *Enterprise* and the *Hornet*, which took part in the Battle of Santa Cruz Island. In this encounter the *Hornet* was lost, but huge losses of aircraft were inflicted on the Japanese. Kinkaid was then made Commander of Task Force 67, a cruiser squadron, and set about improving night-fighting techniques so that he could prevent the Japanese supplying their men by the 'Tokyo Express' by night. After a successful operation as Commander of the Northern Forces in the Aleutian Campaign, Kinkaid was appointed Commander of the 7th Fleet, which was a fleet of transports and converted carriers. It transported the 6th Army to Leyte in October 1944 and during the Battle of Leyte Gulf came under attack from Vice-Admiral KURITA's big cruisers. However his carriers put as many aircraft as possible in the air and held off the Japanese until Kurita lost his nerve and withdrew.

**Kirponos, Colonel General Mikhail, 1892–1941** Kirponos was Commander of the Southwest Front (Kiev District) in June 1941 when the German invasion of the USSR began. He was able to hold up the advance of the German Army Group South at the Polish border with his tank units, but once these had been overrun, his forces withdrew to Kiev. In September he sought STALIN's permission to withdraw further but Stalin demanded that he hold Kiev. As the High Command debated the next step, time ran out for the men in Kiev and Kir-

ponos and his staff were killed while trying to break out of encirclement. Some 500,000 Soviet prisoners were taken by the Germans in this debacle.

**Kleist, Field Marshal Paul Ewald von, 1881–1954** Kleist was a top Panzer Commander in the German Army. In May 1940 he was in command of the Panzer Arm of the Armies of GUDERIAN and HOTH, which crossed the Meuse at Sedan with such masterful efficiency and speed that it was held as a supreme example of mobile warfare throughout the war. Whenever the German High Command counseled caution, the generals were reminded that had it not been for the speed of the crossing at Sedan, France might not have collapsed so easily. In 1941 KLEIST held the command of First Panzer Group which was part of Army Group South's advance into the Ukraine. Kleist's advance was slowed down by tank opposition from KIRPONOS' forces and had to be speeded up by the diversion of Guderian's Panzer Group from Army Group Center. The largest encirclement was achieved at Kiev and Uman and some 665,000 men were taken but valuable time was lost and the advance to Moscow was held up. Kleist's First Panzer Army was given orders in 1942 to take the oilfields in Baku and drive through the Caucasus. Although Kleist's troops reached Mozdok they ran out of gasoline and were forced to withdraw in a hurry leaving equipment behind because VATUTIN threatened to cut off the German troops in the Caucasus. Kleist was then given command of Army Group A which fought in the long retreat in the southern Ukraine in 1943–44. He was taken prisoner by the Soviets and died in jail. Kleist was a reliable Panzer Commander, without the brilliance of Guderian.

**Kluge, Field Marshal Gunther von, 1882–1944** Kluge was a respected figure in the German Army who commanded the Fourth Army with great success in the Polish and French campaigns. In 1941 he led that Army in its advance in the USSR as part of Army Group Center, but he was technically superior to GUDERIAN, who refused to act as his subordinate and did not consult Kluge concerning his actions. Kluge feared HITLER's wrath and in the wake of the Soviet counter-offensive in December 1941 he evolved a technique for dealing with Hitler about the latter's prohibition on retreat. He would telephone Hitler repeatedly and negotiate a limited retreat. A series of repeated 'little retreats' eventually constitutes a full retreat. He managed to keep Hitler's confidence and he was appointed Commander in Chief of Army Group Center, distinguishing himself in the defensive battles to keep his front stable. On 1 July 1944 he became Commander in Chief of the West after Hitler had lost confidence in RUNDSTEDT. Kluge worked hard to mount a counterattack at Avranches but he did not have sufficient forces to stop the US VII Corps breaking out. Kluge became very depressed about the situation on the Western Front and at the same time he was under pressure from STÜLPNAGEL to join the Generals' Plot against Hitler. On the day of the July Plot Kluge refused to commit himself until he had absolute proof of Hitler's death and when this was not forthcoming he refused to join. Hitler was suspicious about his participation and thought that Kluge had tried to negotiate with the Allies. On 17 August Kluge was dismissed and recalled to Berlin but he swallowed poison on the way back leaving a testament in which he affirmed his loyalty to Hitler.

**Knox, W Frank, 1874–1944** Knox was a Republican who held the post of Secretary of the Navy from July 1940 until his death in April 1944. He was an experienced politician and administrator on whom Roosevelt could rely to do the job well. As Secretary of the Navy he supervised the expansion of the Navy and insured that the fleet in the Pacific was supplied.

**Koenig, General Marie Pierre, 1898–1970** Koenig gained some of his military expertise in the French Colonial wars and served as a captain in the Norway campaign in 1940. When the Allies were forced to withdraw from Norway he returned to France only to be compelled to retire to England when France fell. He joined DE GAULLE's Free French Army and was sent to North Africa to command a force largely made up of members of the Foreign Legion. An enthusiastic and dynamic leader he conducted the defense of Bir Hacheim in June 1941. Although he was forced to withdraw, his stand against ROMMEL's Panzers was considered by the Allies to be a victory as he had held the fort for ten days against overwhelming odds and had been able to save most of his troops from being captured. After the invasion of Europe he became Commander of the Forces of the Interior. His major task in this post was to bring the resistance groups under the control of the government of de Gaulle. When Paris was liberated he became the military Governor of the city and it fell to him to restore law and order to the beleaguered city.

**Koga, Admiral Mineichi, 1885–1943** Admiral Koga replaced Admiral YAMAMOTO as Commander in Chief of the Combined Fleet after the latter's death on 17 April 1943. Unflamboyant, efficient and cool, he was nonetheless seduced by the idea of the 'Decisive Battle' with the Allied Fleet, a do-or-die conflict which would decide the nation's fate. He completed plans for this battle (Operation Z) on 8 March 1944 but he knew the chances of victory were slim. On 31 March 1944 he set out to die in a plane which disappeared in a storm without trace.

**Koiso, Lieutenant General Kuniaki, 1880–1950** Koiso, a reserve General with experience in intelligence but not in combat, was appointed Prime Minister after the resignation of TOJO in July 1944. He was to share power with Admiral Yonai (Navy Minister and Assistant Prime Minister) who was associated with KONOYE, KIDO and the Emperor HIROHITO, and therefore with the peace faction. Koiso was never more than an unstable interim leader, having the support of neither the peace faction nor the militarists, and therefore having no influence on the prosecution of the war or on the preparations for peace. He believed Japan could not win the war but felt the US would not give acceptable terms. In this position he presided over defeat after defeat. He had publicly committed his government to victory in Leyte in a radio broadcast on 8 November 1944. The December decision to abandon Leyte, followed by the defeat at Iwo Jima, brought his government near collapse.

Koiso was ignored by the military and not involved in decision-making. When the Americans landed on Okinawa, Koiso demanded that the military structure be reorganized so that he, the Prime Minister, would be consulted. When the Admirals and Generals refused, Koiso resigned in April 1945 and he was succeeded by SUZUKI.

**Kondo, Admiral Nobutake, 1886–1953** In December 1941 Kondo and his Southern Fleet were on patrol off the shores of Malaya and when news reached him that Force Z, the *Repulse* and *Prince of Wales*, was in the vicinity, he sent out the aircraft which sank this British naval presence in the Far East. At Midway he was in command of the Main Support Force for the invasion of the island, but when NAGUMO's Carrier Force had been put out of commission by the US, Kondo's fleet withdrew without seeing any action. Kondo was then given command of a unit of cruisers and given tactical command of the fleet in the battle known as the Eastern Solomons (24 August 1942). Kondo tried to engage the US fleet off Guadalcanal by day in order to give TANAKA a chance to get supplies to the Japanese on the island, but both operations failed. In October Kondo was sent to try to coordinate his fleet with the land offensive and in the Battle of Santa Cruz Island that followed, sank the *Hornet*. The last action in which he was engaged was the naval Battle of Guadalcanal in which his cruisers tried to shell Henderson Field. He did not accomplish this mission because he ran into US forces off Savo Island and although he sank the *Preston* and the *Walke* the main object of the exercise, the reinforcement of Guadalcanal, failed.

**Konev, Marshal Ivan, 1897–1973** Konev attended the Frunze Military Academy and graduated in 1926. An exceptionally competent Commander, Konev served in the Smolensk sector in August 1941 and from October 1941 throughout 1942 he was Commander of the Kalinin Front which stayed the German advance on Moscow. In July 1943 he checked the German attack at Kursk and swept on to take Orel, Belgorod and Poltava. From 1943–44 he led the Steppe Front (which eventually became the 2nd Ukrainian Front) which liberated Kirovograd in January 1944. Konev was responsible for one of the most famous of Soviet victories: he encircled ten German Divisions at Korsun-Shevchenko. Although this was a masterful stroke, the Germans managed to break out but only with terrible losses – 20,000 men. Konev then led the 1st Ukrainian Front and captured Lvov. In February 1944 he was appointed Marshal. Accompanied by ZHUKOV and his

Army, Konev's Front advanced from the Vistula to the Oder and eventually reached Berlin. He continued to the Elbe where he joined US forces at Torgau. He then swept south and entered Prague in May 1945. In 1946 he was appointed Deputy Minister of War and was Commander in Chief of the Warsaw Pact Armies between 1955 and 1960.

**Konoye, Prince Fumimaro, 1891–1945** Konoye was a member of the peace-seeking faction in Japan. In July 1940 he had been recalled to serve as Prime Minister. He had a history of opposition to the militarists but did not have effective political power. Although he had envoys in the USA trying to secure a compromise over the issue of Indo-China and of China itself, he could reach no agreement because the military leaders refused to countenance any withdrawal from China. He was forced to resign in October 1941 and was replaced by TOJO. After the fall of Tojo in July 1944 Konoye began to campaign for an end to the war and was saying in private that Japan had lost the war and there was nothing Japan could do to avoid a total military collapse. Konoye was chosen to lead a peace-seeking delegation to the USSR but MOLOTOV refused to see him as he was preparing to leave for the Potsdam Conference. In the post-war Cabinet Konoye served as Vice-President but the US threatened to try him as a war criminal so he poisoned himself rather than face trial.

**Kretschmer, Commander Otto, 1912–** Kretschmer was the best German U-Boat Commander in World War II and is credited with having sunk more than 200,000 tons of Allied shipping between 1939 and 1941. In 1939 he commanded U.23, a small coastal submarine, which sunk the HMS *Daring* among others. After nine patrols in U.23 he was given command of the ocean-going submarine, U.99. With this U-Boat Kretschmer per-

fected his technique of infiltrating convoys and then committing a surface attack. On one patrol alone he sunk seven ships. He was awarded the Knights Cross with Oak Leaves for his exploits. On 27 March 1941 U.99 and U.100 (the latter commanded by Schepke) were encircled by HMS *Walker* and HMS *Vanos*. Kretschmer and his crew scuttled their U-Boat and surrendered. Kretschmer was incarcerated in Britain and Canada for the duration of the war. He was regarded as outstanding by both sides.

**Krueger, Lieutenant General Walter, 1881–1967** Krueger was a skilled tactician, who was one of MACARTHUR's principal ground Commanders. He took command of the 6th Army in early 1943 and turned it into a superb fighting force which saw action in New Guinea, New Britain, the Admiralties, Biak, Noemfoor and Morotai. The Army was expanded and took part in the reconquest of the Philippines in 1944. In January 1945 the 6th Army landed on Luzon where it faced conditions it had not experienced before. The Army had fought in jungles and swamps and now faced long dusty roads through open spaces, then cities and also mountains. MacArthur was also pressing him to speed up the offensive but Krueger kept his Commanders advancing steadily until they reached Manila, which had to be fought for street by street and was only taken at the beginning of March. The 6th Army spent the last few months of the war clearing the Philippines of the Japanese. Krueger was an extremely competent Commander who did not seek the public eye.

**Krupp von Bohlen und Halbach, Alfried, 1907–1967** At the outbreak of World War II Krupp was one of three deputy directors of the massive Krupp industries which included the Essen armament factories and various mining, energy and steel-making concerns. Between 1939 and 1943 Krupp 'incorporated' industries from occupied countries into the Krupp organization. In some cases processing plants were totally dismantled and then transported to and reassembled in Germany – such as the Mariupol electro-steel works which were reconstructed at Berthewerke in Breslau. Krupp was not selective about the labor he used in his many factories: prisoners of war, civilians from occupied countries and inmates from concentration camps. He even went so far as to establish factories near concentration camps because of the availability of 'cheap' labor. By 1943 Krupp had become the sole owner of the company, had been awarded the Nazi Cross and had been appointed the War Economy Leader. In 1944 he was arrested by an American patrol and in 1948 was tried as a war criminal. He received twelve years imprisonment.

**Kuribayashi, General Tadamichi, 1885–1945** On 30 June 1944 Kuribayashi was appointed Commander of Ground Forces on Iwo Jima. With his 109th Division he set about building a formidable network of caves and pillboxes which made the island immune to aerial bombardment. The Japanese defenses on Iwo Jima were consistently bombed for months before the invasion by the Marines occurred in February 1945. Kuribayashi was a cavalry officer who had lived for three years in the USA and had great admiration for US industrial power but this did not deter him from his desire to fight to the last. He was tireless in his efforts to resist the Marines and bitter fighting continued until 26 March when the final suicidal attack by the Japanese failed. One of his last messages to Japan was sent on 15 March 'Have not eaten or drunk for five days. But fighting spirit is running high. We are going to fight bravely to the last moment' – and this he did.

**Kurita, Admiral Takeo, 1889–1977** Kurita commanded the Close Support Force at Midway but his major engagement was the Battle of Leyte Gulf in October 1944. Here he commanded the formidable First Striking Force. On his way to Leyte Gulf, he was spotted by US forces, attacked and forced to take evasive action losing the *Musashi*. He therefore arrived at Leyte six hours late, but he still took the heavily outnumbered US transports and escorts completely by surprise. Kurita's cruisers went into battle and sank three destroyers and an escort carrier; however when they finally gained the upper hand in the two-hour battle Kurita decided to withdraw. Although his ships might have been able to sink more US ships they would still not have scored the decisive victory required by the weak and outnumbered Japanese Navy.

**Kurochkin, Lieutenant General Pavel, 1900–** In May 1941 Kurochkin, the Commander of the Trans-Baikal Military District, was designated Commander of the 20th Army and transferred to west of Moscow. This move came too late to be implemented before the German invasion and so he was made Commander of the Northwest Front before the end of the year. In January he was able to attack west of Smolensk and encircle seven divisions of the German II Corps in Demyansk. In 1944 he was made Commander of the 2nd Belorussian Front but he failed to take Kovel and was dismissed. However he was then given command of the 60th Army on the Czechoslovakian Front which captured Opava in April 1945.

**Kuznetsov, Admiral Nikolay, 1902–1974** Kuznetsov was the Commander in Chief of the Navy and was a member of the Stavka during the war. Not active in the field he was present at all the planning meetings throughout the war. He participated in the Conferences at

Potsdam and Yalta in 1945. Also in 1945, he fought against the Kwantung Army in China but after the war he was demoted.

**Kuznetsov, General Vasiliy, 1894–1964** Kuznetsov was one of the new generation of Soviet Generals to emerge during the war, in the company of KONEV, GOVOROV, ROKOSSOVSKY, KATUKOV and VLASOV. Kuznetsov fought in defense of Kiev in 1941 and has been held responsible for this disaster by the Soviets, an opinion which left Marshal BUDENNY far too free of blame. Kuznetsov led the 1st Guards Army at Stalingrad. From 1942 to 1943 he was Deputy Commander of the Southwest Front and from 1943 to 1945 he fought in the battles of the Donbass, Warsaw, eastern Pomerania and Berlin.

# L

**Langsdorff, Commander Hans, 1890–1939** Langsdorff was the Commander of the 'pocket battleship' *Graf Spee.* Before he was trapped by the Royal Navy in 1939 he sunk nine British commerce ships totaling 50,000 tons. But on 13 December 1939 the British cruisers *Ajax, Exeter* and *Achilles* cornered the *Graf Spee* near Montevideo Harbor off the coast of Uruguay. The ensuing battle was called the Battle of the River Plate. Realizing that escape was impossible Langsdorff landed his crew and 300 prisoners of war before scuttling his ship and committing suicide. An honorable man, Langsdorff had insured that not one British life was lost on any of the British merchant vessels he had destroyed.

**Laval, Pierre, 1883–1945** Laval first became infamous on an international level when he, as French Foreign Minister, accompanied by Sir Samuel Hoare, the British Foreign Secretary, made a secret agreement with Italy to surrender Abyssinian territory to her. Once the Hoare-Laval Plan was made public both Ministers resigned. Laval surfaced again as Deputy Head of State and Foreign Minister when PÉTAIN was appointed Head of State by the National Assembly on 23 June 1940, after the fall of France. He had reached the conclusion early in the Battle of France that German victory was imminent and thus continued to woo Germany even if it meant having to repress dissident Frenchmen. Accused of plotting, Laval was ousted from office in December 1940 but was reinstated in April 1942. When France was liberated by the Allies he withdrew to Germany accompanied by the now-puppet regime. At the end of the war Laval was found in Spain, was deported, tried in France, found guilty and shot at Fresnes prison. Disliked by the Allies and most Frenchmen and distrusted by his German 'friends' he saw himself as a French patriot, a view which finds little support.

**Laycock, General Robert 'Lucky,' 1907–1968** Laycock was leader of the Commando group known as 'Layforce' which conducted numerous behind-the-line operations from 1940 onwards. It took part in raids in Libya and Crete but after the extremely high casualties resulting from an attack on Crete in May 1941, it was disbanded. Laycock went to North Africa and led another Commando group which attempted to assassinate ROMMEL. The group which included KEYES, attacked Rommel's house in Sidi Rafaa, only to find he was no longer there. Laycock and one other soldier were the only survivors and they had to walk through the desert to reach British lines. After this he went on further operations in Sicily and Italy but returned to England in 1943 to train Commando groups. He succeeded MOUNTBATTEN as Chief of Combined Operations and prepared the plans for D-Day.

**Leahy, Admiral William, 1875–1959** Leahy was ROOSEVELT's personal military representative and Chief of Staff from 1942 onwards. His precise duties were never defined but he presided over meetings of the Joint Chiefs of Staff and acted as a liaison officer between that body and the President. He had daily conferences with the President and made sure that the President's opinions were made known. When Roosevelt died Leahy proved an invaluable adviser to TRUMAN in the last months of the war.

**Leclerc, General Philippe, 1902–1947** An officer in the French Army, Leclerc was captured in May 1940 at Lille. He escaped once, was recaptured and escaped again and joined DE GAULLE in England. He went to Africa as the first military Governor of Chad and Cameroun and General Officer Commanding in French Equatorial Africa. In December 1942 he commanded a Free French force and led it across the Sahara Desert to join the British 8th Army in Libya. In 1944 he led the 2nd French Armored Division for the Normandy invasion and was the official who received the formal surrender of the Germans in Paris in August 1944. He fought in several other campaigns, notably in Alsace and in southern Germany. Always a French patriot, he was unfortunately killed in an airplane accident shortly after the armistice.

**Leeb, Field Marshal Wilhelm Ritter von, 1876–1956** Leeb began his military career as a Bavarian artillery officer as had HALDER, JODL and KESSELRING. An intelligent man, he soon rose to the top of the prewar Army and retired after the BLOMBERG-FRITSCH crisis in 1938. Author of a theoretical text on decisive warfare, he was recalled to command Army Group C in the Polish campaign. In 1940 Army Group C attacked the Maginot Line. In the USSR he led Army Group North in the advance to Leningrad (1941). In January 1942 Leeb was purged and was never recalled.

**Leese, General Sir Oliver, 1894–1978** In 1942 MONTGOMERY brought in Leese to command XXX Corps of the British 8th Army in North Africa. Leese was an exceptionally competent leader distinguishing himself at El Alamein and leading the Allied invasion of Sicily. As Commander in Chief of the 8th Army having succeeded Montgomery in January 1944, Leese went to Italy where he succeeded in pushing KESSELRING into retreat. In November 1944 he gave command of the 8th to MCCREERY and became Commander in Chief of the Allied Land Forces in Southeast Asia.

**Leigh-Mallory, Air Marshal Sir Trafford, 1892–1944** Leigh-Mallory was a controversial figure but a very successful fighter commander. At the outbreak of the war Leigh-Mallory was in command of No 12 (Fighter) Group which was responsible for the defense of the Midlands and the east coast shipping routes. He favored the use of 'big wing' formations in the Battle of Britain, which meant that a massive concentration of intercepting forces had to be available inland. The Commander in Chief of Fighter Command (DOWDING) and the Commander of No 11 Group in the south of England were against this and there were bitter disputes. In December 1940 Leigh-Mallory became Commander of No 11 Group and with DOUGLAS as Head of Fighter Command was able to shift Fighter Command onto the offensive. In November 1942 Leigh-Mallory was appointed Head of Fighter Command and in 1943 Commander in Chief of the Allied Air Forces for the coming invasion of Europe. Again he became involved in a dispute because he wanted control of the British and US strategic bomber forces, but their Commanders HARRIS and SPAATZ insisted on their operating independently. Leigh-Mallory's greatest contribution to Operation Overlord was his Transportation Plan, which advocated a concentrated bombing of German communications prior to the landings. On the whole he was successful in this role and the 9000 aircraft under his command denied free use of the air to the Luftwaffe.

In November 1944 Leigh-Mallory was appointed Commander in Chief of South East Asia Command but he was killed with his wife in an air crash while en route.

**Lemay, General Curtis, 1906–1990** Lemay was the architect of the US bombing offensive against Germany and Japan. He was sent to England in 1942 with the 8th Air Force and instituted a daylight bombing campaign against specific targets. He led many raids himself and devised the best defensive formation: aircraft flying at staggered heights. In July 1944 Lemay went to the China-India-Burma Theater to take command of the 20th Bomber Group and greatly improved the bombing offensive against Japan. He used B-29s and flying long distances from China they were able to hit targets in western Japan and Formosa, providing there was good visibility. In November 1944 the Marianas were ready to be used as air bases and Lemay now sent out missions to bomb the Imperial homeland. Since bomber losses were high in daylight raids, Lemay switched to night-time low-level area bombing using fire bombs. The most spectacular raid was the Tokyo raid on the night of 10 March which destroyed sixteen and a half square miles of the capital.

**Leopold III, King, 1901–1983** On 10 May 1940 Germany invaded Belgium and King Leopold assumed command of the Belgian Army. Leopold requested aid from the Allies who sent troops to aid the Belgian forces. However, after two weeks of difficult fighting which had cornered the Belgians in the northeast of their country, Leopold made the unassisted, arbitrary decision to surrender, 28 May 1940. The army, the people

and the government led by Prime Minister Pierlot opposed this admission defeat and declared his capitulation illegal. But it was too late to reverse the action. The Germans swept into Belgium and confined Leopold to the Palace of Laeken near Brussels. He further antagonized his citizens by contracting a morganatic marriage during the war. When the US invaded Belgium in 1944, Leopold was taken by the Wehrmacht to Germany where he was found by the Americans in 1945. The Belgian people refused to let Leopold return to the throne and would not even allow him return to Belgium until 1950.

**Liddell Hart, Captain Basil, 1895–1970** Liddell Hart was a brilliant military thinker whose ideas were largely ignored by the British Army. He had served in the Army during World War I and had written an official manual *Infantry Training* in 1920. In 1924 he retired from the Army in order to promote and develop his ideas. He became a leading exponent of the use of tank and air power, a complete rejection of the World War I policy of static warfare. He developed ideas using a force of tanks as an independent striking force to make deep penetrations into enemy territory, cutting off enemy troops from their supplies and high command. During the interwar period very few people in Britain listened to him; in fact the Germans seem to have benefited from his results since both GUDE-RIAN and ROMMEL studied his work and called themselves his pupils. For a short time he served as an adviser to HORE-BELISHA, the War Minister, in )37, but during the war he held no fficial appointments. After the war he nterviewed many of the senior German Generals, including RUNDSTEDT, LEIST and WARLIMONT and after years of writing wrote the best one-volume history of World War II available today.

**List, Field Marshal Wilhelm, 1880–1971** List was an engineering officer in the Bavarian Army. In 1939 he commanded the Fourteenth Army and led it into Poland. In 1940 he led the Twelfth Army which led the advance into Belgium by crossing the Meuse between Namur and Dinant. On 19 July 1940 he became Field Marshal and in the spring of 1941 was Commander in Chief of German Forces for Operation Margarita (invasion of Greece). In the USSR he commanded Army Group A (July–October 1942) as it advanced into the Caucasus. His failure to break through the line caused him to be dismissed by HITLER. He was tried for war crimes at Nuremberg and sentenced to life imprisonment but was pardoned and released after five years.

**Litvinov, Maxim, 1876–1952** A Bolshevik from his early days, Litvinov was Soviet Commissar for Foreign Affairs from 1930. He was in favor of Soviet cooperation with the west and advocated the use of the League of Nations, as an anti-Fascist organization. However he was replaced on 3 May 1939 by MOLOTOV who reversed Litvinov's policies and made a pact with Germany. From 1941 to 1943 he was Soviet Ambassador to the USA. At the same time but continuing until 1946 he was Deputy Commissar for Foreign Affairs.

# M

MacArthur, General Douglas, 1880–1964 MacArthur was one of the most colorful and controversial figures in the US Army in World War II. He had served for several years before the war as an adviser to the Philippine government but in July 1941 was recalled to active duty with orders to mobilize forces in the Philippines and prepare for war. By December he had raised the number of men at arms from 22,000 to 180,000; however these consisted mainly of untrained Filipinos who would desert as soon as the fighting broke out. MacArthur was handicapped in his defense of the islands by lack of naval operations. Within a week of the main Japanese landings, MacArthur had abandoned Manila and withdrawn to the Bataan peninsula. The final battle was protracted with the last US troops surrendering in May 1942. MacArthur left the Philippines at the President's request on 11 March with the words 'I shall return.'

MacArthur felt he and the USA had reneged on their word by leaving the Philippines to the Japanese and determined to recapture it as soon as possible. His ambition was fulfilled three years later and these years were spent gradually wearing down Japanese concentrations in the islands to the north of Australia. In the spring of 1942 MacArthur had only 25,000 troops and 260 obsolete aircraft in Australia and he had a tough job persuading the Joint Chiefs of Staff to send reinforcements. The United States' policy was Germany first and the defeat of Japan was not considered as urgent. MacArthur saw the defeat of Japan as an important venture and pressed his views. In this he could count on some support from Admiral KING, Commander in Chief of the Navy, whose main concern was that his Navy win the war in the Pacific. The first operation the Joint Chiefs agreed to undertake was the recapture of Guadalcanal in August 1942 but this first step was allocated to Admiral NIMITZ's fleet; MacArthur would accomplish the next step in the Solomons campaign and also retake New Guinea.

The fight to take Guadalcanal was hard and costly in casualties. In early 1943 MacArthur presented his Elkton Plan which proposed bypassing the major troop concentrations and taking airfields in the Huon peninsula, New Georgia, New Britain, Bougainville and an attack on Kavieng and Rabaul. MacArthur's tactic was known as island-hopping by the Army and succeeded because the Japanese troops lost their air cover and were isolated and left to die. By hopping from coastal town to coastal town, New Guinea was eventually secured by mid-1944 and some 44,000 Japanese troops under General ADACHI were bypassed at Wewak. The Solomons campaign was also protracted and Rabaul was bypassed. By mid-1944 the Joint Chiefs were ready to consider the next step. Nimitz thought this should be the capture of Formosa and destruction of Japanese air power, but MacArthur advocated his long-cherished dream of recapturing the Philippines and in September it was finally agreed on. On 9 January 1945 the US troops landed at Lingayen Gulf on

Luzon and MacArthur waded ashore accompanied by OSMEÑA and Romulo and one month later he entered Manila. The fighting in the Philippines continued until the Japanese surrender and MacArthur spread his activities to the Dutch East Indies. He was convinced the Japanese would fight to the last and advised President TRUMAN accordingly. It fell upon MacArthur to accept Japan's formal surrender on Nimitz's flagship the USS *Missouri* in Tokyo Bay on 2 September 1945.

MacArthur was a flamboyant character who made sure the people back home knew what he was doing to win the war. He was a great publicist but he made many enemies. Generals MARSHALL and EISENHOWER disliked him and even President ROOSEVELT, resentful of his popularity, did not wish him to have the limelight. After the war he ruled Japan as an all-powerful potentate but he overstepped the mark in Korea which led to his downfall.

**McCreery, General Sir Richard, 1898–1967** In 1940 McCreery served with the British Expeditionary Force in its disastrous campaign in France. In May 1941 he was sent by Brooke to North Africa to serve as Chief of Staff to AUCHINLECK; however their relationship was stormy and McCreery was dismissed. He returned to serve as ALEXANDER's Chief of Staff in August 1942 and played a major role in drawing up the plans for the last stages of the Battle of El Alamein.

McCreery went on to a successful career as a Corps Commander with the X Corps of the 8th Army, which he led in the Salerno landings. The Corps played a crucial role in the Battle for Monte Cassino and McCreery was promoted in November 1944 to lead the 8th Army in its final offensive in Italy.

**McIndoe, Archibald, 1900–1960** McIndoe was a New Zealand surgeon who developed advanced techniques for treating bad burns and disfigurements. He began to work with RAF pilots who had been burnt during the Battle of Britain and through plastic surgery was able to repair their physical damage. McIndoe however was also concerned with their mental health and rehabilitation and he insisted that the ninety-day rule which invalided men out of the service after ninety days should be abolished.

**Maclean, Brigadier Fitzroy, 1911–** Maclean was a well-traveled Member of Parliament who was CHURCHILL's personal envoy to TITO in September 1943. He was parachuted into Yugoslavia as leader of the British Military Mission to find out whether Tito's partisans were fighting the Germans. Maclean reported back to EDEN in November and recommended that the British should give Tito more supplies and support. He returned to Yugoslavia and took part in the fighting which drove the Germans out of Belgrade. He continued as the British government representative in Yugoslavia until March 1945.

**McNair, General Lesley, 1883–1944** McNair was a US General who specialized in developing training systems. In 1940 McNair was made Chief of Staff at the US Army General Headquarters and set about extending the training methods. He wanted the ordinary soldier to know more about the conditions which faced him in battle. Men were sent out on exercises which fully simulated battle conditions and were trained to act as a formation. McNair was killed when Allied aircraft accidentally bombed the unit he was visiting in Normandy.

**Maisky, Ivan, 1884–1975** Maisky was the Soviet ambassador to London from 1932–1943. He was well-liked by British politicians and had many close friends among them. He was ambassador during the sensitive period of the German-Soviet Non-Aggression Pact and the fall of France, when he was able to inform STALIN of Britain's resolve to stand firm and continue fighting alone. He had advance knowledge of HITLER's plans to invade the USSR but Stalin did not act on his information. After this Maisky had to badger the Allies on Stalin's orders to open a Second Front in Europe. Maisky persuaded HOPKINS to go to Moscow which resulted in a negotiated US-USSR Lend-Lease agreement. Maisky also negotiated with the various governments-in-exile in London.

In June 1943 Maisky was recalled to Moscow and appointed a Deputy Commissar of Foreign Affairs, a position well out of the limelight. He participated in the Yalta and Potsdam Conferences and chaired the 1945 Allied Reparations Commission in Moscow.

**Malenkov, Georgy, 1902–1988**
Malenkov pursued a successful career working on the security and political aspects of the military from 1920–1941. At the start of the German invasion of Russia he was appointed to the newly formed Committee for the Defense of the State (GKO). This committee was composed of STALIN, MOLOTOV, VOROSHILOV, BERIA and Malenkov. Malenkov was responsible for technical equipment for the Army and Air Force. He was closely involved in the massive Russian evacuation of industrial materials to the east. During the first two years of the war he also served as political Commissar on a number of different fronts. From 1943–45 he served as Chairman of the Committee for the Restoration of the Economy which dealt with countries recently liberated from the Germans. At the end of the war Malenkov became Deputy Chairman of the Council of Ministers and briefly took power after Stalin's death,

to be ousted shortly thereafter by KHRUSHCHEV.

**Malinovsky, Marshal Rodion, 1898–1967** Malinovsky was commanding an army at Odessa at the start of Barbarossa (June 1941) and in December 1941 was given command of the Southwest Front. In December 1942 at Stalingrad, Malinovsky prevented MANSTEIN from freeing PAULUS' encircled Sixth Army. From 1943 to 1944 Malinovsky was Commander first of the Southwest Front and then of the 3rd Ukrainian Front with which he cleared out the Donbass and west Ukraine. Later in 1944 he became Commander of the 2nd Ukrainian Front and, in conjunction with TOLBUKHIN, invaded Rumania, totally defeating the Germans, taking 200,000 prisoners and causing Rumania to defect to the Allies. Malinovsky continued on to Hungary and took Budapest in February 1945. In April 1945 he liberated Slovakia. Malinovsky then led the Soviet Armies in Manchuria in August.

**Mannerheim, Marshal Carl von, 1867–1951** Mannerheim was a Finnish officer in the Tsar's Army at the time when Finland was a part of the Russian empire. He returned to Finland in 1917 to lead the White Army to victory over the Local Red Army. In 1939 Mannerheim was recalled by Finland to resist the Russian invasion. He was not successful in this venture but on surrender did manage to secure terms favorable to Finland by using his considerable diplomatic skill. In 1941 HITLER invaded Russian territory and Finland chose to resume hostilities against the USSR to regain the territory she lost in 1940. When defeat yet again seemed inevitable in 1944 Mannerheim, as Head of State, was able to secure terms for the armistice propitious to Finland. Finland's national hero was a statesman of tact, intelligence and diplomacy.

**Manstein, Field Marshal Erich von,
1887–1973** Generally regarded as the
most successful and certainly most brilliant field commander of the German
Army in World War II, Manstein's reputation rests on two pillars: his ability to
frame excellent plans and his skill at
executing difficult orders in the teeth of
the enemy's opposition. He first made
his name in World War II when, as
Chief of Staff to RUNDSTEDT of Army
Group A in 1939, he proposed an alternative to the High Command's plans for
invading France and the Low Countries.
This was for a drive to the Channel
through the wooded hills of the Ardennes, aimed at separating the British
and French field armies from their static
supporting armies. Already notorious
for his arrogance and tactlessness to superiors, his temerity in challenging the
High Command view brought him demo-
tion to a less influential post but en
route he was called to visit Hitler, to
whom he outlined his scheme and who
thenceforth supported it. As a reward,
he was given command first of LVI
Panzer Corps and then of the Eleventh
Army, which he handled brilliantly in
the capture of the Crimea. In July 1942
he was promoted to command Army
Group Don and in December very nearly
succeeded in relieving Stalingrad in an
operation known as Winter Storm. In
February 1943 he achieved the greatest
German success in counteroffensive operations of the whole war by recapturing
Kharkov. Thereafter, like all German
generals, he was driven steadily into retreat, with the difference that he constantly asked Hitler for permission to
'maneuver,' by which the Führer understood him to mean give up ground when
not under pressure to do so. In fact, his
idea was to force the Soviets off balance
and then counterattack, but Hitler's sus-
picions always overcame the logic of his
arguments. He was eventually dismissed
in March 1944 and spent the rest of the
war on his estate. Friends and enemies
continued to regard him as a master of
modern warfare.

**Mao Tse-tung, 1893–1976** Mao was
Chairman of the Chinese Communist
Party from 1931 until his death.
He broke with STALIN in 1927 after
Commintern directives led to a massacre
of Communists by the Kuomintang
in Shanghai. In 1937 a new alliance
between the Kuomintang and the Communist Party was forged in the face
of Japanese aggression, but only lasted
until 1940 when Mao decided to fight
CHIANG Kai-shek rather than the
Japanese. Mao directed his wartime
operations from Yenan, in Shensi Province. One last attempt at an alliance
negotiated by US Ambassador HURLEY,
between Chiang and Mao failed in 1944.
After the defeat of Japan, civil war
began.

Mao was a brilliant innovator of new
revolutionary techniques and a master
of guerrilla warfare. His strategy was to
base his revolutionary movement on the
peasantry, moving his forces through
friendly territory and organizing these
areas as he progressed. Only TITO led a
comparable resistance movement during
the war with such success.

**Marshall, General George, 1880–
1959** At the outbreak of World War II,
Marshall had just been appointed Chief
of Staff of the American Army, then
only 200,000 strong. He had formerly
acted as aide to Pershing, after World
War I, in which he had fought as a
junior officer, but otherwise had had no
training in the raising of a great Army
for war, towards which America seemed
inevitably to be drifting. Nevertheless
he succeeded, by the time of Pearl
Harbor, in more than doubling the
Army's size and, as soon as war broke
out, on carrying through a major reorganization, which divided it into three:
the Army Ground Forces, the Army Air
Forces and the Army Service Forces. He

proved himself to be more than an organizer. He had already done much to aid American preparedness for war by his prewar planning and appointment of trusted subordinates, like EISENHOWER, to key positions. Immediately after Pearl Harbor, he became chairman of the new Joint Chiefs of Staff Committee to advise the President on strategy, a post he held throughout the war. He consistently supported the principle of 'Germany First' and, though irritated by what he regarded as British prevarication over the invasion of Europe, steadfastly supported the Anglo-American strategic line in the face of American naval opposition. He accompanied the President or represented the Chiefs of Staff at most of the major inter-Allied conferences of the war, and maintained a creative relationship with ROOSEVELT until his death. Despite suggestions that he should eventually take over command of the American armies in Europe, the President eventually decided that he was too valuable in Washington to be spared and remained Chief of Staff until the war's end. In postwar years he became Secretary of State and the architect of the Marshall Plan to rebuild the war-shattered economies of Europe, foe's and friend's alike. A cool and distant figure, with whom few could claim to be intimate, he impressed all who worked with him by his total unselfishness and impartiality of judgement and by a sort of Roman nobility of character.

**Masaryk, Jan, 1886–1946** Masaryk was an important Czechoslovakian statesman and Foreign Minister of the Czech government-in-exile in London. At the time of the Munich Agreement and the partition of Czechoslovakia, Masaryk was Ambassador to London. He became Foreign Minister of the government-in-exile under Edouard BENEŠ. His first major task was to act as mediator between Beneš and the British government

in their attempt to gain full recognition for their government. This was achieved on 19 July 1941 and was followed in 1942 by EDEN's formal renunciation of the Munich Agreement. Masaryk also went on extensive speaking tours of Britain and the United States and made daily BBC broadcasts to Czechoslovakia. These were extremely successful, partly because of the symbolic value of his name; his father, Thomas Masaryk, was the hero of Czech independence. Relations between the Czech government-in-exile and the USSR were extremely good. Masaryk signed a mutual aid agreement with the USSR on 18 July 1941 which provided for Czech units within the Soviet Army and later signed a friendship pact.

Masaryk died having 'fallen' out of a window in Prague under mysterious circumstances in 1948.

**Matsuoka, Yosuke, 1880–1946** Matsuoka was Foreign Minister of Japan from 1940–1941. He was a westernized man, brought up in Portland, Oregon by a Methodist family and holding a degree in law from the University of Oregon. However he was at the same time extremely xenophobic, greatly mistrusted America and Britain, and was primarily concerned with not allowing Japan to lose out in the approaching Great Power crisis. He is best remembered for coining the phrase, Greater East Asia Co-Prosperity sphere.

His main experience was in business but he turned to foreign affairs as Japanese delegate to the League of Nations, 1932–3. He staged a dramatic walk-out when Japan was censored for its invasion of Manchuria. A close friend of KONOYE's, Matsuoka became Foreign Minister in his Cabinet in September 1940. His first achievement was to complete a Tripartite Pact with Germany and Italy (23 September) which was primarily aimed at inhibiting the United States. In the spring of 1941 he traveled to Germany and Russia and was so impressed with STALIN and with the USSR's strength that he signed a neutrality pact with MOLOTOV on 13 April 1941. The Japanese were outraged by the conclusion of such an agreement with their traditional enemy and by Matsuoka's un-Japanese-like direct action. In July 1941 the entire Cabinet resigned in order to get rid of him. Matsuoka was tried and executed by the Allies for his part in initiating the war.

**Menzies, Robert, 1894–1978** Menzies was Prime Minister of Australia from April 1939 until 28 August 1941, as head of the United Australia Party's minority government. Thus it was Menzies who organized Australia's preparations for war, announced its entry into the war (3 September 1939) and deployed three Australian divisions to the Middle East. In August 1940 he formed a coalition government with the Country Party but had only a very small majority over the opposition Labor Party. From January to May 1941 Menzies traveled back and forth to London visiting troops along the way. Menzies resigned on 28 August 1941 and his party only remained in power until 6 October when it was succeeded by a Labor government under CURTIN.

**Meretskov, Marshal Kirill, 1897–1968** Meretskov was Chief of General Staff at the start of the war but was soon superseded by ZHUKOV. In the Russo-Finnish war he had commanded an army on the Vyborg flank and led the breakthrough of the Mannerheim Line. He again made a name for himself as Commander of the Volkhov Front in the defense of Leningrad from 1941–44. He is said to have saved Leningrad in December 1941 by driving the Germans out of the town of Tikhvin, thereby keeping supply lines open. In January he and General GOVOROV broke the German Blockade and reestablished railway lines from Moscow

to Leningrad. In February 1944, Meretskov was appointed Commander of the Karelian Front to drive the Germans out of Finland. He had by this time lost touch with STALIN and was out of favor. In August 1945 he was given command of the 1st Far Eastern Front.

**Merrill, Brigadier General Frank, 1903–1950** Merrill trained and led a long-range penetration group called 'Merrill's Marauders.' They were modeled on WINGATE's Chindits but were considerably more effective.

Merrill was in Rangoon at the start of the war and was STILWELL's most trusted subordinate during his retreat from Burma. In May 1942 Merrill became a Lieutenant Colonel and began training his guerrilla force for operating in jungle conditions behind Japanese lines. Merrill's Marauders set out in February 1944, cut off the Japanese rear at Maingkwan and severed their supply line at the Hukawng Valley by March. Although Merrill himself was hospitalized in April, May and July, his Marauders continued living off the land, harassing the enemy's communications and attacking isolated outposts. On 17 May, together with some of Stilwell's Chinese troops, they captured the Myitkyina airstrip. The town of Myitkyina held out till 4 August 1944.

Merrill then became Deputy US Commander in Burma–India and, later, Chief of Staff of the US 10th Army in the Pacific.

**Metaxas, General Joannis, 1871–1941** Metaxas was the dictator of Greece from 1936 to 1941. He was a staunch royalist who was thought to be pro-German but when MUSSOLINI invaded Greece in October 1940, Metaxas immediately mobilized all his 'reserves. By November the Greeks had gained the upper hand and were able to repel the Italians and occupy half of Albania.

Metaxas died shortly after this success and he did not see the final invasion of Greece.

**Michael, King of Rumania, 1921–** Michael became King when his father CAROL II abdicated in his favor in September 1940. His accession to power coincided with ANTONESCU's seizure of power and Michael could do nothing to prevent it. However in August 1944 Michael was able to turn the tables and had Antonescu arrested and locked away in a closet in his palace. His attendants disarmed Antonescu's bodyguard and a new government was formed that evening, 22 August. The government's first act was to declare war on Germany. Michael remained King until the end of 1947 when he decided he could no longer lead a Communist state.

**Mihajlović, General Draza, 1893–1946** Mihajlović was a Yugoslavian resistance leader who was superseded by TITO in the middle of the war. He was a Royalist Army Officer in charge of the Operations Bureau of the General Staff when the Germans invaded in April 1941. Following the invasion, Mihajlović left for Serbia with a small following and established a resistance group called the Četniks. In the fall of 1941 Mihajlović was widely publicized by the Allied press and was even supported by the Russians. However the Četniks were not only dedicated to Serbian interests but were also staunchly anti-Communist. Attempts at co-operation between Mihajlović and Tito's partisans foundered during the first campaign against the German occupation (fall 1941). Mihajlović and his Četniks attacked Tito in Serbia and were soundly defeated. Mihajlović then decided not to launch an active campaign against the Nazis but rather to wait for the Nazis to wipe out Tito and his partisans. Not only did he decide not to attack the Germans but decided to collaborate with

them as well. In January 1942 he was appointed Commander in Chief of Armed Forces and War Minister of the Yugoslavian government-in-exile. It was not until late in 1942 that the Allies found out what was happening and they soon shifted their support to Tito who rapidly became a national leader. The Yugoslav government-in-exile dismissed Mihajlović in May 1944 and he had no part in the postwar coalition government. Mihajlović was tried and executed in 1946.

**Mikawa, Vice-Admiral Guinichi, 1890–** On August 7 1942, immediately upon receiving information of American landings on Guadalcanal and Tulagi, Mikawa, then Commander in Chief on Rabaul, set out with a force of five heavy cruisers and two light cruisers. He managed to get through the Slot undetected on the next day and that night took CRUTCHLEY's Southern Force and Riefkohl's Northern Force completely by surprise. This was partly due to bad communications between the Americans. The Battle of Savo Island resulted in the Japanese arriving home safely with no casualties while the Americans lost four cruisers and 1023 men. Mikawa however had not attacked the undefended US supply ships believing mistakenly that US carriers were in the area.

**Mikolajczyk, Stanislaw, 1901–1967** Mikolajczyk was a Polish statesman who headed the Polish government-in-exile from 1943–44. He had been the leader of the Polish Peasant Party and left Poland in 1939 to join the Polish National Council in Paris. In 1941 he was appointed Deputy Prime Minister and Minister of the Interior in SIKORSKI's government in London. He was charged with maintaining contact with the Resistance in Poland. After Sikorski's death, Mikolajczyk became Prime Minister but lacked his predecessor's authority both with his own people and with his Allies. In November 1944 he resigned because of the Allied lack of support over the Warsaw Uprising and the question of Poland's Eastern frontier. He was the only major Polish politician in the west to return to Poland after the war where he joined the Lublin Committee. However he was soon purged by the government.

**Mikoyan, Major General Artem, 1905–1970** With mathematician M I Gurevich, Mikoyan produced the Soviet MiG-1 high altitude fighter which first flew on 5 April 1940. This plane was modified into the MiG-3 of which 3322 were produced before production stopped in the middle of the war. It was widely used in the early years of the war for interception and air-to-air combat, being small, maneuverable, with a 750 mile range and outclassing all other planes at heights above 16,000 feet.

**Milch, Field Marshal Erhard, 1892–1972** Milch had been a fighter squadron commander in World War I and had then gone on to work in the commercial aviation industry. In 1926 he was made Chairman of Lufthansa, the newly formed state airline. He used Lufthansa as a cover behind which he developed the skilled manpower and tested the techniques and machinery which would form the new German Air Force. When the Luftwaffe was officially recognized in 1935 it had 1000 aircraft and 20,000 trained men, and Milch was placed at the head of the Air Ministry. Working with UDET and Wever, Milch directed the organizational side of the business for which he had tremendous talent. He had been a close friend of GOERING, but they fell out and Udet was temporarily in the ascendant until he committed suicide in 1941. Milch was the dominant figure in German aircraft production until 1944 when he had to share his power with SPEER. He was convicted of

war crimes and was released on parole in 1955.

**Mitscher, Vice-Admiral Marc, 1887–1947** Mitscher was the US Navy's main aviation expert and a Commander of carrier forces in the Far East throughout the war. In 1941 he was given command of the carrier USS *Hornet* which was used to launch DOOLITTLE's bomber raid on Tokyo (18 April 1942). In June the *Hornet* was one of the three US carriers at the Battle of Midway. Mitscher was made Air Commander of Guadalcanal on 1 April 1943 and had control over the Air Force units of the US Army, Navy, and Marines and of the New Zealand RAF.

In January 1944 Mitscher took command of the Fast Carrier Force, Task Force 58, part of SPRUANCE's Central Pacific Force. From January to October 1944 it was responsible for destroying 795 enemy ships and 4425 planes. This Force had its own fleet train and could therefore remain in operation for long periods at a time. It was used to provide an air umbrella for the invasions of the Marshalls and Hollandia and in June 1944 went to the Marianas. Mitscher and his Force played a crucial role in the Battle of the Philippine Sea where Mitscher made the daring decision to send his planes out although they could only be recovered from the raid after dark. From August to September 1944 Task Force 58 was involved in raids on the Bonin Islands, Palau, Mindanao and Formosa. Finally they provided air cover for the campaigns in Iwo Jima and Okinawa where they had to contend with kamikazes and other enemy planes flown from Japan.

**Model, Field Marshal Walther, 1891–1945** Model represented a new middle-class in the German Army and was one of Hitler's more trusted Army Commanders. He built himself a reputation as an energetic and forceful commander at the head of the Sixteenth Army in France and the 3rd Panzer Division in the USSR. As the older Army Commanders lost HITLER's confidence, Model was given greater responsibilities. He helped plan the great tank battle at Kursk which ended in a defeat for the Germans; however Model held the Front together with his tireless energy. In 1944 Hitler used him as a trouble-shooter, transferring him from front to front. In early 1944 he commanded Army Group North and stopped the Soviet advance into the Baltic States. He also commanded Army Group Center after the opening of the Belorussian Campaign and the collapse of all resistance on that Front. Model succeeded in restoring stability to the front and stopped the Soviet armies outside Warsaw. On 17 August he was transferred to replace KLUGE as Commander in Chief of the west but found there was little he could do to repair the front. In September he was replaced by RUNDSTEDT and given command of Army Group B in Belgium, which was driven back to Holland shortly afterwards. However he was in the vicinity of the British paratroop attack on Arnhem and successfully prevented the Allies gaining an early bridgehead over the Rhine. Through careful reorganization of his forces he was able to mount the Ardennes offensive which nearly broke the back of the Allied advance. However when the offensive petered out, Model found himself trapped in a pocket in the Ruhr. He tried in vain to break out and decided to disband the Army Group on 15 April 1945. He shot himself on 21 April because he felt it was a disgrace for a field marshal to surrender.

**Mölders, Oberst Werner, 1913–1941**
Mölders was one of the Luftwaffe's leading fighter pilots with a score of over 150 planes downed. He commanded Fighter Groups in the Battle of France and the Battle of Britain, using Me-109s,

aircraft about which he complained vociferously. In 1941 he went to the Russian Front as Inspector of Fighter Aircraft. He died in November 1941 when his plane hit a factory chimney on the way to the state funeral of UDET.

Mölders was outstanding both as a tactician and as a pilot. He invented the 'Four Fingers' formation which was later adopted by the RAF.

**Molotov, Viachislav M, 1890–1970**
Molotov succeeded LITVINOV as Soviet Commissar for Foreign Affairs on 3 May 1939 and retained this post until 1952. In August 1939 he successfully negotiated the Nazi-Soviet Non-Aggression Pact which specified the partitioning of Poland between Germany and the USSR and defined their spheres of influence in the Baltic and Balkans. The basis of this agreement was overturned when Molotov received reports of German activities in Finland and Rumania. Molotov confronted HITLER with these reports, negotiations broke down and Hitler's plans for Barbarossa were set in motion in late 1940. On 13 April 1941 Molotov won a diplomatic victory by signing a non-aggression pact with Japan, but he had to announce the news of the German invasion on 21 June 1941. He was appointed to the five-man State Defense Committee shortly afterwards.

Throughout the war Molotov attended all the major Allied conferences and many meetings with Heads of State in Moscow. He took on many of STALIN's responsibilities at various times due to the latter's overwork or ill-health. In May 1942 he visited Washington and London charged with pressuring the Western Allies into opening up a Second Front in Europe at the earliest possible date and resuming the sending of convoys of equipment to Russia. ROOSEVELT actually promised Molotov that an Allied invasion of Europe would take place in 1942 but had to back down later in the year. Molotov also signed a

20-year treaty with England at this time, pledging support against Hitler.

In June 1943 Molotov was engaged in secret negotiations with RIBBENTROP through intermediaries. Though they did not come to an agreement, news of the Russian attempt to make a separate peace leaked to the Western Allies. It was not allowed to disrupt their relations however, and convoys to Russia were resumed in November 1943. Molotov hosted the Foreign Ministers' Conference in Moscow in October 1943 and was the USSR's first delegate to the United Nations in San Francisco in June 1945.

**Montgomery, Field Marshal Bernard, 1887–1976** Montgomery's wilfulness, egocentricity and arrogance were noticeably dominant traits of his character as a young officer. Despite them, he had risen at the outbreak of World War II to general's rank and to command 3rd Division, which he took to France in 1939 and evacuated from Dunkirk, battered but intact, in June 1940. He was one of the last officers to leave the beaches, and brought home an enhanced reputation, which won him command first of V and then of XII Corps. His rise to fame began in 1942 when he was chosen by CHURCHILL to replace AUCHINLECK in command of 8th Army in the Western Desert. He had the good luck to take over at a time when the 8th Army was receiving its first plentiful consignment of modern equipment and reinforcements and when Rommel's forces had almost outreached their own supplies by the speed and depth of their advance. It was Montgomery's remarkable ability to infuse his new command with confidence and belief in his powers of command, as much as these material benefits, which fitted it, however, to undertake the task of defeating the enemy for good at the Battle of El Alamein. Montgomery's conduct of the battle, and particularly of the pursuit towards Tunis which ensued, has been criticized. But he was the undoubted victor and thus, to that date, the first British general to have defeated a major German Commander in open battle. The British people accepted him as a hero overnight and he never subsequently lost that cachet. After the landing of the Anglo-American armies in French North Africa he became subject to EISENHOWER's command and fought successfully to destroy what remained of the German-Italian army in Africa, particularly at the Battle of Mareth. In the invasion of Sicily he commanded in competition with the Americans for the capture of the island, and subsequently led the 8th Army in the invasion of Italy as far as the line of the River Sangro. In January 1944 he was recalled with Eisenhower to plan the invasion of Europe, in which he was to command the ground forces under the latter's supreme direction. He rightly insisted on the amplification of the original landing force from three to five divisions and, once they were ashore on 6 June, conducted a well-judged offensive against the Germans which culminated in the breakout of the Allies from the bridgehead in July. In September he surrendered control of the ground forces to Eisenhower, but continued in charge of the British 21st Army Group until the end of the war. During the Ardennes campaign, he was once again summoned by Eisenhower to take charge of an Anglo-American force on the northern flank of the break in, which he handled with great skill if less tact. His organization of the Rhine Crossing was his last major command achievement before the end of the war, when he accepted the surrender of all German forces in northern Europe. After the war he was Chief of the Imperial General Staff and Deputy Supreme Allied Commander in Europe. He had been made Viscount Montgomery of Alamein for his great victory of 1942.

**Morgan, General Sir Frederick, 1894–1967** Morgan was the chief planner of the Allied invasion of Normandy. In January 1943 he was appointed Chief of Staff to a Supreme Allied Commander who was not yet appointed, and was ordered to produce a detailed plan for an invasion of Europe. Morgan was not given sufficient resources, especially landing craft, and could not get any until EISENHOWER was appointed Supreme Allied Commander. Morgan's final plan was adopted at a conference in June–July 1943 and for the next year, until D-Day 4 June 1944, the plans for Operation Overlord were worked out in great detail under Morgan.

**Morgenthau, Henry, 1891–1967** Morgenthau was President ROOSEVELT's Secretary of the Treasury from 1934 until the end of the war. During the war his one overriding task was to finance a mammoth war economy and war production without prompting correspondingly great inflation. This he did by maintaining high taxes and by selling Defense (later called 'War') Savings Bonds. Morgenthau was also responsible for the freezing of Japanese assets before the war in the Far East and for organizing economic measures against the Axis Powers. He also put the Lend-Lease Program into operation.

At the Quebec Conference of September 1944 Morgenthau put forward a plan to settle the long-disputed fate of postwar Germany. The Morgenthau Plan advocated enforcing agrarianism on Germany, in which most industry would be dismantled and the sites turned into arable land. This plan actually had the support of CHURCHILL and Roosevelt but not of their Cabinets. Thus when the plan was leaked to the public they abandoned it quickly. The fact that Morgenthau was a Jew allowed GOEBBELS to use both him and his plan for anti-Allied propaganda – a warning to Germans of what would happen should Germany surrender.

**Morrison, Herbert, 1888–1965** Morrison was a member of CHURCHILL's Cabinet throughout the war, first as Minister of Supply and then simultaneously as Home Secretary and Minister of Home Security.

In 1939 Morrison was a leading member of the London County Council and chairman of its General Purposes and its Civil Defense Committees. He was also a leader of the Labour Opposition in Parliament and was responsible for the 'No-confidence' motion which felled CHAMBERLAIN's government on 8 May 1940. Churchill then made Morrison Minister of Supply in his new government with special emphasis on securing raw materials. In October 1940 he was made Home Secretary and Minister of Home Security. Morrison organized the National Fire Service and a system of fire watching, the Civil Defense and the Home Guard. As Home Secretary he had to take responsibility for decisions regarding censorship of news and internment and arrest of suspected enemies of the state. In January 1945 he played a large part in organizing and giving direction to the Labour election campaign. The new government adopted his proposals on nationalization, health and education.

**Morshead, Lieutenant General Sir Leslie, 1889–1959** Morshead was the Commander of the Australian 9th Division in North Africa and the Far East. It was the 9th Division which held Tobruk against ROMMEL from April 1941 until they were slowly replaced by elements of SCOBIE's 6th Army during September and October. In October 1942 Morshead and the 9th Division took a major role in the Battle of El Alamein. They were then transferred to the Far East where they took part in the invasion of New Guinea, particularly in the amphibious attack on Lae. In 1944 Morshead became General Officer Commanding New Guinea Force and Commander of the 2nd Australian Army. In the last months of the war he was directing operations to reconquer Borneo.

**Moulin, Jean, 1899–1943** Moulin was an important French resistance leader responsible for fusing dozens of rival guerrilla groups into one organization loyal to DE GAULLE. Moulin was prefect of Chartres in which capacity he entered a dispute with the Germans in the summer of 1940 over certain arrests. He tried to commit suicide on 17 June but was saved and retired to Provence. There he made contact with resistance groups and managed to unite three of them under the name of *Combat*. In late 1941 Moulin managed to get to London to confer with de Gaulle as representative of *Combat*. He could have presented himself as a major rival to de Gaulle but instead gave him his complete loyalty. He was parachuted into France on 1 January 1942 as de Gaulle's delegate-general and spent the next eighteen months on the move throughout France discussing, negotiating and persuading in order to bring about a unified resistance. By March 1943 he had achieved a fusion of all non-Communist groups in the former Vichy areas into the *Mouvements Unis de Résistance*, and in May 1943 succeeded in effecting a national link-up called the *Conseil National de la Résistance*, all loyal to de Gaulle, whose first meeting he chaired on 27 May 1943. However at a meeting of 21 June at Caluire, near Lyons, Moulin was arrested by the Germans and died after being horribly tortured. Moulin had been one of the most talented and politic of resistance leaders and there was no one who could completely take his place.

**Mountbatten, Vice-Admiral Lord Louis, 1900–1979** Mountbatten was an expert in communications in the Royal Navy when the war began. In 1939 he was given command of the 5th Destroyer Flotilla assigned to the defense of Britain, and participated in the evacuation of Allied troops from Norway. In April 1941 he took his fleet to Malta and in May saw action off Crete, in which his flagship, HMS *Kelly*, was sunk. Shortly after he became Adviser on Combined Operations and was involved in preliminary planning for the projected invasion of Europe. He continued his planning activities as a member of the Chiefs of Staff Committee, working on the raids at St Nazaire (March) and Dieppe (August) and the Allied North Africa Landings of November 1942. Mountbatten also attended the Casablanca Conference in January 1943 and the Quebec Conference (July) at which the Allied command in Southeast Asia was reorganized.

Mountbatten became Supreme Allied Commander of this new Southeast Asia Command in October 1943. He lacked ships, landing craft and other equipment and therefore decided to concentrate on a land campaign. He spent the remainder of 1943 building up a secure base in India with improved communications which could be used for the campaign in Burma which began in December 1943. Mountbatten carried out these preparations with flair and a real feeling for public relations which enormously increased morale. The campaign itself, directed by General SLIM, was very successful despite limited resources, highlighted by the countering of a major Japanese offensive at Kohima and Imphal in February-March 1944 and the capture of Mandalay in March 1945. Burma was completely reconquered by May 1945. In September Mountbatten accepted the surrender of 750,000 Japanese at Singapore.

Mountbatten was a popular General because of his showmanship and a successful one because of his great capability, belief in science and technology and his ingenuity in confronting problems.

**Murphy, Robert, 1894–1958** Murphy was an American diplomat who acted as ROOSEVELT's political representative in North Africa from 1941 to 1943. In this capacity he gathered much useful intelligence and set up an intelligence network in preparation for EISEN-HOWER's landings at Casablanca in January 1943. On 22 November 1943 Murphy was appointed member of the Advisory Council to the Allied Control Commission for Italy.

**Mussolini, Benito, 1883–1945** Mussolini's international importance was already in decline by the outbreak of World War II. His seizure of power in 1924 had inspired HITLER by its demonstration of what a Fascist party, properly led, could achieve, and by his seizure of Ethiopia in 1935 and massive intervention in the Spanish Civil War in 1936, he succeeded in making himself seem the equal, if not the superior, of his German dictator on the international stage even after Italy's real power had begun to wane. But, as he himself knew all too well, Italy was industrially too weak and geographically too exposed to wage aggressive war against the Western Allies, and he carefully avoided involving himself in World War II until both had been brought to the brink of defeat by the blitzkrieg of May, 1940. Thereafter he was cast as Hitler's junior partner.

His desert army was humiliatingly defeated by a minor British force, in December 1940 and the invasion of Greece which he launched from Albania in November came to an even more shameful end. He had to be rescued from the debacle, by then an embarrassment to Hitler himself, in April 1941 and thereafter played no independent role in the war. He lost the greater part of his field army in the Tunisian defeat of 1943, when his expeditionary force in Russia was also almost completely destroyed at Stalingrad. By July, when it was clear that the Allies were preparing an invasion of mainland Italy, his position at home had been fatally weakened and he was deposed at a meeting of the Fascist Grand Council on 24 July. Imprisoned on the Gran Sasso in the Abruzzi, he was rescued by a parachute coup de main, led by Otto SKORZENY, on 12 September and taken to the north of Italy, where he attempted to refound a sovereign government at the head of a so-called Italian Social Republic. Germany had by then, however, taken Italy under effective military government and Mussolini wielded little power. In April 1945 he was captured, with his mistress, Clara Petacci, by partisans and executed. Their bodies were exhibited, hung by the heels, in a Milan square. It was a squalid end to a life which, though marred by much miscalculation, great vulgarity and some cruelty, compared in no way with the calculated inhumanity of Hitler's.

# N

**Nagumo, Admiral Chuichi, 1887–
1944** Nagumo commanded First Carrier Strike Force *Kido Butai*, from his
flagship the *Akagi* for the first eleven
months of the war. This was the Japanese Navy's corps d'élite, but Nagumo
was a torpedo expert, not an aviation
specialist, unhappy in his position and
overcautious. He led his force at Pearl
Harbor in December 1941 and decided
against sending his planes in for a third
attack, though it could have been decisive. He then commanded *Kido Butai*
at Midway where he showed hesitation
and an inability to adapt to this new
form of battle in which enemy fleets
never made contact. Nagumo then
fought two unsuccessful naval battles
of Guadalcanal: the Battles of the Eastern Solomons and of Santa Cruz Islands. He was relieved of that command and posted to the Marianas.
There he organized the defense of
Saipan. He committed suicide on 6 July
1944 when it was clear that all was
lost.

**Nebe, Artur, 1896–1945** Nebe had been
a policeman and eminent criminologist
in the Weimar Republic and a member
of the Nazi Party since 1929. By the
start of the war he was a top SD official
and head of KRIPO, the Criminal Investigation Department. In January 1942 he
was put in the charge of an *Einsatzgruppe* ordered to exterminate the Jews
of Russia. It is uncertain to what extent
he carried out his orders. Nebe was
involved with the conspirators against
HITLER for a long time and in July 1944
was involved in the bomb plot. He was

arrested soon after and executed on 3
March 1945.

**Neurath, Konstantin von, 1873–
1956** Neurath served as HITLER's Foreign Minister from 1932 to 1938. He
was not a Nazi but a conservative appointed to the Cabinet by Hindenberg,
who resigned his post in opposition to
Hitler's aggressive policies leading to
war. In 1939 Neurath was appointed
Reich Protector of Bohemia-Moravia, a
post which involved enforcing Berlin's
'advice' onto the satellite government of
the region. He was forced to retire because of his leniency and was replaced
by HEYDRICH. Neurath was tried at
Nuremberg for his complicity in starting
the war, but was given only fifteen years
imprisonment because he had opposed
and prevented various activities of the
Gestapo and SD in Czechoslovakia.

**Nimitz, Admiral Chester, 1885–
1966** Nimitz was Commander in Chief
of the US Pacific Fleet from 17 December
1941 until the end of the war. An outstanding strategist, he was responsible
for bringing the US Fleet from its weak
and dejected situation after Pearl Harbor
to a position of initiative and offense
within the first year of the war in the
Far East. Taking command shortly after
Pearl Harbor, Nimitz's first task was to
protect the US Hawaiian bases and maintain communications with the mainland.
To this purpose he gathered the large
Midway Fleet. At the Battle of Midway
Nimitz was considerably aided by the
cracking of the Japanese Fleet code some
months earlier and by the American

victory at Coral Sea in May 1942. After Midway, Nimitz had a considerably freer hand.

Commands in the Pacific were now rationalized, in order to ease interservice tensions. MACARTHUR was given command of the Southwest Pacific up to 160° East longitude and Nimitz commanded the Central Pacific from 160° East including Guadalcanal, the site of his next offensive. Here the Japanese showed their superiority in night fighting and by October 1942 the US had only one carrier left. However Vice-Admiral HALSEY was able to rally US forces and regain the initiative as the US increased war production and superior resources were taking effect.

Nimitz was a great believer in amphibious operations and felt that these would be more successful if used not to attack central Japanese troop concentrations directly but to take less well-defended islands behind the Japanese main lines thereby cutting them off, a strategy known as leapfrogging to Navy men. This was to be organized as an approach to Japan by way of the Central Pacific Islands. The Joint Chiefs of Staff agreed to this in 1943 and the operations opened up with November 1943 assaults on Makin and Tarawa in the Gilbert Islands and in February 1944 on the Marshalls. Nimitz then divided his fleet into two teams which he employed alternately: SPRUANCE's 5th Fleet and Halsey's 3rd. After the taking of the Marianas it was agreed that Nimitz should aid MacArthur's landings at Luzon and Okinawa, later adding Iwo Jima, which could be used immediately for direct attacks on Japan. One of the mainsprings of Nimitz's strategy throughout the war was his rivalry with MacArthur: Nimitz and his superior, KING, were always arguing that the Navy should have priority in the Pacific campaign and the lion's share of the resources available. The Joint Chiefs gave way to MacArthur's campaign to recapture the Philippines; Nimitz had argued for the taking of Formosa. However Nimitz's Central Pacific route to Japan was accepted for the final assault. In the last months of the war Nimitz's staff were planning this operation. The two rivals joined together in the final ceremony of victory: MacArthur accepted the formal surrender of the Japanese on board Nimitz's flagship the USS *Missouri* in Tokyo Bay on 2 September 1945.

**Nomura, Admiral Kochisaburo, 1877–1964** Nomura was Japanese Ambassador to Washington in the last days before the war. He was given little leeway to negotiate with Cordell HULL and was out of touch with Japanese political developments. Nomura presented the Japanese declaration of war to Hull about eighty minutes after the attack on Pearl Harbor began on 7 December 1941.

**Novikov, Colonel General Aleksandr, 1900–1976** Novikov was Commander in Chief of the Soviet Air Force (VVS) from 1942 until 1946. After serving as Chief of Staff to Leningrad VVS from 1938–1940 and as Chief of Staff of VVS on the Karelian Front during the Russo-Finnish War, Novikov became Commander in Chief and undertook the major reorganization of the Air Force following serious defeats by the Luftwaffe. During the war Novikov attended most Stavka meetings and was in charge of all air operations at the Battles of Stalingrad, Kursk, Belorussia and Königsberg and in the 1945 operations against the Kwantung Army in Manchuria. In 1946 he was dismissed from his post and possibly imprisoned.

**Nye, General Archibald, 1895–1967** Nye served as Vice-CIGS (Chief of Imperial General Staff) to General BROOKE, the CIGS, from 1941 to 1946. After commanding the Nowshera

Brigade and serving as Director of Staff Duties in the early stages of the war, he was suggested as a possible CIGS himself. He had an excellent working relationship with Brooke and was often delegated to act in his place.

# O

**O'Connor, General Sir Richard, 1889–1981** In September 1939 O'Connor was in command of the 7th Division and was Governor of Jerusalem. In June 1940 O'Connor and his Division were sent from Palestine to Egypt where he was appointed Commander of the Western Desert Forces, under the overall command of his friend, General WAVELL. In September 1940 Marshal Graziani's Italian forces from Libya invaded Egypt. Within two months Wavell had launched an offensive which was to take Tobruk and to reach Benghazi and El Agheila by 5 February 1941. O'Connor led the northern flank in this successful mission and was appointed General Officer Commanding British troops in Egypt under General Neame. In March 1941 ROMMEL launched a counteroffensive and shortly afterwards Neame and O'Connor were captured and sent to Italy. In December 1943 when Italy capitulated they were freed and by June 1944 O'Connor was again in command, this time of VIII Corps for the invasion of Normandy. O'Connor was a brilliant Commander. His operative motto was 'offensive action wherever possible.' Many of his colleagues and comrades-at-arms felt that it was only the fact that he was captured that prevented him from being declared one of the top Desert Commanders.

**Olbricht, General Friedrich, 1886–1944** Olbricht was the Head of the Supply Section of the Reserve Army and personal Deputy to FROMM. He was above all an administrator and prepared the detailed planning for Operation Valkyrie – to disrupt communications of the Third Reich under cover of an operation to put down a foreign worker uprising. On the day STAUFFENBERG's bomb exploded at Rastenburg, 20 July 1944, HÖPNER and Olbricht were ready to take over the War Office and put Valkyrie into motion; however the message that the bomb had exploded did not come through. Olbricht vacillated and did not launch the operation until 1600 hours by which time communications with HITLER's entourage had been re-established. Olbricht arrested Fromm whom he could not win over, but when news that Hitler was alive reached him he lost his nerve. Fromm was able to reassert his authority and he arrested Olbricht. Fromm had Olbricht, Stauffenberg and the other conspirators shot in the courtyard on that day.

**Oldendorf, Rear Admiral Jesse, 1887–** Oldendorf was the Commander of Task Group 77.2 at the Battle of Leyte Gulf. His task was to prevent the Japanese forces from passing through the Surigao Strait. Early in the morning of 25 October 1944 Oldendorf's ships were able to devastate Vice-Admiral Nishimura's force with torpedo and radar-controlled gunfire. This was the first clear victory achieved by the Americans in surface action against the Japanese. Oldendorf remained as Commander of Combat Formations of the 7th Fleet and when on duty off Luzon in January 1945 bore the brunt of the kamikaze attacks.

**Onishi, Admiral Takijiro, 1891–1945** Onishi was a fanatical Japanese militarist and something of a cult figure among his staff. In 1941 as Chief of Staff of the Eleventh Air Fleet under YAMAMOTO, Onishi and his friend, Commander Minoru GENDA, carried out an important feasibility study on Pearl Harbor in preparation for the attack. In the first days of the war Onishi led an attack on Clark Field near Manila, and despite bad weather and against the advice of his subordinates, destroyed all US air power in the Far East.

In October 1944 Onishi was made Commander of the Fifth Base Air Force on Luzon which was to support Admiral KURITA's attack on the US invasion force at Leyte. He had only 100 planes at his disposal and, wanting to maximize their effectiveness, he set up the Special Attack Group – the first formal Kamikaze Corps. Their first operations proved remarkably effective and for a time the Japanese looked on them as the answer to all their problems, which put Onishi very much in the limelight. Onishi was a die-hard to the end and adamantly opposed surrender. After the Japanese surrender of 15 August he committed suicide.

**Oppenheimer, J Robert, 1904–1967** In 1936 Oppenheimer was a professor of atomic or nuclear physics at the University of California. In 1942 when the USA joined the war he was appointed Director of the government laboratory at Los Alamos and Head of the team which was to build the first atomic bomb. A dynamic leader with a brilliant mind, Oppenheimer was able to complete his project in time to use it against Japan. Some have argued that this was done in the 'nick of time' as many lives were spared because the Allies did not have to invade the Home Islands.

**Osmeña, Sergio, 1878–1961** Osmeña was Vice-President of the Philippines under QUEZON and accompanied him to the USA after the Philippines fell. There he took over many Presidential duties because of Quezon's ill health. Osmeña sat on the Pacific War Council and attended many other conferences and board meetings which discussed military and other matters of concern to the Philippines. He also lectured throughout the USA on the Philippine situation. When Quezon died in August 1944 Osmeña became President.

Because of his intense dislike of MAC-ARTHUR, it took much persuasion to get Osmeña to accompany the Luzon invasion of January 1945. However, he did return and with Romulo and MacArthur helped to integrate the Filipino guerrilla forces with the US Army. Osmeña became head of the new civilian government after the liberation.

**Ozawa, Vice-Admiral Jisaburo, 1896–1966** Ozawa was Commander of the Japanese Mobile Fleet from November 1942 until the end of the war. The ablest strategic thinker of the Japanese Navy and one of the first to realize the possibilities and significance of carriers, Ozawa did not take over the Carrier Force until after Japan had lost its superiority at sea and most of its trained aviators. Appointed after the dismissal of NAGUMO, Ozawa was Commander at the Battle of the Philippine Sea in which he lost his flagship, the carrier *Taiho*, and 340 planes. Two other carriers were damaged and on the next day Ozawa made the mistake of lingering near the battle site which cost him three more ships. The Japanese could never again face the Allied Navy with equal strength; Ozawa wanted to resign but was persuaded to stay.

At the Battle of Leyte Gulf, 24 October 1944, Ozawa's Mobile Force was to act as a decoy to lure Admiral HALSEY's Fleet away from the San Bernardino Strait. This Ozawa accomplished with tremendous skill, but the battle had already been lost – the Japanese Navy could no longer challenge the US.

# P

**Papagos, General Alexander, 1883–1955** Papagos was the Commander in Chief of the Greek Army on 28 October 1940 when the Italians invaded Greece from Albania. He repelled the attack and sent the Italians back to Albania. The Allies instructed General WAVELL to send large reinforcements to help Papagos. At a joint meeting between the Greek and British military leaders it was agreed to defend the Aliakmon Line on 22 February 1941 but a week later the British, under Anthony EDEN, found that Papagos and his Army had not withdrawn to the Aliakmon Line but were waiting to see what position Yugoslavia was going to take. On 9 March the Italians attacked and in early April the Germans arrived to reinforce them. The British-Greek Armies were forced to retreat. On 21 April General Tsolacoglou had overthrown Papagos and by 27 April Greece was under German control. Papagos was taken to Dachau concentration camp as a hostage in 1943 and was freed by the Americans in 1945. He returned to his original position as Commander in Chief to wage war against the left-wing guerrillas in northern Greece in the years immediately following World War II.

**Park, Air Marshal Sir Keith, 1892–1975** Park was an extremely inventive and energetic British Air Marshal who commanded in the Battle of Britain, Malta and the Far East. A New Zealander, Park became Air Officer Commanding (AOC) No 11 Fighter Group under DOWDING in 1939. In June 1940 he was in charge of providing air cover for the Dunkirk evacuation and with only 200 planes managed to gain air superiority over the German bombers. In the Battle of Britain Park's tactics were much criticized and led to great tension with Air Vice-Marshal LEIGH-MALLORY, but they were generally successful. In particular he urged that the RAF should meet attacking German planes well before the German planes reached their targets; this put the RAF fighters at great risk but protected civilians and led to higher scores.

In the fall of 1941 Park became AOC at Allied Headquarters Egypt and on 15 July 1942 was appointed AOC Malta. Malta was a vital strategic base for the Allies but from late 1941 it had been on the defensive and was constantly short of supplies. Park pushed the campaign onto the offensive by attacking German convoys and aircraft at sea. In November 1942 he provided air support for Allied landings in North Africa, as he did for landings in Sicily, July 1943, and Italy, September 1943. In January 1944 Park became Supreme Commander of Air in the Middle East and in February 1945 he was appointed Air Commander in Chief of Southeast Asia Command, in which capacity he provided vital air support for the British offensive on Rangoon.

**Patch, General Alexander McCarrell, 1889–1945** In 1941 before the Americans had joined the war, Patch commanded the Infantry Replacement Center at Camp Croft in North Carolina. In spring of 1942 he was sent to help the French defend New Caledonia in the South Pacific and was appointed Commander of that Task Force. In the very early days of 1943 Patch, as commander of American Forces, led his troops to their first major land victory at the Battle of Guadalcanal. In March 1944 he became Commanding General of the US 7th Army which landed between Cannes and Toulon on 15 August as part of the invasion of France (Dragoon). Fighting steadily, the 7th Army advanced up the Rhône valley capturing Alsace in the winter and the Saar by 15 March 1945. The German Army Group G was now in retreat and Patch crossed the Rhine on 26 March. He then prevented the Germans from forming a national redoubt by making a headlong advance into southern Germany. On 5 May 1945 Patch received the formal surrender of BALCK's Army Group G.

**Patton, General George, 1885–1945**
Patton belonged to the small band of American officers who cherished a belief in the future of the tank through the long years of interwar stagnation. He had seen action in the American tank corps in World War I, and distinguished himself. He had also impressed by his ability in the more conventional activities of army life and had been appointed Superintendent of West Point. But Patton was not at heart conventional. His manner was extrovert, his appearance flamboyant and his dealings with people emphatic to the point of theatricality. He was given command of II Corps in the Torch landings in North Africa in 1942 and then promoted to lead the 7th Army in the invasion of Sicily, where he lost patience with EISENHOWER's plan, which allotted the decisive role to MONTGOMERY, and took over the lead himself. Unfortunately, he also lost patience not once but twice with soldiers whom he found in hospital for 'combat fatigue' and on the second occasion was reported in the newspapers for having slapped a man's face. As a

result he was demoted and, when re-employed for the invasion of Europe, had to serve as Commander of the 3rd Army under his old subordinate, Bradley. He nevertheless succeeded in making himself the star of the Breakout of Normandy by the speed and force of his advance to Lorraine and the German frontier in July-September. It was an advance conducted against the background of a bitter strategic debate with Eisenhower over the advisability of allotting Montgomery an equal share of the available supplies. And though it is now thought that Eisenhower's strategy was broadly correct, Patton remained convinced that he had been robbed of the chance to invade Germany and perhaps end the war in 1944. He spent the winter of that year fighting a bitter battle of attrition on the frontier, interrupted by his decisive intervention in the Battle of the Bulge, conducted a masterly crossing of the Rhine in the spring and repeated his whirl-wind success of the previous summer by the audacity of his advance to Czechoslovakia, from which he withdrew, under political pressure, with the greatest reluctance. He was killed in an accident in December 1945. Patton was no great theorist of tank tactics, but he was the founder of the armored tradition in the American army.

**Paul, Prince Regent of Yugoslavia, 1893–1976** Paul served as Regent for King PETER II from 1934 until he was deposed on 27 March 1941 in a bloodless coup. Paul worked for Yugoslav neutrality, believing the country militarily unfit to fight the Germans. However despite Allied pressure and contrary to the sentiment of both his people and armed forces, Paul bowed to German threats and signed a secret pact with the Axis on 25 March 1941. Two days later the leader of the Yugoslav Armed Forces, SIMOVIĆ, put into operation plans for a military take-over and gave Peter II power to rule the country. Paul and his family left for Greece that night.

**Paulus, Field Marshal Friedrich, 1890–1957** Paulus was a bright young staff officer who served as Chief of Staff of the Sixth Army in its campaigns in Poland, Belgium and France. He was picked out and made Deputy Chief of General Staff to HALDER with the brief to examine the possibilities of an attack on the USSR, and was responsible for the detailed planning of Operation Barbarossa. In January 1942 he was made Commander of the Sixth Army and led it on the advance to Stalingrad. He planned to surround the city and encircle the Soviet troops within it. Although he succeeded in encircling the troops in November 1942 he was running short of supplies and his men were exhausted but HITLER insisted that he continue to fight and promised that GOERING's Luftwaffe would keep him adequately supplied. These promises were never kept and the Soviet troops under CHUIKOV fought street by street, giving Paulus' no respite. In December MANSTEIN launched an offensive to try to relieve Paulus' Army but Paulus refused to break out because Hitler had given him orders not to withdraw. In recognition of his bravery Hitler made him a Field Marshal on 30 January but on the next day he surrendered, much to Hitler's anger. He was kept in captivity for the remainder of the war. In mid-1944 he began giving broadcasts urging German soldiers to give up and his name became synonymous with traitor. He decided to settle in the Soviet zone of Germany after the war and appeared as a key witness for the Soviet prosecution at the Nuremberg trials.

**Pavlov, General Dimitry, d. 1941** Pavlov was Commander of the Western Front when the Germans invaded Russia. A tank expert who had served in Spain and in Finland on the Mannerheim Line, he believed that tanks had a merely subsidiary role as infantry support. In 1940 Pavlov was appointed Commander of the Western Military District (renamed the Western Front on 23 June 1941) which covered Northeastern Poland, and the Bialystok and Brest-Litovsk regions. In June 1941 Pavlov faced GUDERIAN's 2nd and 3rd Armored Groups with equal infantry strength but low numbers of tanks, one half of which he lost in the first day's encounter. By 28 June his defenses had collapsed and he was replaced by YEREMENKO. Pavlov, his Chief of Staff, and his Fourth Army Commander, Korobkov, were all shot for incompetence.

**Peirse, Air Marshal Sir Richard, 1892–1970** Peirse was a British Air Marshal who served as Deputy Chief of Air Staff at the beginning of World War II, becoming Vice-Chief in 1940. In the same year he succeeded PORTAL as Commander in Chief of RAF Bomber Command but inadequate radar equipment, lack of crew training, and a high casualty rate which resulted from night operations under such conditions led to his leaving the post in January 1942.

He was subsequently appointed Air Officer Commanding in India where his initial task was to plan the reorganization and expansion of his units. A new Bengal Command was established to facilitate operations in Northeast India. On his return from the Washington Conference in May 1943, he speeded up preparations for the China airlift in Assam. In November 1943 he was appointed Allied Air Commander in Chief of Southeast Asia Command and coordinated air transport and supplies for the British offensive to retake Burma. He retired in November 1944.

**Percival, Lieutenant General Arthur, 1887–1966** Percival was GOC (General Officer Commanding) Malaya when the Japanese invaded on 8 December 1941.

After serving in France under General DILL, Percival was sent to Malaya in July 1941. British defense of the area depended on command of sea and air, yet Percival had insufficient aircraft and on 10 December 1941 lost his entire fleet, Force Z. On the other hand Singapore was protected by its big guns, which were effective against sea attack but not against land attack. Unfortunately Japan invaded by land from the north. Percival had been aware of these problems when he had served in Malaya in 1936–38 but nothing had been done since to rectify the problem as the European fronts had top priority. Furthermore Percival's troops were ill-trained and badly led, and their defense in North Malaya was simply a series of retreats. By 27 January Percival ordered a general withdrawal to Singapore Island and on 8 February the Japanese landings began. CHURCHILL ordered Percival to fight to the death, but Singapore was rapidly running out of water supplies, had no hope of reinforcements or air support and the troops were quite demoralized. Percival and 85,000 men surrendered to General YAMASHITA on 15 February 1942 in what was considered the most shameful blow to English arms in history. Percival was interned in Manchuria throughout the war but was flown in to be present at the Japanese surrender in Tokyo Bay on 2 September 1945.

Peron, President Juan Domingo, 1895–1975 In 1943 Peron began his climb to power by joining a military coup to make sure Argentina remained pro-Axis. Argentina stood apart from the rest of Latin America in its support of the Axis powers – both because of strong nationalist distrust of US interference in internal affairs and because of the belief that Germany would win the war. Despite fears in the British Foreign Office that trading links with Argentina would be damaged and that information on Brit-

ish shipping movements might be passed on to the Germans, in February 1943 Argentina again reaffirmed her neutrality.

On 26 January 1944, in the face of Argentina's increasing isolation in comparison with Brazil, and the realization that a German victory was less likely, the government broke off relations with Germany and Japan. Any hopes amongst the Allies that a more democratic and co-operative regime might overthrow the increasing power of Colonel Peron were quickly shattered; in fact it only strengthened his position. In 1945 Peron became Vice-President and Minister of War. His aim was to achieve undisputed power based on the support of the underprivileged laborers and on his popularity and authority in the Army. He was elected President in 1946.

Pétain, Marshal Henri Philippe Omer, 1856–1951 A remarkable and patriotic soldier, Pétain was much honored for his defense of Verdun in 1916. In 1939 he was appointed Ambassador to Spain but was recalled to Paris by REYNAUD in 1940 after the German invasion of France and appointed Vice-President of Council. Convinced that Britain was destined to lose the war he rejected Reynaud's proposal (which was supported by DE GAULLE and DARLAN) to ally with Britain and continue to fight the Axis invasion. Pétain was heard to utter 'To make union with England was fusion with a corpse.' LAVAL and some Cabinet ministers supported Pétain and Reynaud resigned on 16 June 1940. Pétain assumed the Presidency and offered the Germans an armistice on 22 June. Laval petitioned the National Assembly to grant Pétain emergency powers. Pétain established his government at Vichy in the unoccupied part of France and pursued a policy of collaboration with the Germans who allowed him to have 10,000 men to keep the peace in his sector. In December 1940 Pétain dismissed Laval because Laval not only wanted to be on peaceful terms with Germany but wanted to support the Axis actively and declare war on the United Kingdom. Although Laval's influence was partially curbed, Laval was reinstated on the Germans' insistence in April 1942. In November the Allies invaded French North Africa and the Germans occupied the Vichy-ruled part of France; Pétain's government became a puppet. At 86 Pétain was unable to administer his government efficiently and his power declined. He was removed to Germany in August 1944 but voluntarily returned to France in April of the following year to stand trial. He was sentenced to death but de Gaulle commuted the sentence to life imprisonment as they had served in the same regiment in World War I. Pétain died on the Atlantic island, Ile d'Yeu, at the age of 95. Pétain was not a treacherous leader but one who suffered rather from defeatism; he inevitably chose the policy he thought best for France.

**Peter II, King of Yugoslavia, 1923–1970** Peter ruled through his Regent, Prince PAUL, from 1934 until SIMOVIĆ's coup of 27 March 1941 which placed Peter on the throne. The coup was a reaction to Paul's collaborationist policy with the Nazis, embodied in a pact with the Axis signed on 25 March. However Germany invaded on 6 April and all resistance collapsed within two weeks. Peter and his government went to Athens and then to London where they spent the duration of the war. Peter supported the non-Communist guerrilla force in Yugoslavia called the Četniks, which were led by MIHAJLOVIĆ. The Allies, however, seeing that the Četniks spent most of their time fighting other partisans and collaborating with the Germans, supported TITO's partisans. Peter was therefore a diminishing force in Yugoslav and Allied affairs. Peter bowed to the inevitable and signed an agree-

ment with Tito on 1 November 1944 which involved representing himself through a Regency council. However Tito declared a Republic on 29 November 1945 and Peter never returned to his country.

**Petrov, General Ivan, 1896–1950** Petrov was an eminent Soviet General who fought mainly in the Crimea and Caucasus. At the start of the war he was stationed with the 2nd Cavalry Division defending Odessa and was evacuated to the Crimea when it could no longer be held. Petrov was in charge of the defense of Sevastopol when the rest of the Crimea had been captured. He managed to keep the city for many months until the Germans launched a major assault in June 1942. Petrov continued to fight until July when Russian supplies and reinforcements failed to get through. Petrov was evacuated before the city fell on 3 July.

In the winter offensive of 1942–43 Petrov was Commander of the Black Sea Front which attacked the Germans in the Caucasus only to come to a standstill. Petrov finally managed to take Novorossiysk and the Taman and Kerch Peninsulas in September and October 1943, forcing the Germans back into the Crimea. He commanded the 2nd Belorussian Front but was removed after a short time. From August 1944–April 1945 Petrov then commanded the 4th Ukrainian Front with which he crossed the Carpathian passes from the north into Ruthenia in October and then turned west towards Slovakia where he was ordered to aid the partisans. However he was held up by difficulties afforded by the mountainous terrain. In the January 1945 offensive he turned north towards Poland and ended the war liberating parts of that country.

**Phillips, Admiral Sir Tom, 1888–1941** Phillips was the Commander of Force Z which was sunk off Malaya in the first days of the war against Japan. In July of 1941 CHURCHILL decided to cut off oil supplies to Japan and to provide a deterrent force in the area. Rather than send a large fleet he sent the *Prince of Wales*, which was a new-style battleship, and the *Repulse*. Phillips arrived in Singapore on 3 December to take command and set off on 8 December to attack a large Japanese convoy which had been reported unloading at Singora and Kota Bahru. Phillips had no aircraft carrier and no air support from land bases. On 9 December the weather cleared and Force Z was spotted by Japanese planes. Phillips turned south to return to port but then turned toward Kuantan when he received reports (which turned out to be false) of a Japanese landing there. Force Z was attacked by the Japanese elite 22nd Air Flotilla on the morning of 10 December and the *Prince of Wales* and the *Repulse* were both sunk by midday. Most of the men were rescued but Admiral Phillips was one of those lost.

**Popov, General Markian, 1902–1969** Popov began the war as Commander of the Leningrad Military District (which became the Northern Front in late 1941). He took part in the Battle for Stalingrad in 1942 as a Commander of Armored Divisions. On 11 February 1943 as part of TIMOSHENKO's drive after Stalingrad, Popov captured Kharkov but was driven out by the massive German counterattack. In July 1943 at the Battle of Kursk, Popov commanded the Bryansk Front which with SOKOLOVSKY's Western Front was to wait in reserve until after the German offensive had been repulsed. On 12 July, two days after KLUGE ordered the German Army onto the defensive, Popov came down from the north onto Kluge's Army in the Orel area and delivered a mighty blow. Popov advanced from Orel in the second half of August to Bryansk. In 1944 Popov was given the command

of the 2nd Baltic Front which with two other Fronts could only advance slowly because of the fortifications they encountered in the north. He was replaced by YEREMENKO when he failed to take Riga. Although he was a competent General he was never really trusted by STALIN.

**Portal, Air Chief Marshal Sir Charles, 1893–1971** Portal was the British Chief of Air Staff from 1940–45. Formerly Chief of Bomber Command, Portal was a wise and competent Commander of the RAF and his chief contribution to the winning of the war was the influence he wielded both over CHURCHILL and in Anglo-American strategic decision making. He was much liked by the Americans, to whom he was remarkably successful in presenting the British point of view at the major inter-Allied conferences. Portal was a firm advocate of strategic area bombing and this brought him into conflict with the Americans who advocated daylight precision bombing. However diplomacy and the respect with which Portal was regarded led to the formulation of a compromise: the Combined Bomber Offensive determined at the Casablanca Conference.

In early 1944 Portal's views on area bombing changed and he felt the bombers should play a more auxiliary role in Allied offensives in Europe. This put a tremendous strain on his relations with HARRIS who threatened resignation. Portal had to modify his demands because he realized that this would be a tremendous blow to Bomber Command morale.

**Pound, Admiral Sir Dudley, 1877–1943** In 1939 Pound was promoted to Admiral of the Fleet and First Sea Lord, and he also acted as Chairman of the British Chiefs of Staff Committee until March 1942 when BROOKE succeeded him. His regime as First Sea Lord was marked by increasing centralization which often worked to his good. However he worked too hard and his judgment was sometimes called into doubt. In July 1942 he took the decision to order the convoy PQ-17 to scatter because it was threatened by a powerful German surface force. The decision to scatter left the convoy vulnerable and only ten ships reached the USSR out of 33. Pound was criticized for interfering but his intervention was unusual; on-the-spot decisions were more usually taken by Commanders at sea. He held the office until he was taken ill and died three weeks after resigning his post. His record in office was highly successful and he earned CHURCHILL's admiration and confidence.

**Prien, Lieutenant Günther, 1908–1941** During the first two years of the war Prien was a U-Boat Commander who became a German national hero. As Commander of submarine *U.47* he was ordered by Admiral Doenitz to plan and execute an attack on Scapa Flow, the British anchorage in Scotland. In the early morning of 14 October 1939 Prien's U-Boat penetrated a narrow passage into the anchorage. Though most of the fleet had been removed to Loch Ewe, Prien managed to sink the HMS

*Royal Oak* with 833 men on board. Occurring only six weeks after Britain had entered the war, it was a blow to morale but led to a tightening up of anchorage defense which was much needed.

Prien went on to fight in the Atlantic and Channel until on 7 March 1941 *U.47* was sunk with all hands by the corvettes *Arbutus* and *Camellia* and destroyer *Wolverine*. The news of his death was kept secret for a long time because of his enormous popularity.

**Pyle, Ernest, 1900–1945** Pyle was a famous American war correspondent who spent more than three years in combat areas in Europe and the Far East. Already a successful and syndicated columnist before the war. Pyle was stationed in London in 1941 where he covered the 'Blitz.' He went on to cover the campaigns in North Africa, Sicily, Italy and France. He also accompanied the assaults on Iwo Jima and Okinawa. He was killed by Japanese bullets on 18 April 1945 while visiting the island of Ie Shima. Pyle won many awards including the Pulitzer Prize for his vivid eye-witness accounts which concentrated on the experiences of the ordinary soldier.

# Q

**Quezon, Manuel, 1878–1944** Quezon was President of the Commonwealth of the Philippine Islands from 1935 until his death in 1944. He was strongly in favor of US-Philippine co-operation. When war began the Philippines (an American possession) were a prime Japanese target and they made their first landings on the mainland on 22 December 1941. Quezon, who did much to raise Philippine morale throughout this time, left for Corregidor on 24 December on MACARTHUR's advice. He kept in close contact with the struggle however and was inaugurated into his second term of office as President in an air-raid shelter in Corregidor. In March 1942 Quezon left for Australia and then went on to the US where he spoke before the House of Representatives on 2 June, and offered assurances of Filipino determination to fight to the end. Quezon was ill with tuberculosis and died on 1 August 1944 at Saranac Lake, New York, a few months before the liberation of his country.

**Quisling, Vidkun, 1887–1945** A former Army officer and government minister, Quisling was the leader of the Norwegian Nazi Party, the *Nasjonal Samling*. On 14 December 1939 he visited HITLER and showed him his plans for a coup in neutral Norway. Hitler, while stalling Quisling, prepared his own plans for an invasion of Norway which would depend not on the ability of the Norwegian Nazi Party followers but on the strength of the German Army for its success. On 9 April 1940 the Germans invaded Norway and Quisling became the Head of the puppet government; most Norwegian ministers and officers in the government resigned within a week of his appointment. In September even the Germans were having difficulty agreeing with him and he was ousted. In February 1942 he was reinstated by Reichskommissar Terboven as Minister President but he had no real authority. At the end of the war he surrendered himself to the police and was tried for high treason. He was found guilty and executed on 24 November 1945. Considered by the Norwegians, the Allies and most of the world as a traitor of the worst type, there is little doubt that he regarded himself as a patriot who tried to achieve the best 'deal' possible for Norway.

# R

**Radolfi, Alexander 'Rado'** Rado was the resident director of a Soviet intelligence network in Switzerland during World War II. He was a professional scientist and worked as a cartographer for a press agency. He recruited RÖS-SELER to his network and provided first-class military information to the USSR. In October 1943 the Swiss began to pick up members of his group and he panicked and fled to Paris. He re-emerged at the end of the war and was extradited by Moscow from Egypt as Soviet intelligence wanted to question him about his misuse of funds.

**Raeder, Admiral Erich, 1876–1960** Raeder was Commander in Chief of German Naval Forces until 1943 and was the architect of the German Navy of World War II. He had the 'pocket' battleships built and paid the foundations for the German U-Boat fleet. In October 1939 he put forward a plan to rival British naval supremacy in the North Sea using bases in Norway and shortly afterwards was planning the naval aspects of the Norwegian campaign of April 1940. The next operation he was given to plan was the invasion of England, which Raeder thought was far too ambitious a project for the German Navy. For the next two years HITLER and Raeder were involved in a constant argument over how the German Navy should be used. Hitler did not wish to spend any money building more battleships and would not risk the forces he had, except in operations off the Norwegian coast. When even the Arctic con-voys of the Allies were getting through without trouble, Hitler put pressure on Raeder to step up a harassing campaign. After the failure of the Battle of Barents Sea Hitler dismissed Raeder and replaced him by DOENITZ in January 1943. Raeder was found guilty of war crimes at Nuremberg and sentenced to ten years' imprisonment.

**Ramsay, Admiral Sir Bertram Home, 1883–1945** As Flag Officer at Dover in 1940, Ramsay organized the evacuation of soldiers from Dunkirk. Ramsay was an expert in amphibious operations at every level. In 1942 he was appointed Naval Force Commander for the invasion of Europe but was transferred in July to command the Algerian landings in North Africa which began in November of that year. In July 1943 he prepared the amphibious landings in Sicily as Naval Commanding Officer, Eastern Task Force. In 1944 he was appointed Naval Commander in Chief for Operation Overlord, much to EISENHOWER's relief as he thought Ramsay an exceptionally able Commander. Operation Overlord officially began on 6 June 1944 and one million soldiers disembarked on the coast of France, a marvelous testimony to Ramsay's ingenuity. His next project involved the invasion of the Isle of Walcheren. On 2 January 1945 Ramsay was on his way to meet MONT-GOMERY in Brussels when his plane crashed killing all hands. Ramsay was a brilliant Admiral who commanded the respect of both his superiors and his men.

**Rashid Ali, el-Gaylani, 1892–1944**
Rashid Ali seized power in Iraq on 1
April 1941 and immediately pledged his
loyalty to Britain. However his leanings
were pro-Axis so Rashid Ali was determined to try to get help from HITLER
and was able to extract a promise of air
support and supplies from the Vichy
regime via Syria. The British, aware of
his political leanings, told Rashid Ali
that they were sending in more troops
in accordance with the Anglo-Iraqi
treaty terms. Rashid Ali agreed but on
27 April said no more troops could enter
the country. The British continued to
send in troops and Rashid Ali led an
attack on the British camp at Habbani-
yah on 29 April. However the superior
air power of the British defeated the
greater numbers of the Iraqis. On 30
May Rashid Ali fled to Persia.

**Reichenau, Field Marshal Walther von,
1884–1942** Reichenau was one of the
few Army Commanders who was a defi-
nite supporter of HITLER and his Nazi
regime. In fact Hitler had considered
making him his Commander in Chief of
the Army after FRITSCH's dismissal, but
RUNDSTEDT managed to talk him out
of this. In 1939 he led the Tenth Army
into Poland and then in 1940 the Sixth
Army into Belgium, entering Brussels in
triumph. In 1941 he led the Sixth Army
in the invasion of the USSR and his
Army accomplished the encirclement of
Kiev, although this took longer than
anticipated. After the purge of the eastern Generals in December 1941, following the failure of the offensive against
Moscow, Reichenau was made Commander of Army Group South. However
he had a heart attack at his Headquarters and died after being flown back to
Leipzig – a premature death for such a
skillful Commander.

**Reynaud, Paul, 1878–1966** Reynaud
was Prime Minister, Foreign Minister
and Minister of War of France until 16
June 1940. He had succeeded Edouard
DALADIER as Head of State on 21
March 1940. One of his first acts was to
meet CHURCHILL and on 28 March to
issue a declaration in which both England and France pledged not to make a
separate peace with Germany. However,
shortly afterwards the Germans crossed
the Meuse and the French Army's fiasco
under General GAMELIN began. On 19
May 1940, four days after the German
breakthrough at Sedan, Reynaud reorganized the Cabinet and the High Command, replacing General Gamelin with
the aged WEYGAND and appointing the
even more aged PÉTAIN as Deputy
Prime Minister. Reynaud was to regret
this decision for both Weygand and
Petain were strongly in favor of surrendering to Germany. Reynaud wanted to
continue the fight but there was little he
could do except negotiate with Britain
for aid which it could not give. On 13
June he asked Britain to release him
from his pledge not to make a separate
peace. Two days later he proposed
moving the government, Air Force and
Fleet to North Africa but no action was
taken. On 16 June Reynaud finally resigned and Pétain took over.

Reynaud was arrested by the Vichy
government on 6 September 1940. Early
in 1942 he was one of the defendants at
the famous show trial at Riom in which
the Vichy government tried former government leaders for their alleged failure
and negligence during the fight against
the Germans. The defendants managed
to turn the tables on their accusers
whom they showed to have been the
true traitors. Reynaud was deported to
Germany in 1943 and released at the
end of the war.

**Ribbentrop, Joachim von, 1893–
1946** Ribbentrop became HITLER's Foreign Minister in 1938 because he had
impressed the Führer with his veneer
of social graces. In fact his arrogant
airs made him many enemies within

Germany and abroad. CIANO, Italy's Foreign Minister, despised him and said he was 'vain, frivolous and loquacious.' He laid the foundations for the German-Soviet Non-Aggression Pact partitioning Poland, which he signed with MOLOTOV in August 1939. However Ribbentrop warned Hitler that the invasion of Poland would probably lead to war with England and he was proved right. His influence declined steadily during the war but Hitler retained him; however in 1943 Ribbentrop had secret discussions with Molotov at Kirovograd about ending the war on the Eastern Front. The discussions faltered on the question of where to draw a new frontier. Ribbentrop maintained a low profile throughout the war and disappeared after the fall of Berlin. He was captured by the Allies, put on trial at Nuremberg and hanged as a war criminal.

**Ridgway, General Matthew Bunker, 1895–1993** Ridgway was a daring Commander of airborne infantry operations in Sicily and in northwestern Europe. Assigned to the US 82nd Infantry Division, he organized the first Allied airborne assault. This operation which took place on 10 July 1943 involved parachuting from a glider regiment as part of the initial invasion of Sicily. Ridgway successfully accomplished the aims of his mission, but the casualties were high; bad weather and insufficient training of the glider pilots forced a large number of the planes to land in the sea. On 12 September he was brought with his Division to Salerno immediately following the Italian capitulation and fought his way up to Naples.

Ridgway was then sent to Britain to participate in the preparations for D-Day. During the invasion Ridgway and his 82nd led the assault on the Cotentin peninsula on 6 June 1944. Ridgway was then put in command of the XVIII Airborne Corps which fought in the airborne invasion of the Netherlands at Eindhoven, in the defense against the Germans' Ardennes offensive and in the Allied offensive against the Siegfried Line. His last engagement was the crossing of the Elbe.

**Ritchie, General Neil, 1897–1983** Ritchie was the Commander of the British 8th Army when it suffered its major defeat by ROMMEL in 1942. Until mid-1940 Ritchie was Chief of Staff to General BROOKE in Belgium and France and went to the Middle East in 1941 as Deputy Chief of Staff to AUCHINLECK, the Commander in Chief. Ritchie replaced CUNNINGHAM in command of the 8th Army on 26 November 1941 in the middle of the battle for Tobruk. By December Rommel was forced to withdraw to the west of Cyrenaica and the British gained much territory and relieved Tobruk from its ten-month siege. However on 21 January Rommel launched his counterattack with tremendous force and had captured Cyrenaica by 28 January. He now stood at Ritchie's El Gazala-Bir Hacheim line, a defensive wall of outposts connected by heavily mined strips. Ritchie's Army was spread over a considerable area with a concentration of force in the north. Rommel concentrated his troops an offensive in the south and attacked on 26 May catching Ritchie offguard Ritchie and Auchinleck now decided to leave a garrison of 35,000 men at Tobruk even though it was indefensible while the rest of the force retreated towards El Alamein. Rommel attacked Tobruk on 20 June and it the next day, with almost the entire on garrison captured and a large cache of supplies falling to Rommel who could now into Egypt within the month. Ritchie was removed from his post on 25 June and replaced by Auchinleck himself.

Ritchie was unlucky to be posted to North Africa in the middle of a difficult situation without any experience in desert warfare facing Rommel. He went on to command the XII Corps of the British 2nd Army in north-west Europe after D-Day and did this very capably.

**Roey, Cardinal Joseph van, 1874–1961** Primate of Belgium and Archbishop of Malines, van Roey courageously faced the impossible situation in his country and actually tried to influence events from his important position. A strong advocate of Belgian neutrality, he supported the King's surrender in May 1940 when that neutral policy proved untenable. During the occupation he tried to insure that the Church and the schools could not be used as Nazi instruments. He arranged homes for Jewish children elderly people and helped those in hiding. In June 1943 he issued a Pastoral Letter calling for a stop to attacks on German soldiers because of the fierce reprisals which ensued. He also spoke out publicly against Allied night bombing which was causing heavy civilian casualties and turning people's opinion against the Allies. This had some influence on Allied policy.

**Rokossovsky, Marshal Konstantin, 1896–1968** Rokossovsky was one of Russia's most able successful Front Commanders of the war. A veteran of the Far East, he was arrested during the purges of 1938 but was subsequently released and reinstated. In 1941 after the German invasion he led the first tank counterattack in the Ukraine. Transferred north, he helped the trapped inexperienced 16th and 20th Armies to break out of their encirclement at Smolensk on 6 August. He distinguished himself in November and December in the defence of Moscow as Commander of Southern Section, Siberian Army.

In 1942 Rokossovsky served as Commander of the Don Front at the defense of Stalingrad. Here his Armies achieved a decisive breakthrough against the Rumanian and Italian Armies enabling the

Soviets to move southwards to encircle PAULUS' Sixth Army and later to mount an offensive against it. At the Battle of Kursk Rokossovsky commanded the Central Front while VATUTIN commanded the Voronezh Front. Opening the battle on the night of 4 July with an artillery barrage, the Central Front held its ground throughout the Germans' week-long onslaught until on 10 July Field Marshal KLUGE and General MODEL went onto the defensive leaving behind them 50,000 German dead, 400 tanks and mobile guns and 500 aircraft. In the counteroffensive beginning 3 August, Rokossovsky broke through to the Dnieper and in the fall continued through to the Pripet Marshes.

In June 1944 Rokossovsky was given command of the 1st Belorussian Front which moved against the German Center to take Lublin and Brest-Litovsk. On 29 June Rokossovsky trapped two German Panzer Corps and took Bobruisk with 24,000 prisoners. By July 1944 he had advanced to Warsaw but was unable to continue due to supply and transport problems and to the weariness of the troops. However in August the city of Warsaw rose against the Germans assuming that the advancing Russians would soon come to their aid. Rokossovsky not only did not aid them in any way but did not allow the Western Allies to use Soviet airfields to supply the Warsaw insurgents. The uprising was put down by late September. In January 1945 the Fronts were reorganized and Rokossovsky, now commanding the 2nd Belorussian Front, resumed his advance, first taking Warsaw and then heading north to sweep through northern Poland and take Danzig on 26 January. This trapped the Germans in east Prussia. On May 1945 his troops made contact with the British at Wittenberg. After the war Rokossovsky became Chief of Armed Forces in Poland.

**Rommel, Field Marshal Erwin, 1891–1944** Rommel excelled at every level of command he held, from platoon to army group commander. As a lieutenant in World War I, he led his platoon with great dash in the Battle of the Frontiers. As a company commander he won the *Pour le mérite*, Germany's highest decoration for bravery, in the Battle of Caporetto. Between the wars Rommel wrote an important textbook on infantry tactics, in which the theory or doctrine of 'forward control' was first developed, and at the outbreak of war he was given command of a Panzer Division, the 7th, which he commanded in the Battle of France. He perhaps owed his command to a lucky acquaintanceship with HITLER, but he justified his appointment by the brilliance with which he handled the division in the field (slightly marred by his unsure reaction to the British counterattack at Arras on 21 May 1940). In February 1941, when the rest of the German Army was preparing for the invasion of Russia, he was chosen to lead the Afrika Korps which Hitler had decided to send to the rescue of Mussolini's Army in Libya, and his handling of it in the next eighteen months laid the foundation of a military legend. On his arrival he immediately halted and then turned back WAVELL's advance into Cyrenaica and, until Alamein, retained the initiative throughout the almost continuous fighting of the next year. He was halted by AUCHINLECK in July 1942 but found the strength to renew his attack towards Cairo in August. It was only because he had exhausted his supplies and reinforcements and overextended his lines of communication that he was so soundly beaten at El Alamein in October and he then made MONTGOMERY pay a high price for his victory. His retreat to Tunisia was a well-conducted delaying action and his defense of the territory when he arrived far stronger than the Allies had expected. He was ordered home by Hitler before the final collapse and then sent to prepare France against the threat of Allied Invasion. His strengthening of the coastal defenses made the landings, when they came, costlier than they would have been, and he conducted a tenacious defense of the German lines around the lodgment area, even though he had not been allowed by RUNDSTEDT to deploy his troops as he wished. On 17 July however, he was wounded by a British fighter's attack on his car and evacuated. He then came under suspicion of implication in the Bomb Plot and was offered by Hitler the choice of standing trial, with the inevitable danger that threatened his family, or of committing suicide. He took the proffered poison and was given a state funeral, having, it was announced, died of his wounds.

**Roosevelt, Eleanor, 1884–1962** Eleanor Roosevelt was the wife of President ROOSEVELT and an extremely popular public figure in her own right. In September 1941 she was made Director of the Office of Civilian Defense. Throughout the war she traveled widely on goodwill trips to build morale, visiting Britain, Australia and the South Pacific. She was several times a delegate to the United Nations General Assembly and was Chairman (1947) of the UN Committee on Human Rights.

**Roosevelt, President Franklin Delano, 1882–1945** Roosevelt had been President of the United States for nine years before Pearl Harbor, years which he had devoted chiefly to leading America out of economic collapse. His political interests were domestic, his instincts pacific, and he was conscious of the extent and intensity of American unwillingness to become involved in the European war of 1939–41. He nevertheless felt it of vital interest to the United States that Britain and her Allies be saved from defeat and he was able, notably by the

Lend-Lease Act of March 1941, to assure her supplies of whatever war material she needed. He also began to agree with Winston CHURCHILL, an old acquaintance, on a common set of war aims, formalized by their meeting in Argentia Bay, Newfoundland, in August 1941, and known as the Atlantic Charter. When war came, through Japan's surprise attack on Pearl Harbor, America was materially unprepared for it, but Roosevelt at any rate had decided the broad lines on which it should be fought. Germany was to be defeated first, since only she among the Axis powers possessed the industrial and technical capability to win a victory single-handed; Britain was to be preserved from defeat at all costs, since her territory provided the essential springboard for an invasion of Europe; America would support all enemies of the Axis, whatever their political creed; she would make a massive military effort on land, sea and in the air, but would principally work for victory by making herself the 'arsenal of democracy.' Roosevelt, crippled by polio, seemed physically unfitted for the effort of a war Presidency, but he sustained the burdens with remarkable vitality. He won a fourth Presidential election in 1944, by a vast majority, and devoted much time to maintaining effective relations with Congress. But he also traveled to meet Churchill and the other wartime leaders at a succession of exhausting and widely-scattered conferences: Casablanca in January 1943, Quebec in August, Cairo in November, Teheran in December, Quebec again in September 1944, and Yalta in February 1945. Roosevelt played an independent role throughout, often at odds with Churchill over means, if not over long-term ends. His diplomacy was, in particular, designed to diminish the scope of the colonial system in the postwar world, and to tame the USSR by the administration of sympathy and concessions. Churchill felt, but did not say,

that he found Roosevelt's estimation of Soviet intentions naive. Postwar opinion in the west has tended to support Churchill's point of view. There was a generosity in Roosevelt's philosophy of international relations which nevertheless commands respect, and he was clearly more far-sighted on the colonial issue, particularly in the Far East, than the British leader. His worldwide appeal was enormous, his character, opinions and achievements in themselves a demonstration to neutral opinion that right was on the Allied side. When he died, on 12 April 1945, he was mourned throughout the Allied and neutral nations, and perhaps nowhere more than in Britain.

**Rosenberg, Alfred, 1893–1946** Rosenberg was born into one of the overseas German communities at Reval in Tsarist Russia, and trained as an architect in Moscow before the revolution. On its outbreak he made his way to Germany, filled with violent anti-Bolshevik and anti-Semitic sentiments, to which he was able to give full vent when he joined the Nazi Party and became editor of its newspaper, the *Völkischer Beobachter*. During HITLER's imprisonment after the 1924 Munich Putsch he was temporarily party leader. He lacked executive skills, however, and was relegated to theoretical and educational activities when Hitler resumed the leadership. Hitler had, nevertheless, a sort of reflexive respect for him as an intellectual and old comrade, and made him Minister for the Occupied Eastern Territories in 1941, on the grounds of his special knowledge of and interest in the region. But Rosenberg exercised little real power there. It was GOERING and HIMMLER who put into practice the theories of racial superiority and exploitation that he had advanced. As a prophet of the excesses of Nazism, and an accessory to its crimes, he was tried and executed at Nuremberg.

**Rösseler, Rudolf 'Lucy,' 1897–1958** Rösseler was a German publisher whose contacts in the German High Command were able to supply Moscow with invaluable information. Rösseler was a Bavarian protestant who left Germany for Switzerland when HITLER came to power. When war broke out, the contacts he had developed in the Wehrmacht during his service in World War I suddenly supplied him with information on the German invasion of Belgium, Holland and northeast France to take place on 12 November 1939. Hitler postponed the invasion, but the Allies refused to believe Rösseler's information. Eventually RADOLFI recruited him by an intermediary and Rösseler worked for the USSR. Rösseler supplied STALIN with advance warning of Barbarossa, the strength and composition of the Army and its morale. Stalin ignored this but later information helped the Red Army anticipate pincer movements by Generals GUDERIAN and HOTH. Information on the German build-up at Kursk made an invaluable contribution to the Russian victory in July 1943. After Radolfi's ('Rado') network was liquidated in November 1943, 'Lucy' went out of operation. After the war Rösseler continued to work for the USSR and died in 1958, but he never revealed the source of his information in Germany.

**Rotmistrov, Marshal Pavel, 1901–1982** Rotmistrov was a successful Russian Tank Army Commander. On 19 December 1942 as Commander of the VII Tank Corps in the Stalingrad counteroffensive, he was involved in the defense of the River Myshkova line and inflicted heavy losses on the Germans, helping to halt von MANSTEIN's advance. At Kursk, Rotmistrov commanded the V Guards Tank Corps which was part of KONEV's Steppe Front. On 11–12 July he had to make a forced march of 210 miles to reach Prokhorovna which he executed brilliantly and arrived well-camouflaged. However Russian forces in the area were hard pressed and Rotmistrov had to counterattack on his own with no support. Over 1500 tanks and mobile guns were involved in this engagement in which Rotmistrov's fierce assault left the Germans unable to dislodge him from the position he had established. The Germans lost 10,000 men and 300 tanks. Rotmistrov was then involved in the counterattack on Kharkov on 3 August.

In January 1944 Rotmistrov served in the Ukraine, again under Konev and was then promoted to Marshal of Armored Troops and Deputy Commander of the Red Army's Armored Forces.

**Rundstedt, Field Marshal Gerd von, 1875–1953** Rundstedt had retired from the German Army after the FRITSCH-BLOMBERG crisis but returned to command Army Group A which invaded Poland in September 1939. In May 1940 he held the same command for the invasion of France and it was his Panzer spearhead which broke through at Sedan and cut off the British Expeditionary Force. He persuaded HITLER to allow Army Group A to halt its offensive and to leave the reduction of the Dunkirk pocket to the Luftwaffe. This crucial decision allowed the evacuation of the BEF. In 1941 Rundstedt was given command of Army Group South which moved through the Ukraine in September but was relieved of the command two months later when Hitler refused to allow him to withdraw. In 1942 he was reinstated and made Commander in Chief of the west and was responsible for the defense of Fortress Europe. When the Allies finally landed in Normandy, Rundstedt was caught unprepared: his troops were deployed over the Channel coast and his Panzer Divisions were well in the rear. On 1 July 1944 he was replaced by KLUGE, who was then dismissed on 17 August, and replaced by MODEL. Rundstedt was recalled in

September but at that point there was little he could do to stop the Allied advance over northwest France. However he planned the Ardennes offensive, sometimes known as the Rundstedt offensive, in which he did not have much confidence. He retired in March 1945 after its failure, but to the end Hitler respected his judgment. It has been said that this was because Hitler was impressed by his aristocratic presence, and the Prussian military tradition which he represented.

**Rybalko, General Pavel, 1894–1948** Rybalko was an able Commander of Tank Armies who is credited with liberating Prague. A military instructor from 1941–42, he was appointed Commander of the 5th Guards Tank Army in the summer of 1942 and then of the 3rd Guards Tank Army. He was involved in the Stalingrad counteroffensive where he crossed the Don in December 1942 to defeat a German-Hungarian Army in the Voronezh region. After the Battle of Kursk, Rybalko managed to cross the Dnieper and establish a bridgehead on the western bank. He was also involved in the liberation of the Ukraine and in the capture of Lvov in July 1944.

**Rydz-Smigly, Marshal Edward, 1886–1943** Rydz-Smigly was the virtual ruler of Poland and Commander in Chief of the Polish Armed Forces when the Germans invaded in 1939. He did not mobilize his country in time and then conducted a defense which did not take account of the Germans' speed of advance. His Army was in confusion within a week and unable to mount any delaying actions. Two weeks after the invasion, Rydz-Smigly ordered a withdrawal into south-eastern Poland hoping to establish a concentrated center of resistance which could wait until British or French aid arrived. However at this point the Soviets invaded eastern Poland and the Army caved in. Rydz-Smigly and his government escaped to Rumania where they were imprisoned. Rydz-Smigly was dismissed from his posts by SIKORSKI and his government-in-exile in London. He escaped from Rumania in 1941 and returned to Poland to join the underground. He was probably killed by the Germans in 1943.

# S

**Saito, General Yoshitsugu, 1890–1944** Saito led the defense of Saipan when 127,600 American troops invaded the island on 15–17 June 1944. Although the official Commander in Chief was Admiral NAGUMO, it was General Obata who built the defenses and Saito who commanded the 32,000 strong garrison. He was not an able commander nor did he have much experience of combat. By the 22 June the Marines had cut the island in half and though there was much intense fighting it was essentially a clearing operation. On 6 July Nagumo and Saito both committed suicide in order to encourage their troops to fight to the last, which they did in two suicidal counterattacks. Likewise, thousands of civilians killed themselves en masse. Only 1000 Japanese soldiers survived; 22,000 civilians died; and the Americans suffered 14,000 casualties of which 3500 were deaths.

**Salazar, Prime Minister Antonio, 1889–1972** Salazar, a former Professor of economics, was Prime Minister and Foreign Minister of the Fascist Portuguese State from 1932 to 1972. Portugal had been allied with Britain continuously since 1373, and at the outbreak of war Portuguese public opinion was extremely pro-British. Nonetheless Salazar began the war with a policy of strict neutrality which he adopted with British agreement as the closure of Portuguese ports to all combatants hurt Germany far more than the Allies. In August 1941 Salazar approached the American government for military aid in case of German invasion, but would only allow foreign troops on Portuguese soil after the initiation of a German attack. The Allies suggested that in the event he should withdraw his government to the Azores. Salazar held to the same policy with regard to Timor, but when it was invaded by the Japanese in February 1942 there were Dutch and Australian troops present.

The Portuguese islands off the Azores were strategically vital to the Allies particularly for the war in the Atlantic. Salazar refused to allow them to be used by either side until an agreement of 8 October 1943. CHURCHILL was strongly in favor of invading the Azores if or even before Salazar refused but was restrained by his Cabinet. The Allies used the Azores for air bases but Salazar remained officially neutral.

**Sansom, Odette, 1912–** Odette Sansom was Peter CHURCHILL's wireless operator and was awarded a George Cross after the war for her bravery. She was French-born but had married a British subject and was living in Somerset with her three little girls when the war broke out. In spring 1942 she answered a call for snapshots of the French coast to help Commando raids and these were sent to the SOE (Special Operations Executive) who recruited her. Her first mission was to set up a circuit at Auxerre but it was only after three unsuccessful attempts to get to France that she was landed by felucca on the Riviera in November 1942. She made contact with Churchill who asked her to stay on as a relief operator but his circuit, *Spindle*, had been penetrated by the Gestapo so they transferred to Annecy. Sergeant BLEICHER convinced Sansom that he was an Allied sympathizer but London warned her to avoid him. Churchill returned to France in April 1943 and was met by Sansom, who was on his reception committee. The next morning Bleicher arrested them but she pretended that they were married and that Churchill was not an agent but had merely come to France to visit her. She was handed over to the Gestapo and kept in Fresnes Prison for a year. There she was tortured and on one occasion she was branded on the base of the spine with a red hot poker. In May 1944 she was transferred to Ravensbruck concentration camp where she was under sentence of death. However the Commandant of the camp, Suhren, decided to keep her alive because he thought she was a relation of Winston CHURCHILL; thus she survived the war.

**Sauckel, Fritz, 1894–1946** Sauckel served as Nazi Plenipotentiary General for the Allocation of Labor from 1942 until the end of 1944. He organized the deportation of over five million people to Germany to maintain the war effort and himself estimated that perhaps only 200,000 of these came voluntarily. He had enormous problems after 1943 when all available manpower was used up and he resorted to bypassing local governments to kidnap labor off the streets. In one affair his men kidnapped 1000 French police officers in Marseilles while they were out on exercises. He encountered great resistance in which men in many occupied areas took to the hills and forests. Nonetheless Sauckel managed to produce enough labor to actually increase war production until 1944 when the German economy began its final collapse. He was tried at Nuremberg after the war and executed for crimes against humanity.

**Schacht, Dr Hjalmar, 1877–1970** Schacht was HITLER's brilliant Minister of the Economy who engineered Germany's recovery and rearmament in the 1930s. In 1923 he was appointed special commissioner to restore Germany's currency and managed to defeat inflation by the summer of 1924. He warned against the shaky foundations of the 1920s' prosperity and accurately foresaw the advent of the economic world crisis. In the winter of 1928–29 Schacht was one of two chief delegates to the Young Committee on reparations and protested violently against the resulting Young Plan. He joined Hitler's camp (though he never joined the Nazi Party) in 1930 as an economic adviser and brought with him his enormous prestige and the support of his many influential industrial contacts. A respectable bourgeois conservative he believed that Hitler would bring stability to Germany but that he could be controlled and was therefore instrumental in bringing him to power. He became President of the Reichsbank in 1933 and Economic Minister in 1935 in which capacities he masterminded German economic recovery without inflation, especially through fiscal and foreign trade operations. Though he believed that rearmament was essential to Germany he disagreed with Hitler in the subordination of all other matters to this objective. On these grounds he resigned in 1937 as Economic Minister and his functions were taken over by GOERING. Similarly in 1939 he was dismissed as bank president after protesting against Hitler's extravagant military expenditure. Schacht also maintained that Germany could not hope economically to sustain a prolonged war. In 1943 he left the Cabinet and public affairs completely.

Schacht had been involved in German opposition circles since his participation in the Abortive military coup of 1938 and the Nazis had never trusted him. After the July 1944 Bomb Plot he was arrested on suspicion and imprisoned in Flossenberg. Released by the American advance, he was later tried and acquitted at Nuremberg.

**Schellenberg, General Walther, 1911–1952** Schellenberg was an SS General and secret service officer who became Head of Combined Secret Services in 1944. A law graduate of Bonn with a strong interest in and Command of several languages he was much prized by the SS and SD for his culture and intelligence. This won him the patronage of HEYDRICH, Head of the SD (Intelligence and Security Service), when Schellenberg joined in 1934. He was involved in a vast number of plots and subterfuges which he enjoyed enormously and performed well. In 1938 he organized the *Einsatzgruppe* (Combat Troops) of combined SS, SD and Gestapo under Heydrich's orders. He was one of the first to enter both Austria and Poland after their take-overs, to carry out operations planned by HIMMLER. In 1939 he was involved in investigating British intelligence operations, an operation in which he posed as a resistance agent to gain the confidence of three MI5 agents in Holland. This led to their kidnap by SS troops on neutral territory.

In 1944 Schellenberg became Head of all the secret services after the arrest of CANARIS and the dismantling of the Abwehr. In 1945 he took a leading role in Himmler's attempt to arrange an armistice with the Western Allies. Schellenberg arranged meetings between Himmler and Count BERNADOTTE in April 1945. When the Reich finally fell Schellenberg was in Denmark still trying trying to arrange a surrender.

**Schirach, Baldur von, 1907–1974** Schirach was the leader of the Hitler Youth movements from the late 1920s until August 1940 when, too old for this job, he was made Gauleiter and Defense Commissioner of Vienna to re-

place an incumbent veteran member of the Austrian Nazi Party. HITLER gave Schirach this position reasoning that Vienna was a good city for a man of his cultural pretensions. However he was a total disaster for the party, rejected by everyone and exerting no influence in Vienna. No suitable replacement could be found however and he therefore remained in his post until the end of the war. As Gauleiter, Schirach organized the forced deportation of thousands of young people from eastern occupied countries to Germany and the deportation of 60,000 Jews from Vienna. He claimed not to have known about the extermination camps. Though he successfully escaped after the liberation and was working for the Allied occupation forces, Schirach surrendered in June 1945, unable to live with his guilt. He was sentenced to twenty years imprisonment.

**Scholl, Hans and Sophie, 1917–1943 and 1920–1943** The Scholls, brother and sister, were the leaders of a naive but tragic group of anti-Nazis. Their movement, called the White Rose, founded their objections to HITLER's regime on devout Christianity and saw Hitler as the anti-Christ. Their activities at Munich University consisted of circulating anti-Nazi letters. These came to the attention of the Gauleiter of Bavaria who harangued the students on 16 February 1943. On 19 February the Scholls openly distributed leaflets which they had published to students between lectures. They were arrested and tried on 22 February 1943 by Judge Roland Freiser in a dramatic mockery of justice. The Scholls immediately confessed in order to spare their associates, but these were already known to the Gestapo. One hundred were arrested and in addition to executions many died after torture. Hans was 25 years old and Sophie 22 at the time of their death.

Even though their activities were

pathetic, the public and the police were shocked to see the extent of opposition in existence in the universities and intellectual circles. Furthermore many were deeply moved by the Scholls' deaths and they were seen as political martyrs by the opposition.

**Schörner, Field Marshal Friedrich, 1892–1973** Inordinately ambitious, Schorner was also an able leader, but feared as well as admired by his men because of their suspicion that they would pay with their lives for his offensive zeal. It nevertheless brought him rapid advancement in the German Army, which accelerated as prominence allowed him to display his ostentatious Nazism and ready agreement to obey impossible orders – which both commended him to HITLER. By July 1944 he had been appointed to command Army Group North, at the head of which he remained unprotestingly until January 1945, though it had by then been surrounded for several months without reason or hope of rescue. He then moved to the command of Army Group Center in Czechoslovakia, but in the last ten days of the war, following Hitler's suicide, inherited the title of Commander in Chief, which he had always thought his due.

**Scobie, General Ronald, 1893–1969** In October 1941 Scobie was sent as General Officer Commanding (GOC) 6th Division (later 70th Division) which replaced the besieged Australian garrison at Tobruk. In the major winter offensive to reconquer Cyrenaica, Scobie under CUNNINGHAM's command led the break-out from Tobruk on 21 November 1941. In 1942 Scobie became GOC at Malta which was strategically crucial because of its use as a base to attack German supply convoys to North Africa. In 1943 he was given the post of Chief of Staff, Middle East Command. Finally, in 1944 Scobie became GOC in

Greece and directed the final operations leading up to the German withdrawal from Athens on 12 October. However when the British entered the capital two days later they found the Communist National Liberation Front (EAM) and its military wing (ELAS) ready to take over the government. This was a particularly sensitive issue to England and France who were at the time faced with the imminent Soviet occupation of all eastern Europe and the Balkans. Scobie was ordered by CHURCHILL to hold Greece at all costs and found himself in the middle of a civil war by December. EAM however was not receiving any external aid because they constituted a purely indigenous group and because the Soviets had promised not to interfere. They were forced to make a truce on 11 January 1945. A constitutional regime was set up and the Communists brutally repressed.

**Scoones, General Sir Geoffrey, 1893–1975** Scoones was a British Corps Commander involved in the intense fighting in Burma in 1944. From 1939 to 1941 he was on the General Staff at Allied HQ in India and then Director of Military Operations and Intelligence. On 19 July 1942 he was given command of the IV Corps stationed at Imphal near the Burmese frontier. The British were unable to mount an offensive however as command and communications were being reorganized and the Burma front was low on the list of Allied priorities. In November 1943 SEAC was established and Scoones was placed under STILWELL's command, assigned to cross the Chindwin River into Burma. However – the Japanese were planning an offensive on Imphal in January 1944 and in February Scoones put forward a plan to withdraw to Imphal which was strategically strong. Against all odds he got all his forces there by April and possessing only five weeks' worth of supplies managed to defend the area until the Japanese ran out of supplies. Scoones began his advance into central Burma on 23 June.

On 7 December Scoones was appointed General Officer Commanding, Central India Command and on 14 December was knighted.

**Scott, Rear Admiral Nicholas, 1889–1942** Scott commanded a Striking Force of two heavy cruisers, two light cruisers and five destroyers at the Battle of Cape Esperance. Scott was escorting a supply convoy and trying to clear the 'Slot' (in the Solomon Islands) when he surprised a Japanese fleet under Rear Admiral Goto. Scott attacked and although the result was inconclusive it was the first time an American fleet had successfully challenged the Japanese.

At the Naval Battle of Guadalcanal, 12–14 November 1942, Scott was put under CALLAGHAN's command but was killed when his flagship, the *Atlanta*, was hit when caught between the American and Japanese cross-fire.

**Senesh, Hannah, 1921–1944** Senesh was a Hungarian Jewish girl who worked with Partisan forces in eastern Europe. In 1939 she left Hungary for Palestine but she wanted to participate in the war so she volunteered to go on a mission to help Jews in Nazi countries in 1942. On 15 March 1944 she was parachuted into Yugoslavia and joined a Partisan group. After three months she crossed into Hungary and joined resistance workers. She was captured before she could begin her mission and was interned in the Horthy Miklos Prison where she was tortured. In jail she kept the spirits of the other prisoners up by singing out snippets of information she picked up. She was sentenced to death and executed on 7 November 1944.

**Serov, General Ivan, 1905–1968** Serov was a secret police Commander responsible for many mass deportations and executions throughout the war. In 1939–40 he took charge of the 'Sovietization' of the Baltic States of Estonia, Latvia and Lithuania, deporting undesirables to labor camps. He then served as Commissar for Internal Affairs (under KHRUSHCHEV) heading the NKVD and was responsible for the mass deportation of 3.5 million Ukrainians to the east. In 1941 he became Deputy Commissar for State Security under BERIA and in 1943–44 organized the deportation of dissident ethnic groups to Siberia. Serov became Deputy Supreme Commander of Soviet forces in Germany in 1945 and Head of 'Smersh.'

**Seyss-Inquart, Artur von, 1892–1946** Seyss-Inquart was an Austrian Nazi who prepared the way for the Anschluss and later became Reich Commissioner of the Netherlands from 1940 until 1945. Acting as secret Austrian representative for the Nazis while the party was still illegal, Seyss-Inquart finally came to the fore in 1938 when HITLER demanded on threat of invasion the legalization of the Nazi Party and the appointment of Seyss-Inquart as Minister of Interior with control over the police. This was accomplished in February 1938 and Seyss-Inquart began taking his orders directly from Berlin, acting independently of the Austrian Chancellor. On 11 March 1938 with German troops at the Austrian border, he was appointed Chancellor and organized the Nazi take-over of power.

In October 1939 Seyss-Inquart was made Deputy Governor-General of the Polish General Government which comprised territories not officially annexed by Germany or Russia. In May 1940 he became Reich Commissioner of the Netherlands with total control of the entire Dutch administration which he subordinated completely to the demands of the German war effort. Directly responsible to Hitler and without interference from even the Dutch Nazis whom he excluded from government, in March

1941 he was given power of summary justice in any case of suspected resistance or dissension. He issued heavy collective fines and reprisals, confiscated the property of Jews and all enemies of the Reich. He deported 117,000 Jews, forced five million Dutch to work for the Germans and in 1943 seized textiles and consumer goods for Germany. In May 1945 Seyss-Inquart was arrested by the Canadians and executed for war crimes after a trial.

**Shaposhnikov, Marshal Boris, 1882–1945** Shaposhnikov was a brilliant military theorist, who at various times in the war was a member of the Stavka and Chief of General Staff. Throughout the 1930s he was extremely influential as Deputy People's Commissar for Defense. In 1940 he was made Head of the Stavka with ZHUKOV as his deputy and in August of that year was put in charge of fortifications. He put forward a plan to withdraw the Red Army behind the old borders, the Stalin Line, rather than allow them to be thinly spread over the new Polish frontier. This plan was overruled and Shaposhnikov was dismissed as Chief of Staff and replaced by MERETSKOV. On 10 July 1941, following the German invasion STALIN reformed the Stavka and once again included Shaposhnikov who was also reinstated as Chief of General Staff. However he counseled withdrawal as part of a policy of strategic defense and thereby courted Stalin's anger. After a tour of duty in Belorussia, Shaposhnikov fell ill and was replaced by VASILIEVSKY in November 1941, but nevertheless helped plan the defense of Moscow and the counterattack which followed. In June 1942 Shaposhnikov advised against an offensive at Kharkov considering it premature and once again argued for strategic defense. In the same month he was again appointed Deputy People's Commissar of Defense in charge of revising military regulations. From June 1943 until his death, Shaposh-

nikov served as Commandant of the Voroshilov Military Academy.

**Shawcross, Sir Hartley, 1902–** Shawcross was Britain's Chief Prosecutor at the Nuremberg war crimes trials. He was made a King's Counsel in 1939 and at the start of the war was appointed Chairman of the Enemy Aliens Tribunal. During the war his most important posts were Deputy Regional Commissioner of the South Eastern Region and Regional Commissioner of the North Western Region. In 1945 Shawcross was made Attorney General in the new Labour government and it was in this capacity that he went to plead the Allied case before the International Military Tribunal in Nuremberg. This Tribunal had been authorized by the US, UK, USSR and provisional French governments in August 1945 although it had been publicly announced from the beginning of the war that war criminals would be tried. Shawcross was at the first and most famous of the trials which began in November 1945 and continued for ten months. There were 22 defendants including political and military leaders, Gestapo, SS and SA, most of whom were found guilty. The Tribunal did not accept Shawcross's case that the German Army and Navy were themselves criminal organizations.

**Sherman, Rear Admiral Frederick, 1888–1957** Sherman was Commander of the Carrier Task Forces in the Pacific Theater from November 1942 to March 1944 and from August 1944 to September 1945. Stationed at Bougainville in 1940, he went on to command the *Lexington* in the Battle of Coral Sea in May 1942. During the battle the *Lexington* was hit by dive-bombers and had to be abandoned. Sherman then commanded the *Saratoga-Princeton* task force which fought in the co-ordinated attacks on Rabaul, part of MACARTHUR's offensive in that region. At the Battles of the

Philippine Sea and of Leyte Gulf, Sherman commanded the 5th Fleet losing the *Princeton* in the latter battle.

**Shigemitsu, Mamoru, 1881–1957** Shigemitsu was the Japanese Foreign Minister from 1943 to 1945. He was Minister to China from 1930–36 where he lost a leg to a Korean terrorist's bomb in 1932, an injury which was painful for the rest of his life. He served as Ambassador to the USSR from 1936–38 and to Britain from 1938–41. In London he tried to appear anti-militarist and to put forward the case that the Japanese alliance with Germany need have no effect on Japanese relations with Britain. Two days after Pearl Harbor Shigemitsu was appointed to the Nanking puppet government and in 1942 became Ambassador to France. Supported by TOJO from 1941, he became Foreign Minister in 1943. He was replaced by TOGO in April 1945 but was called on to attend the Japanese surrender on board the USS *Missouri* with UMEZU. After several years imprisonment for war crimes he returned to active politics as Deputy Prime Minister and as Foreign Minister from 1954–56.

Shigemitsu was a strong opponent of the occupation of China on the grounds that it contradicted Japan's anti-colonialist propaganda. He pursued this line of argument and advocated the abolition of the unequal treaties with Nanking and the provision of unrestricted economic aid to China. As Foreign Minister he called for political freedom for Japanese satellite nations and the withdrawal of military occupation forces in line with a 'good neighbor policy.'

**Sikorski, General Wladyslaw, 1881–1943** Sikorski was head of the Polish government-in-exile and Commander in Chief of Free Polish Forces from 1939 until his death in 1943. He was refused a command in the Polish Army when the Germans invaded because RYDZ-SMIGLY distrusted him. Sikorski was in Paris when Poland collapsed and became Premier of the provisional government and Commander of the Polish Armed Forces now in France, an Army which grew to a body of 100,000 by the spring of 1940. When France fell Sikorski went to England with his Army and government.

In England Sikorski opened negotiations with the Allies for recognition and aid for the underground movement. He also established close rapport with CHURCHILL which was to be of much use. In July 1941 when Russia was at its lowest point, following the opening of Barbarossa, Sikorski began negotiations which led to the Sikorski-MAISKY agreement. This was a joint Soviet-Polish declaration of alliance which included a recognition of Poland's pre-1939 borders and a repudiation of the Soviet-German partition. It also provided an amnesty for Polish prisoners and deportees in Russia and permission for General ANDERS to form a Polish Army in the USSR from the Polish population in Russia. The central issue at this time and throughout the war was the fate of the 14,500 Poles who had been deported in 1939, 8000 of whom disappeared into Russian camps after April 1940. Anders was unable to trace the vast majority of these and tension between the Polish government-in-exile and Russia increased by the year. In 1943 Sikorski presented Churchill with evidence that the 3000 Polish officers buried at Katyn had been murdered by the Russians. CHURCHILL however wanted to keep his relations with STALIN smooth at all costs and therefore smothered the issue. Sikorski died in a plane crash at Gibraltar on 4 July 1943 and the Polish government in London became progressively impotent. Sikorski was the only Polish leader who had sufficient stature and skill to secure the confidence of his people and to achieve the close relations with both Churchill and Stalin, which were necessary to maintain a united and effective Polish government with substantial influence in Allied affairs.

**Simonds, Lieutenant General Guy, 1903–1974** Simonds was an extremely versatile Canadian Corps commander operating in the European Theater. He commanded an infantry division in Sicily and an armored division in Italy achieving remarkable advances with low casualties. Commanding the Canadian II Corps following D-Day, he led a technically inventive offensive on Falaise on 8 August 1944 (Operation Totalize) which made use of armored infantry carriers operating by night. Simonds also led his Corps in the Scheldt campaign in which he meticulously destroyed the German defenses along the waterways around Antwerp and then Nijmegen. Simonds commanded the Canadian 1st Army twice during the Scheldt campaign and again in the latter stages of the advance into West Germany.

**Simović, General Dušan, 1882–1962** Simović was head of the Yugoslav government when Germany invaded in 1941. A staunch Serbian nationalist and anti-German, he became Chief of Army General Staff in 1939 and then Chief of Air Force Staff in 1940. From December 1940 he became a leader of resistance both to the Germans and to the impotent policies of the Yugoslav government then headed by the Regent, Prince PAUL. Urged by the Allies to resist and to attack the Italians in Albania and pressured by the Germans to join the Tripartite Pact, events came to a head when in February 1941 HITLER demanded the right to move military materials across Yugoslavia. Simović openly warned Paul that the Serbian people would not accept his deferring to Hitler's pressure. However the government signed a secret pact with the Axis on 25 March. Two days later in an efficient and bloodless coup the Army put Simović at the head of the government and declared PETER II King.

The Allies immediately pledged their support to Simović and renewed their attempts to bring Yugoslavia into the war. Simović however wanted to concentrate on internal problems and maintain strict neutrality so as not to antagonize Hitler. Hitler, on the other hand, decided to invade as soon as he heard news of the coup and postponed Barbarossa in order to send an Army which included seven Panzer divisions and 1000 aircraft to invade Yugoslavia on 6 April, two days after CHURCHILL's personal appeal to Simović to prepare a resistance. Belgrade fell on 13 April after intensive bombing and heavy casualties; the government fell on 17 April and resistance was over by 20 April. Simović fled to Greece with Peter and served as Premier of the government-in-exile in London until his resignation in 1942. Although nominated by Peter to head his government after the war, he was rejected by TITO. He retired in May 1945.

**Skorzeny, Lieutenant Colonel Otto, 1908–1975** Skorzeny was one of HITLER's most successful irregular soldiers. He had been invalided out of service in December 1942 and found himself appointed to organize a special commando unit. As an unknown he had been appointed by the German Army High Command to sabotage the outfit which Hitler had specially requested, but in fact, he succeeded in establishing a most successful unit. Their first coup was in September 1943 when Skorzeny and about 90 soldiers landed on the plateau of the Gran Sasso in the Abruzzi mountains and succeeded in abducting MUSSOLINI. His unit was expanded and his next mission was to bring the Hungarian dictator, HORTHY, to heel. Skorzeny decided the best method to accomplish this would be to kidnap Horthy's son, who was negotiating an armistice with Soviet Russia. Once he had sent Horthy's son to Berlin, Skorzeny brazenly marched into Castle

Hill, the citadel of Budapest and took control of the city. Horthy was forced to abdicate and a pro-Nazi regime was established. All this had been done for the loss of only seven Germans killed. In December 1944 Skorzeny took part in another daring raid when he and his men dressed up as US troops and went behind the lines during the Ardennes Offensive. Although they could not turn the battle into a victory their actions severely shook the Americans, who instituted stringent security measures which only confused the situation more. After the war Skorzeny was tried at Nuremberg but he was acquitted.

**Slessor, Air Marshal Sir John, 1897–1979** Slessor was an RAF Commander who played a major role in the battle against the German U-Boats. When war broke out he was director of the Plans Branch of the Air Ministry. In 1940 he participated in a conference of US and British Army, Navy and Air Force officers in the United States. The conference confirmed the 'Germany first' policy. Slessor then became Air Officer Commanding No 5 Bomber Group, RAF Bomber Command. In 1942 he was given the newly formed post of Assistant Chief of the Air Staff (Policy) and attended all the major Allied conferences. In 1943 Slessor became head of RAF Coastal Command, co-operating with the Royal Navy and the US forces in an intensive effort to defeat the U-Boats in the Battle of the Atlantic. The use of aircraft in this fight turned out to be crucial. Convoys escorted by planes were rarely attacked because they made it impossible for the German boats to operate in wolf-packs and air to sea rockets scored many hits. Victory in this struggle was essential both to maintain the merchant fleet and to make an Allied landing in France possible. In January 1944 Slessor became Commander in Chief of RAF units in the Mediterranean and Deputy Commander in Chief of Allied Air Forces in that theater. In his capacity as Deputy Commander in Chief he was involved in the Riviera landings of August 1944.

**Slim, General Sir William, 1891–1970** Slim was the British Commander who built up the morale of his troops after their 900 mile retreat from Burma and led them back to reconquer Burma.

At the beginning of the war Slim was given command of the 5th Indian Division in the Sudan where he led the offensive against the Italians at Gallabat. He was wounded in this engagement but returned to command the 10th Indian Division in Iraq in 1941. On 8 June 1941 he conducted a successful campaign in Syria and then led a force into Iran (25 August) to enforce Allied demands for the removal of German agents operating there. He routed the enemy and continued on to Teheran where he joined Russian troops. In 1942 he was sent to command the Burma I Corps (Burcorps) which comprised virtually all of ALEXANDER's forces. He arrived in the middle of a desperate situation in which he had to maintain order and morale during a 900 mile fighting retreat from Rangoon to India and to accomplish this before the monsoons began. Once in India he commanded XVIII Corps and his main task again was to build morale.

Late in 1943 Slim was put in charge of the newly formed 14th Army which was organized to mount an offensive in Burma, although this was low on the list of the Allies' priorities. The campaign opened in December 1943 and the British forces struggled to take and retain Arakan. The Japanese mounted an impressive counterattack to take Kohima and cut off the road to Imphal. Slim's Army held them off and forced them to withdraw when their supplies ran out. The Japanese did not collapse but withdrew to Mandalay and Meiktila. Slim followed them through the jungle, crossed the Irrawaddy and took Mandalay in late March 1945 and raced to reach Rangoon before the monsoon. He arrived in May to find the Japanese had already evacuated.

Slim's campaign made extensive use of guerrilla groups: MERRILL's Marauders and WINGATE's Chindits. He achieved his successes by using air supply to maintain communications with his rapidly moving troops. He was greatly admired and liked as a Commander and achieved the greatest land victory over the Japanese in World War II. Late in the war, Slim was made Commander in Chief of Allied Land Forces in Southeast Asia, and was made a General in August 1945.

**Smith, General Holland, 1882–1967** Holland 'Howlin' Mad' Smith is considered the father of amphibious warfare. As Marine Commander of the V Amphibious Corps, he trained and led his troops in the assaults on Kiska and Attu in the Aleutians, Tarawa and Makin in the Gilbert Islands, Kwajalein and Eniwetok in the Marshalls, and Saipan and Tinian in the Marianas. In August 1944 he was made Commanding General of Fleet Marine Force Pacific, directed operations at Guam and led Task Force 56 on Iwo Jima.

Smith developed the techniques that became the standard for amphibious assaults involving the complex co-ordination of land, sea and air forces. All of his operations resulted in extremely high casualty figures which did not deter Smith at all. He was a very tough and hard driving leader. However after the enormous losses on the Gilbert Islands, Smith maintained that the struggle was unnecessary and the islands could have been bypassed. Smith often had problems obtaining co-operation between the Army and the Marines, a difficulty which came to a head during the Iwo Jima invasion. However Smith's skillful administration of amphibious tech-

niques he had developed, rendered the differences unimportant and the landings and battle at Iwo Jima successful.

**Smuts, Prime Minister Jan Christiaan, 1870–1950** A South African soldier of the old school, Smuts had been a member of the British War Cabinet during World War I and had been present at the signing of the Peace Treaty at Versailles in 1919. In the decade before the outbreak of World War II South African politics had rested on the mutual co-operation between the two major parties: the National Party with Hertzog as Prime Minister and the Union Party with Smuts serving as his Deputy. When Poland was invaded in 1939, the coalition divided. Smuts, who was in favor of South African involvement, won a difficult parliamentary debate on the subject and soon was elected Prime Minister. By 1940 he had assumed the leadership of South Africa's war effort including her Armed Forces. South African soldiers fought bravely on many fronts especially in the Ethiopian, North African and Italian campaigns. Smuts supported CHURCHILL in his policies and decisions at every turn. He attended the San Francisco Conference in 1945 to draft the United Nations Charter and was present for the signing of the Peace agreement at Versailles in 1946, the only person to attend both Versailles Peace Conferences.

**Sokolovsky, Marshal Vasiliy, 1897–1968** Sokolovsky served as Chief of Staff of the Western Front under General KONEV from 1941 to 1943. He took part in the planning of Operation Kutuzov (the Battle of Kursk) and commanded the Western Front there. He led the Western Front to Smolensk which he captured on 25 September 1943. He was also involved in the campaigns at Lvov and the Vistula-Oder. From 1944 to 1945 Sokolovsky was Chief of Staff of the 1st Ukranian Front and was held responsible for this Army's failure to advance north from the Pripet Marshes. He was nonetheless posted to serve as Marshal ZHUKOV's Deputy Front Commander on the 1st Belorussian Front in its final assault on Berlin. After the war he was made Commander of the Soviet forces of occupation in Germany. He received an OBE from Great Britain.

**Somervell, General Brehon, 1892–1955** Somervell served as US Commanding General of Army Service Forces from 1942 until the end of the war and as a Presidential adviser. He was involved in problems of mobilization and war production and attended all major planning meetings. He was responsible during the war for supplies, equipment and for the allocation of resources.

**Somerville, Admiral Sir James, 1882–1949** In 1940 Somerville was appointed Commander of Force H in the Mediterranean based at Gibraltar. In July of that year it was his unpleasant task to threaten the French Fleet under Admiral GENSOUL at Oran and Mers-el-Kebir with annihilation unless it proceeded to sail out of range of Axis control. The French government had promised the Allies that no French ship would fall into enemy hands. Somerville delivered an ultimatum and when the French failed to respond, the British were obliged to fire and 1297 French lives were lost. In 1941 Somerville shelled Genoa and was active in the pursuit and ultimate defeat of the *Bismarck*. As Commander of Force H he was instrumental in helping convoys reach their destinations, including, for example, accompanying the convoy which took the tanks and equipment through the Mediterranean to General WAVELL's forces in the Western Desert. Between 1942–44 Somerville was Commander in Chief of the Eastern Fleet which was based in Ceylon. In 1943 he attended the Washing-

ton Conference with CHURCHILL and ROOSEVELT and in 1944 he was Head of the British Naval delegation in Washington.

**Sorge, Richard, 1895–1944** Sorge was a German journalist who ran a very successful spy network for the USSR in Japan. Sorge had been a field commander of Soviet spies in the Far East as early as 1929. As a journalist for the *Frankfurter Zeitung* he made contacts in the German Embassy, first through Herbert von Dirksen and then through the military attaché, Colonel Eugen Ott. In 1934 Sorge built up a network of agents who collected intelligence throughout Japan. His most important agent was Ozaki Hozumi, who was an expert on Chinese affairs and adviser to Prime Minister KONOYE. Ozaki was able to photograph top secret documents and Sorge would exchange information with his friend Ott who was promoted to ambassador in 1935, and thus receive confirmation. He sent advance warning of Barbarossa to STALIN, and although this was ignored he received a note of thanks from Moscow. Sorge supplied the USSR with the important information that Japan would not invade the USSR and Stalin was able to move his Siberian divisions to the defense of Moscow. By 1941 the Japanese secret service had intercepted the transmission of a signal and knew about the network. The Japanese arrested one of Sorge's organizers who confessed and implicated Sorge and Ozaki. They were both arrested in October 1941 and tried and hanged on 9 October 1944.

**Spaak, Paul Henri, 1899–1972** Spaak was Foreign Minister of Belgium before and during the war. Before the war he stood firmly for Belgian neutrality and refused to allow Allied troops into his country. When the Germans invaded on 10 May 1940 he called on Britain and France to fulfill their treaty obligations.

Spaak and Pierlot, the Prime Minister, urged King LEOPOLD, who was in personal command of the Armed Forces, to go to France and continue resistance from there when they saw their imminent defeat. The King, however, stayed in Belgium when Pierlot and Spaak left for England. They mistakenly accused him of treating with the Germans but were later reconciled and kept the Belgian government-in-exile in operation through the war, returning to Belgium after liberation in September 1944. Spaak played a major role in negotiating the Benelux customs agreement of 1944 and in the founding of the United Nations.

**Spaatz, General Carl 'Tooey,' 1891–1974** Spaatz was the US General commanding Air Forces in Europe and the Pacific. Spaatz was an official observer in London during the Battle of Britain. In July 1942 he arrived in London again as Commander of the 8th Air Force, which was to be the principal arm of the strategic air offensive against Germany. He favored day-time precision bombing which brought him into conflict with the British Air Staff which had opted for night-time area bombing. He set the 8th Air Force campaign on its way and was then sent to the North African Theater to co-ordinate air operations of Eastern Air Command and the 12th Air Force. He then became Commander of the Northwest Africa Air Force during the Tunisian campaign and later in Sicily. In January 1944 he returned to Britain as Commanding General of the Strategic Air Force, whose campaign in northern Europe was now in full swing. He directed the aerial preparation of the Normandy landings and then switched to the destruction of the synthetic oil plants, followed by the transportation system within Germany itself. By March 1945, when Spaatz left Europe, production of oil and movement of inland transport in the Reich had

been almost completely halted. In July he took command of the Strategic Air Force in the Pacific and directed the bombing of Japan's major cities. His planes also carried the atom bombs which fell on Hiroshima and Nagasaki.

**Speer, Albert, 1905–1982** Speer is generally recognized as the most able of HITLER's subordinates and the most interesting, in that he retained throughout his membership of Hitler's court, a clear-sighted understanding of its essentially Byzantine character. An architect by training, he first came to Hitler's notice in the planning of the Nuremberg party buildings. In 1942 on the death of the armaments minister, Todt, in an air crash, he was promoted to succeed him at the age of 37, and at once began to demonstrate the most remarkable talent for the administration of war industry. Despite the rising tide of the Allied Bombing Offensive on the armaments factories, he was able, through a policy of rationalization and dispersal, to make output rise for every month until September 1944, and to maintain a flow of war material, if on a diminishing scale, to the very end of the war. It was the destruction of the transportation system, rather than of his dispersed factories, which eventually defeated his efforts. Tried at Nuremberg, he was sentenced to twenty years for his use of slave labor in war industry, and wrote during his captivity the most revealing of all the Nazi memoirs.

**Speidel, General Hans, 1897–1984** Speidel was a key behind-the-scenes figure in the Generals' Plot against HITLER. He was in the position of influence, serving as Chief of Staff to the military commander of occupied France from 1940 to 1942. In 1944 he was assigned to be ROMMEL's Chief of Staff in France and at this point the Generals' plans were well advanced. Their main concern was to get an armistice with the Allies without killing Hitler. Speidel arranged for STÜLPNAGEL to talk Rommel into supporting the plot, however a similar attempt to recruit RUNDSTEDT was not successful. The Allied invasion of Normandy and the replacement of Rundstedt by KLUGE led to a change in plans. Most of the senior generals in France did not support an attempt to assassinate Hitler but if Hitler was dead they would have helped the plotters. Speidel was one of the generals who supported STAUFFENBERG's attempt on 20 July 1944 and after the debacle he refused to obey Hitler's order to destroy Paris. He was arrested and imprisoned, and refused to give any information under interrogation. He escaped after seven months and lived in hiding until the end of the war.

**Sperrle, Field Marshal Hugo, 1885– 1953** Sperrle was Commander of the Luftflotte III, one of several self-contained air units of the Luftwaffe. After commanding the German Condor Legion in the Spanish Civil War, Sperrle became General of Aviators in 1937. Appointed to the command of Luftflotte III in January 1939 he provided air support for the 'Blitzkriegs.' During the Battle of Britain, from July 1940 to May 1941, the Luftflotte III were stationed in northern France and Sperrle in Paris. His unit was given the operational sphere of eastern Britain and KESSELRING's Luftflotte II stationed in northeast France and the Low Countries were assigned to western Britain. Both being self-contained, co-ordination between the two was poor. After heavy losses through the summer they settled down to constant night bombing from high altitudes.

Luftflotte III took the brunt of the Allied air offensive before and during D-Day and therefore took little part in opposing the invaders.

**Spruance, Vice-Admiral Raymond, 1886 – 1969** Spruance was probably America's greatest and most successful naval commander from the historic victory at Midway to his triumph at the Philippine Sea. He began the war as Commander of a cruiser division at Midway Island and was promoted in June 1942 to Commander of Task Force 16 assigned to prevent any invasion of Midway Island. At the Battle of Midway Spruance took over direction of the battle when FLETCHER's flagship, the *Yorktown*, was put out of action and later sunk. His brilliant execution of bomber attacks on the Japanese fleet disabled ten of their ships including four carriers. After this decisive battle, Spruance was appointed Chief of Staff to NIMITZ and was involved in strategic planning.

In August 1943 he returned to active combat as Commander of the 5th Fleet (Central Pacific Fleet) and in November of that year commanded the bombardment of Tarawa in the Gilbert Islands prior to its reconquest. In January 1944 Spruance led the successful leapfrogging operation which resulted in the capture of Kwajalein in the Marshalls. This was followed by his attack on Truk in the Carolines which was co-ordinated with TURNER's attack on Eniwetok, 17 February 1944.

Spruance conducted the naval bombardment which opened the campaign in Saipan on 10 June 1944. His fleet was stationed off the Marianas to protect the invasion force. On the 18 June he was attacked by Japanese aircraft but these were shot down by MITSCHER's planes. On the next day Spruance ordered Mitscher to send out a strike force against the Japanese fleet including OZAWA's carriers. This engagement was known as the Battle of the Philippine Sea; after it the Japanese Navy could no longer challenge the Allied Fleets. Spruance was criticized for being overcautious in not deploying Mitscher's strike force earlier which might have finished off the Japanese Fleet.

Spruance directed the naval side of the Allied invasion of Iwo Jima in mid-February 1945 and then went on in the same month to conduct the first carrier strike on Tokyo. At the end of the war, he was involved in planning the invasion of the Japanese mainland.

Spruance was cautious but effective and always achieved his victories at the minimum cost. He pioneered many naval techniques including the fleet train (which enabled carrier forces to remain in operation for long periods at a stretch) and the circular formation of carriers. Spruance was an unassuming man, unshakable in battle.

**Stalin, Joseph, 1879–1953** Stalin was the Dictator of the USSR and Commander in Chief of the USSR's Armed Forces. Stalin was suspicious of the army and its commanders and in order to get their complete loyalty in 1937 he had purged all those he considered suspect. In 1939 Stalin knew that the USSR was not ready for war, so he made a non-aggression pact with Germany. He abandoned his traditional allies in eastern Europe and in September 1939 annexed part of Poland. Stalin's dreams of expansion received a setback in November 1939 when the invasion of Finland ran into unexpected opposition. The lesson that was learnt was that the Red Army was not the formidable fighting unit it was previously thought to be.

HITLER's invasion in June 1941 went smoothly and Stalin's mass Armies could not stop the German troops who had superior weapons, tanks and training. In the first months of the war Stalin's lack of experience as a war leader showed. He relied on his friends from the 1st Cavalry Army of 1920: BUDENNY, VOROSHILOV and TIMOSHENKO and they were not brilliant army commanders. Finally ZHUKOV was called in and he executed the counterattack which saved Moscow in December 1941. Stalin's tactics had been to rely on

scorched earth policy and the Russian winter. As much industrial plant as possible was moved east of the Urals and the Ukraine and Belorussia were left ravaged. Millions of people had perished in the first six months but the USSR recovered as its armies became more experienced and because the T-34 tank which appeared on the battlefield in 1941 was vastly superior to anything the Germans had produced. The second turning point in the war on the Eastern Front was at Stalingrad where the Russians cut off General PAULUS' Sixth Army and scored a tremendous victory.

Stalin's confidence as a military commander grew and he relied heavily on his staff officers VASILIEVSKY and ZHUKOV, who prepared plans and issued directives. It is unlikely that Stalin originated operational concepts but the choice of plans was his. If Stalin disliked a front Commander he would dismiss him without warning and this meant some Generals were reluctant to report set-backs. In 1944 the Soviet Armies swept over the Ukraine, Belorussia and the Baltic states and eventually took Berlin in April 1945.

Stalin's other main role was as a political negotiator and he showed great cunning in his dealings with CHURCHILL and ROOSEVELT. From the first Moscow Conference held in December 1941, Stalin kept up the pressure on the Western Powers to open up a second front in Europe as soon as possible. At various points he threatened to make a separate peace with Hitler and maintained that if Britain and France had opposed Hitler more effectively, the USSR would not have had to suffer such terrible losses. These constant demands for a second front created much suspicion among the Allies: Churchill thought that as few concessions as possible should be made while Roosevelt thought he could reason with Stalin and accommodate him. In mid-1944 it became clear that Stalin wished to settle the political future of eastern Europe. In Poland he promoted the Lublin Committee and recognized it before attending the Yalta Conference (February 1945). At Yalta Churchill and Stalin divided up countries into spheres of influence and Stalin made promises to hold free elections in Poland which he never kept. At the Potsdam Conference he also staved off pressure to hold elections in Poland from the inexperienced TRUMAN and eventually set up puppet Communist regimes in eastern Europe, the last country to fall being Czechoslovakia.

Stalin was a violent man, bent on acquiring as much for the USSR as he could get. The eastern European countries were milked for equipment and supplies after the war to pay back the USSR for all its suffering. Stalin insured that the USSR was a force to be reckoned with in world politics, not to be isolated as in the first years of the revolution. Her military might was feared the world over.

**Stangl, Franz, 1908–1971** Stangl was Commandant of the Treblinka death camp situated near Warsaw. All those who were sent there were exterminated: only 40 people were known to have survived. At one point Treblinka received 1000 Jews a day, many of them from as far afield as Holland and Belgium. A total of 700,000 were murdered there. At the end of the war the Germans attempted to destroy all trace of Treblinka by demolishing the camp and sending the SS guards to die in Yugoslavia fighting partisans. Stangl managed to survive and return to Austria where he was arrested by the Americans who had no knowledge of his past career. He was turned over to Austrian authorities but managed to escape to South America.

**Stark, Admiral Harold, 1880–1972** In 1939 Stark was appointed Commander of Naval Operations and was in charge

of the immense expansion of the American Navy immediately prior to the war. At this time he also took part in secret discussions with the British regarding the coming war and organized naval patrols to protect US shipping from German submarine and surface ships. Towards the end of 1941 as Japanese-American negotiations reached a critical point, Stark put the Navy on war alert and it was able to move into action immediately after Pearl Harbor. However he failed to give Admiral KIMMEL of Pearl Harbor sufficient warning and was criticized in the government inquiry. In March 1942 Stark was made Commander of all US Naval Forces in the European area. This post was an administrative and diplomatic one, involving him in all the Allied conferences and planning sessions during the rest of the war. Stark was from the start one of the principal advocates of giving the war against the Germans top priority. In the lead up to Operation Overlord, Stark played a major role in keeping Anglo-American relations smooth and cooperative.

**Stauffenberg, Colonel Claus von, 1907–1944** Stauffenberg was a brilliant young officer who had served with great bravery in the Polish campaign, France and North Africa. In April 1943 he was severely wounded by bullets from a low-flying aircraft in the Western Desert. He lost an eye, his right hand and forearm and some fingers on his left hand, but as he lay in hospital he told his wife 'I feel I must do something now to save Germany. We General Staff officers must all accept our share of the responsibility.' When he left hospital he was given a staff appointment at the Reserve Army Headquarters and as Chief of Staff to OLBRICHT was drawn into the conspiracy against HITLER. In June 1944 he was promoted and had to attend briefing sessions at Hitler's Headquarters at Rastenburg. He decided to use this opportunity to try to assassinate the Führer and after several false alarms left a bomb in his briefcase during a staff conference on 20 July 1944. No one had thought to search the briefcase because Stauffenberg was a cripple but the explosion failed to kill Hitler, mainly because the conference was taking place in a temporary hut rather than in the usual concrete bunker so the blast was diffused and because an officer had knocked the briefcase away from Hitler. Stauffenberg left for Berlin (at 1240 hours) as soon as he heard the explosion and arrived at the War Office to find Olbricht, HÖPNER and BECK unable to take decisions. Stauffenberg assured them that Hitler was dead but the conspirators had lost the initiative and at 2250 hours they were overpowered by loyal officers and FROMM took control. He had Stauffenberg shot in the courtyard. Stauffenberg will long be remembered for his courage and valor and as the personification of the German resistance against Hitler.

**Stettinius, Edward, 1900–1949** Stettinius was an American industrialist (Chairman of US Steel) who became a leading government adviser on industrial problems in a war economy and eventually became Secretary of State. He was first brought into government affairs as Chairman of the War Resources Board which investigated the industrial problems which would occur in case of war. In May 1940 he was made a member of the National Defense Advisory Commission and in January 1941 was made director of the Office of Production Management. From October 1941 to September 1943 Stettinius was special assistant to ROOSEVELT on matters concerning war production, allocation of raw materials and war economy. He was also a Lend-Lease administrator. In 1943 he was appointed Under-Secretary of State and was involved in Anglo-American negotiations in London in April 1944.

He also helped organize the Dumbarton Oaks conference. In November 1944 Roosevelt appointed Stettinius Secretary of State to replace Cordell HULL. Stettinius remained in this position until July 1945 when he was replaced by BYRNES but he became the first US delegate to the United Nations, a body he worked with great diligence to promote.

**Stilwell, General Joseph, 1883–1946** Stilwell served as CHIANG Kai-shek's Chief of Staff from 1942–44 and commanded Chinese and American forces in Burma. Stilwell had a long experience of the Far East, having served as military attaché to the US Embassy at Peking from 1932 to 1939. In 1941 he was appointed by the War Department to command US forces in China, Burma and India and to improve the fighting efficiency of the Chinese Army, which meant insuring the proper use of American aid. On 10 March 1942 he became Chief of Staff to Chiang. At this time Stilwell campaigned in Burma with the Chinese Fifth and Sixth Armies, unsuccessfully attempting to hold the Burma road against the Japanese. Stilwell rescued the Chinese garrison which was encircled at Toungoo but after intense fighting Stilwell retreated into India. In August 1943 the Southeast Asia Command was organized and Stilwell was appointed Deputy Supreme Allied Commander under Vice-Admiral MOUNTBATTEN. Stilwell had been extremely critical and mistrustful of the British and this appointment enabled them to keep him under control. It also gave the Chinese some official recognition and insured a minimum of co-operation in the attempt to recapture Burma and restore overland communications with China.

During 1943 Stilwell prepared an offensive into Burma and on 21 December he took personal command of the operation to take Myitkyina which only fell in the following August. Stilwell blamed the British units, WINGATE's Chindits for not fighting well yet they had to be sent home suffering from battle fatigue and in need of hospitalization. In China the air offensive conducted by CHEN-NAULT had provoked the Japanese to launch operation Ichi-Go and they overran US air bases in East China. The Joint Chiefs decided to appoint Stilwell Commander of all Chinese troops in order to deal with the crisis. However Chiang used the opportunity to have Stilwell recalled in October 1944. Stilwell had one last command: he replaced BUCKNER as head of the US 10th Army on Okinawa.

Stilwell was a brilliant soldier who would disappear for months into the Burmese jungle, but he was too independent a Commander and not tactful or diplomatic in dealing with people he disliked. He thought his mission was to press a reluctant Chiang into direct military action against the Japanese. However Chiang did not have the political power he sought and preferred to use US aid to fight the Communists. Stilwell understood this, mistrusted Chiang and yet had to contend with strong, unrealistic sinophile sentiments in the USA and among his superiors. At the same time he had a low opinion of the British and saw no reason to help them re-establish their empire. Stilwell, nicknamed 'Vinegar Joe,' roused controversy and antagonism wherever he went.

**Stimson, Henry, 1867–1950** Stimson was American Secretary of War throughout World War II. He had been Hoover's Secretary of State from 1929–1933 and was appointed to ROOSEVELT's Cabinet in July 1940 despite being a Republican and already 72 years old. His initial preoccupations were overseeing mobilization and training. Stimson was strongly against America's isolationist tradition and championed Lend-Lease and increasing aid to Britain. He sought the repeal of the Neutrality Act which

would enable merchant ships to be armed and introduced the US's first compulsory military service in peacetime in 1940. After Pearl Harbor Stimson was in favor of putting Germany first and was especially vocal in advocating the initiation of a 'second front' in northwest Europe as soon as possible. However in 1943 he bowed to CHURCHILL's arguments to postpone Operation Overlord. Stimson attended all the major Allied conferences.

Stimson was also very active in organizing scientific research during the war. In particular he was involved in exploring the possibilities of atomic warfare from a quite early date and was personally responsible for the Manhattan Project. Stimson strongly recommended the use of the Atom bomb in Japan. He resigned in September 1945.

**Stirling, Colonel David, 1915–1990** After Dunkirk Stirling, transferred from the Scots Guards to the newly-raised Commandos, was sent to the Middle East and there hit upon the idea of organizing deep penetration raids into the enemy lines with the object of destroying aircraft. He received official backing and a small allotment of men and, first by parachute, then by Long Range Desert Group, began a series of descents on enemy airdromes. By 1942 this unit had been transformed into a regular regiment, called the Special Air Service (SAS), and he had become a Lieutenant Colonel and a legend to both sides in the desert, where he was known as 'the Phantom Major.' Early in 1943, however, he was captured by a unit of German soldiers especially trained in anti-SAS operations, and, despite numerous attempts at escape which eventually consigned him to Colditz, remained in enemy hands until the end of the war. While active, he had seen to the destruction of 250 enemy aircraft, and created a novel and now much imitated form of military organization.

**Stopford, General Sir Montagu, 1892–1971** Stopford commanded the XXXIII Indian Corps which reopened the Imphal Road into Burma and captured Mandalay. He was posted to this command in November 1943 and was sent into action when the Japanese mounted their offensive across the Chindwin on Manipur in early 1944. Stopford was ordered to this new front and mobilized and transported his men there with enormous speed. The Japanese had successfully cut the Kohima-Imphal road which stopped communications and supplies to British troops in that part of Assam. Furthermore the British garrison at Kohima, a small force of 1500, was outnumbered four to one and subjected to an intensive barrage. Stopford arrived in time to clear out the road-block, raise the siege of Kohima and continue along the Imphal road at great speed despite monsoons to join SCOONES' IV Corps and help relieve the siege of Imphal. Stopford immediately pressed into Central Burma to take Meiktila and then into the Burmese mountains to attack Mandalay from the north in March 1945. The XXXIII then followed the Irrawaddy River to capture the Yenangyaung oilfields. When SLIM left Burma, Stopford became commanding officer of the Fourteenth Army and accepted the Japanese surrender in Burma. Stopford was a highly respected General and very successful in this, the most intense campaign of the Far Eastern Theater.

**Streicher, Julius, 1885–1946** Streicher was one of the most violent and crude Jew-baiters of the Nazi Party. His career began when he helped to found the Nuremberg German Socialist Party immediately following World War I. This party was a major rival of HITLER's fledgling National Socialist Party until Streicher was persuaded by Hitler to change sides with a large body of supporters. Hitler was extremely grateful for this and remained loyal to Streicher for the rest of his life. Streicher played a role in the Beer Hall Putsch of 1923 and in the same year founded *Der Stürmer* which he edited until 1943. This paper had a semi-official status and specialized in the most scurrilous and pornographic sensationalism, mainly directed against Jews and Communists. In 1935 Streicher staged the Nuremberg rallies.

Though dedicated to Hitler and always protected by him, Streicher was too corrupt and disreputable to be given high government posts. In 1940 he was tried and found guilty of misappropriating confiscated Jewish property. Streicher was removed from his position as Gauleiter of Franconia, but Hitler allowed him to spend the duration of the war on his farm. Streicher was tried for war crimes after the war, was found guilty and executed.

**Strydonck de Burkel, General Victor van, 1876–1953** A distinguished veteran of World War I, Strydonck de Burkel was Commander in Chief of the Free Belgian Forces throughout the war. He commanded the First Military Area from September 1939 until the fall of Belgium in May 1940 after which he went to Britain to command the Free Belgian Forces. He returned to Belgium in September 1944 after the liberation as head of the Belgian Military Mission to the Supreme Headquarters of Allied Expeditionary Force, later becoming Chairman of the Belgian ex-Serviceman's association. He was a competent leader who worked closely with his government-in-exile.

**Student, General Kurt, 1890–1978** Student had flown as a pilot in the German Air Force in World War I and joined the

Luftwaffe on its formation in 1934. GOERING, who was much impressed by the potentiality of the parachute and the success the Soviets were having in adapting it to military use, chose him to raise an experimental force of parachute infantry (*Fallschirmjäger*), which was soon expanded to divisional size. He also oversaw the development of gliders for the transport of air landing troops. This airborne force contributed considerably to the success of the Blitzkrieg in 1940, particularly by its descents in Holland, at Eben Emael and the crossing of the Meuse which opened the way for the German armored forces to penetrate deep into the Low Countries. The descent on Crete in the following year, though brilliantly conceived and executed, was far more costly in lives and forced HITLER to forbid large-scale parachute operations in future. The parachute force continued to grow, however, since it was valued for its high morale, and in 1944 numbered ten divisions. By then Student, who had had the good fortune to be present at the Arnhem Operation and to read its character correctly, had been appointed to command Army Group G in Holland, which he held until May 1945.

**Stülpnagel, General Karl von, 1886–1944** Stülpnagel, the Military Governor of occupied France, was a leading member of the military opposition to HITLER and a key participant in the attempted putsch of 20 July 1944. He had been an active opponent of the Nazis since 1938. In 1939 he was made Quartermaster General and then Deputy Chief of Staff, in which capacity he argued strongly, but without effect, on military grounds against Hitler's proposed Western Offensive. Stülpnagel planned the abortive coup in November 1939, which collapsed when BRAUCHITSCH defected. Stülpnagel continued his search for upper echelon Army support throughout 1940 and 1941. In 1941

he was sent to the Eastern Front where he commanded the encirclement of Kiev and in 1942 went to France.

Stülpnagel's next venture was planned in May 1944 with ROMMEL and SPEIDEL and its purpose was to arrange an armistice without Hitler's consent. It faltered when RUNDSTEDT, the Commander in Chief in the West, refused to take part in it. By July Rundstedt had been replaced by KLUGE who gave his conditional agreement to participate: he would move only if Hitler was definitely dead. On 20 July 1944 STAUFFENBERG's bomb went off at Rastenburg but Hitler escaped injury. The signal for Operation Valkyrie (to take over the state) went out and Stülpnagel began rounding up SS, Gestapo and Nazi officials in Paris; however when Kluge heard Hitler was still alive he refused to help the coup and Stülpnagel tried to cover his steps. He claimed he had rounded up the SS and Gestapo for their own security but he was summoned to Berlin and en route shot himself. He was found floating in a river and rescued. He lived in spite of his terrible head wounds and was put on trial with other conspirators and hanged.

**Sugiyama, General Hajime, 1880–1945** Sugiyama was Commander of the First Imperial Army and of the Home Defense Army and was Army Chief of Staff from 1938 to 1944. He attended the Disarmament Conference in Geneva from 1926 to 1928 and became a member of the Japanese Supreme War Council in 1935. As War Minister from 1937 to 1938 he oversaw the 1937 China campaign and was then appointed Army Chief of Staff. He was an extremely militant member of the Strike South faction of the military and along with Nagano, the Navy Chief of Staff, played a critical role in bringing Japan and America to the point of war. During the Japanese negotiations with the US in the fall of 1941, these two set deadlines as to when war must begin. Throughout the war Sugiyama directed operations from Tokyo. In February 1944 he was made a Field Marshal and resigned as Chief of Staff in favor of TOJO who was then attempting to consolidate his power. Following Tojo's fall, Sugiyama was appointed War Minister under KOISO, a post he held until the end of the war. After the surrender he played an important part in getting the Army to lay down its arms. He committed suicide on 12 September 1945 despite appeals from the Emperor to put national interest first.

**Sukarno, Dr Achmed, 1901–1970** Sukarno was the leader of the Indonesian National Party who after the war became President of independent Indonesia. Before the war, Sukarno was thought to be a Japanese agent by the Dutch government, which refused to negotiate with him. He was released from confinement after the Japanese overran the Dutch East Indies in 1942. During the war Sukarno and Hatta headed the *Putera* from which was developed the Volunteer Army, the *Peta*. By 1944 the Japanese became aware that the *Peta* was being used to further the interests of nationalism rather than their own and they disbanded it. Sukarno was then placed at the head of a new organization set up by the Japanese.

On 1 June 1945 Sukarno made a speech putting forward the five basic principles which would form the basis of a free Indonesia. Anti-Japanese feeling in Indonesia was mounting because the Japanese had not fulfilled their promise to make Indonesia independent and on 7 August 1945 an Indonesian Independence Preparation Committee was set up. Underground independence fighters did not want independence as a gift from the Japanese; Sukarno was pressured by national leaders into declaring an Indonesian Republic on 17 August 1945. Sukarno was thus able to preempt the Allies and prevent a return to colonial rule.

**Sultan, General Daniel, 1885–1947** In April 1942 Sultan was appointed Deputy Commander in Chief of US troops in the China–Burma–India Theater. After General STILWELL's recall in November 1944 Sultan succeeded him as Commander in Chief of that Theater. He led the advance from Myitkyina in February 1945 and re-opened the Burma–Ledo Road. He reached Lashio in March 1945 and took part in planning the reconquest of Malaya, an operation which never took place because of the Japanese surrender in August 1945.

**Suzuki, Prime Minister Kantaro, 1867–1948** Suzuki was an anti-militarist and symbol of peace who led the Japanese peace-seeking Cabinet from April 1945 until the end of the war. A veteran of Korea in the 1890s and of the Russo-Finnish War, Suzuki was already in retirement by 1927. Nonetheless as a military man who was involved in neither the Army nor Navy cliques he was already a valuable compromise figure at that time. In 1929 he was appointed Grand Chamberlain, an advisory post quite close to the Emperor, and was made a member of the Supreme War Council. He was a prime target of the 1936 coup in which he barely escaped death.

In August 1944, after the fall of TOJO, Suzuki was appointed President of the Privy Council as a first step to bringing him back into public affairs. When KOISO's government fell on 5 April 1945 following the American invasion of Okinawa, Suzuki was made Prime Minister. Although he was a universally popular figure, committed to peace and convinced the war was lost, he was extremely old and perhaps too respected a figure to conduct a vigorous leadership. However he was also engaged in a difficult juggling act in which either Japan would be annihilated or the military would mutiny in order to pursue their fight to the death. Suzuki nonetheless made two grave mistakes. One was to try to negotiate via STALIN. The other was to issue an extremely ambiguous answer to the Potsdam Declaration which seemed to say that the Japanese would not even consider it seriously. This was not in fact his intention. On 14 August 1945 Suzuki obtained agreement to take the revolutionary step of asking the Emperor to decide the question of war or peace. He resigned the same day as the surrender was confirmed.

**Szabo, Violette, 1918–1945** Szabo was a half-English, half-French Special Operations Executive agent, whose life was told in the film 'Carve her Name with Pride.' Szabo applied to join the French Section of the SOE after her husband's death in North Africa in October 1942. She was a brilliant student and was selected to set up a network in Rouen to prepare for the Allied invasion. On 6 April 1944 she parachuted into Paris and traveled to Rouen to find that her chief's cover had been broken and his photograph was on posters all over Rouen. Both of them returned to England but on 6 June 1944 Szabo was dropped in the Limoges area for another mission. This time she set out with 'Anastasia' (Local leader of the Maquis) to co-ordinate groups and alert them to action. After successfully completing one mission they ran into a Gestapo patrol and as they tried to escape she twisted her ankle. Szabo had orders to protect 'Anastasia' so she held off the Germans for as long as possible and allowed her companion to escape. She was sent to Paris for interrogation but did not reveal the identity of any of her contacts. She was sent to Germany with two other agents, Denise Bloch and Lilian Rolfe. All three were executed on 26 January 1945.

# T

**Tanaka, Rear Admiral Raizo, 1892–1969** Tanaka was a Commander of destroyer flottillas, the most highly trained units of the Japanese Navy, and particularly expert in night action. Commanding from his flagship, the *Jintsu*, he was involved in every major battle of the first 18 months of the war. At Midway, Tanaka commanded the transport group of the Midway Occupation Force. He was especially notorious for running the 'Tokyo Express' which operated nighttime supply runs to the Japanese on Guadalcanal and regularly slipped through the greatly superior American naval forces equipped with radar. At the Naval Battle of Guadalcanal 12–14 November 1942, Tanaka escorted by KONDO attempted to land eleven transports at Guadalcanal. He was only able to land 2000 soldiers and paltry amounts of rice and ammunition. On 30 November while trying to float barrels of supplies ashore to Guadalcanal, Tanaka was surprised by a larger American force and was able to inflict a humiliating defeat on them due to the superior training and experience of his men in night action. In July 1943 Tanaka was still trying to reinforce, troops on Kolombangara in the Solomons. US methods of nightfighting had improved and Tanaka's flagship was devastated by gunfire and sank. Shortly after, Tanaka protested about the waste of resources in trying to supply these islands; in reply he was dismissed.

**Tedder, Air Marshal Sir Arthur, 1890–1967** Tedder was a British Air Marshal who served as Deputy Supreme Commander of Operation Overlord. In 1941 he came to the fore when he was appointed Commander in Chief of the Middle East Air Force. He stressed the importance of gaining air superiority in the Desert War, feeling particularly vulnerable because it was easier for the Axis forces to receive reinforcements from other fronts. CHURCHILL found him too cynical and nearly sacked him in October 1941 but he had the full confidence of General AUCHINLECK and retained his command. By the time of the Battle of El Alamein, Tedder's Air Force had achieved air superiority and he had designed a system of pattern bombing, 'Tedder's Carpet,' to soften up Axis defense positions prior to an offensive. He also learned of the need to establish good relations with Army Commanders and won their respect in the North African campaign.

After the Casablanca Conference, January 1943, Tedder was appointed General EISENHOWER's Army and Air Force Deputy in Tunisia and thereafter was responsible for co-ordinating land and air operations in the invasions of Sicily and Italy. In 1944 he returned to Britain to become Eisenhower's Deputy in the run up to the D-Day landings. He was also the Supreme Air Commander and had to co-ordinate LEIGH-MALLORY's air offensive with the strategic bombing offensives of HARRIS and SPAATZ. Tedder favored Leigh-Mallory's plan to knock out the German transportation system and was able to get Harris' and Spaatz's co-operation. In November 1944 he took over the direction of the Tactical Air Force when

Leigh-Mallory left for the Far East. On Eisenhower's behalf he signed the instrument of surrender of the German forces in the west in May 1945. His real talent was as a strategist rather than a commander and his great contribution to winning the war in Europe was to isolate the Normandy battlefields from the hinterland of France.

**Terauchi, Field Marshal Hisaichi, 1879–1945** Terauchi was Supreme Commander of the Japanese Southern Army throughout the war. He took the command on 6 November 1941 with instructions to seize all American, Dutch and British possessions in the 'southern area' starting on 8 December. The invasions were accomplished more quickly than anyone expected, enabling Terauchi to order the invasion of Java a full month ahead of schedule. In 1942 Terauchi was given responsibility for constructing the 250-mile Burma Road. Though it would normally have taken five years to build, he resolved to build it in 18 months. Living in appalling conditions a full third of his work force of 50,000 POWs died (as well as a considerable number of Japanese). Terauchi at one point censured HOMMA, responsible for the Bataan Death March, and Immamura of pursuing too liberal a policy regarding natives.

In May 1944, Terauchi moved his HQ from Saigon to Manila and was charged with defending a vast area from New Guinea to Burma with his Southern Army. In July 1944 he was one of the three men suggested to replace TOJO as Prime Minister. Terauchi also commanded at Leyte, where he refused to surrender a lost battle despite a shortage of troops on Luzon and the loss of a convoy of 10,000 men sunk by Allied aircraft. In September 1945 Terauchi suffered a stroke and was therefore unable to attend the surrender ceremony of Southeast Asian troops on 12 September in Singapore.

**Ter Poorten, General Hein, 1887–1948** Serving as Commander in Chief of land forces in the Dutch East Indies from October 1941, Ter Poorten had to organize its defense against the Japanese, who invaded Sarawak, the Celebes and Tarakan (Borneo) in January 1942. Ter Poorten had 125,000 well-trained men and American backing but he had insufficient artillery, planes and transport and the US bombers were of little use because of the lack of fighter support. Aware of this in advance, he blew up all the oil wells in these territories and surrendered in April 1942 near Bandung.

**Tibbets, Colonel Paul, 1915–** Tibbets commanded and trained Crew 15, the men who dropped the atom bombs on Hiroshima and Nagasaki, and himself piloted the *Enola Gay* which dropped 'Little Boy' on Hiroshima on 6 August 1945. As a bomber pilot he had been decorated many times and was of the first to fly a B-17 mission over Europe, at a time when the Luftwaffe still ruled the air. He was then transferred back to the US to lead modification work on the new B-29s. In September 1944 at the age of 29, he was called upon to train Crew 15. He did not accompany Crew 15 to Nagasaki on 9 August. That mission was piloted by 'Chuck' Sweeney flying *Bock's Car.*

**Timoshenko, Marshal Semyon, 1895–1970** Timoshenko was an experienced and effective General who took the full brunt of the German invasion of Soviet Russia in 1941. A man of peasant origins with a long career in the Cavalry and a friendship with STALIN dating back to the Civil War, he participated in the occupation of Poland and commanded Karelian troops in the Russo-Finnish War. In May 1940 he was made a Marshal and replaced the less able VOROSHILOV as Commissar of Defense in charge of reorganizing the Red Army with special reference to the training and discipline of recruits. On 23 June 1941 Stalin called the Stavka (a large committee of Soviet High Command) and Timoshenko initially chaired it. He was given command of the Western Front when the Germans invaded, but at first could do little to halt their advance and at one point his Army was encircled by the Germans at Smolensk. Nonetheless he was able to delay the Germans which prevented them from reaching Moscow before winter. In September 1941 Timoshenko was transferred to the command of the Southwestern Front but failed to prevent the Germans from breaking through to either Stalingrad or the Crimea and was unable to mount a counteroffensive. In May 1942 he mounted a major offensive at Kharkov unaware that the Germans had planned their own offensive a week later and were consequently well-prepared. Timoshenko was routed and transferred to the much quieter North-western Front. He played no further major role in the war except in planning and as Stavka representative in the Baltic and the Balkans.

**Tiso, President Joseph, 1887–1946** Tiso served as the President of separatist Slovakia from 1938 to 1944. Slovakia was included in the new Czechoslovak Republic after World War I but was underdeveloped economically and politically and felt the Czechs were doing nothing to alleviate their problems. When Monsignor Tiso became leader of the Slovak People's Party they pressed for full independence rather than autonomy. The Czech government tried to arrest Tiso but HITLER saw that a satellite state would be useful to him in dismantling the Czech government. He therefore forced them to give up control of the new Slovak state which was then given recognition by the USSR, France and Great Britain. Tiso signed a pact with Germany in March 1939. He constructed

a number of concentration camps but did not use them to intern Jews until forced to by Hitler. In August 1944 Tiso was deposed during a partisan uprising preceding Slovak liberation by the Red Army. Tiso was tried and hanged on 3 December 1946.

**Tito, Marshal (Josip Broz), 1892–1980** Tito was the Communist leader of the Yugoslav resistance during the war. He was able not only to become a national leader and maintain a large and well-disciplined army throughout the occupation but also to keep thousands of badly needed Axis troops tied up in Yugoslavia.

Tito was almost fifty at the outbreak of war and had gained experience in the Russian Revolution, Spanish Civil War and Comintern. When Germany invaded Yugoslavia he organized resistance quickly, and was able to mount sabotage attacks by July 1941 and a full-scale campaign in Serbia in the fall. He succeeded in capturing a number of Serbian towns, including Uzice, where he set up an arms factory and printing press. However he soon came to blows with the rival resistance group, the Četniks, led by Mihajlović who collaborated with the Nazis in order to try to defeat left wing forces. Tito defeated Mihajlović but was then driven out of Serbia by the Germans. This was the first of seven major Axis offensives against the partisans. In each case, Tito followed a policy of fighting as long as he was able, then disappearing into the hills still maintaining tight communication and organization and assuming governmental functions in areas under his control. In November 1942 he held an assembly in Bihač. In May 1943 Tito was attacked by forces six times his size, lost a quarter of his men and half his equipment but managed to keep his men together.

The Allies had little idea of what was happening in Yugoslavia throughout this period. They had given their support to MIHAJLOVIĆ early in the war, but late in 1942 they obtained better intelligence and began shifting their support to Tito. After Fitzroy MACLEAN's clandestine visit to Partisan head-quarters, Tito became the single largest item in the Allied aid program. His fortunes further improved when the Italians pulled out of the war in September 1943. This occasion allowed him to obtain Croatia, the Dalmation coast and a vast quantity of Italian arms. Tito now had an army of a quarter of a million men. In May 1944. the Yugoslav government-in-exile dismissed Mihajlović and began negotiating with Tito. In the same month the Germans launched another massive assault on the partisans but with adequate Allied air support and the approach of the Red Army. Tito managed to take Belgrade by the 20 October 1944. Tito then took part in a coalition government under a temporary regency, but the Communists won the first elections with a large majority and abolished the monarchy.

Tito was one of the greatest and most successful leaders of the war. Because of his aggressive policies, he became the symbol of his country's unity and was able to institute an indigenous Communist government without Soviet support or control.

**Tizard, Sir Henry, 1885–1959** Tizard was a British scientist and an important adviser to the government throughout the war. From 1933 he was chairman of the Aeronautical Research Committee and was one of the pioneers in the development of operational radar, a technique of great importance to the war effort. He was also a member of many other committees which dealt with air warfare. He served as scientific adviser to the Chief of Air Staff for the first year of the war, but resigned this and most of his other posts in June 1940 because of his opposition to Lindemann (known as Lord CHERWELL), the scien-

tific adviser to the new CHURCHILL government. Nonetheless Tizard was active throughout the war. He led a group of scientists to America to initiate profitable Anglo-American scientific cooperation for war purposes. From June 1941 he represented the Ministry of Aircraft Production on the Air Council. In 1943 he spent three months in Australia giving advice on the use of scientific techniques. Later in the war he was a strong opponent of Lindemann's and Churchill's advocacy of area bombing of German towns, believing this to be less successful than more limited operations such as those waged against the U-Boats.

**Togo, Shigenori, 1882–1950** Togo was twice Foreign Minister: at the start of the war and at the end. He was vigorously anti-militarist and anti-war and while he was Minister under TOJO he made every effort in his negotiations with the Americans to avoid war. However he was not able to do anything in the face of the entrenched power of the military leaders and in reality served as little more than a cover for Tokyo's preparations for Pearl Harbor. [It was in accord with this interpretation of his actions that he was tried and convicted as a war criminal despite the sincerity of his efforts.] He resigned shortly after war was declared.

Togo lived in retirement throughout the war until SUZUKI appointed him Foreign Minister in April 1945. He only accepted the job when assured that his sole task would be to seek peace. In this pursuit he was still severely hampered by die-hards in power and was in fear for his life throughout the summer. He was opposed to negotiating through the Russians and his mistrust was justified. He favored publication of the Potsdam Declaration in Japan to show that it was taken seriously and advocated its immediate acceptance providing the Emperor's status was guaranteed. He resigned from the Cabinet in August 1945, after the surrender had been agreed on. He was a brilliant intellectual, extremely blunt, independent and harsh.

**Tojo, General Hideki, 1884–1948** Tojo was the Japanese Prime Minister who initiated the war in the Pacific and directed it until 1944. A military man with tremendous support among the Army as the man who would give them the opportunity to fulfill all their ambitions, his first important post was as Chief of Staff to the Kwantung Army in Manchuria in 1937. In 1938 he was given a special Imperial dispensation to hold a military and a cabinet post simultaneously. He served as Vice-Minister and then in 1940 Minister of War, under KONOYE. It was in 1940 that he played a leading role in negotiating the Tripartite Pact with Italy and Germany. On 17 October 1941 Tojo became Prime Minister on the resignation of the more moderate Konoye.

Tojo's task was to bring Japan into the war. As a first step he forced the French Vichy government to allow Japan to occupy all of French Indo-China. This was accomplished with the aid of Germany, who was afraid however that Japan might not enter the war. They were already disappointed by the fact that Japan had decided to strike south rather than attack Russia, but RIBBENTROP nonetheless offered any number of incentives for Japan to start its offensive. At the same time Tojo was negotiating with the Americans up till the last moments before Pearl Harbor.

Tojo had concentrated onto himself the three posts of Prime Minister, War Minister and Chief of Army Staff and was therefore wholly responsible for the conduct of the war. Thus his position became increasingly more tenuous as events turned against Japan. He tried to diffuse some opposition by handing over the Ministry of War to UMEZU, but when the Marianas fell he could no

longer hold on. He resigned on 18 July 1944, the day that Saipan fell, to be succeeded by KOISO.

Tojo attempted suicide after Japan surrendered but survived to be one of the seven Japanese war criminals to be hanged by the Allies. Nicknamed 'the Razor,' he was a hard-working and authoritarian man whose regime was indistinguishable from a military dictatorship. However as Professor Butow put it 'He somehow failed to fit the pattern. Unlike the Führer or II Duce, Tojo was a selector not a creator, of national thought. His word was not law. It was not his to command or dictate. He was one among equals. He was a militarist – misguided, naive and narrow in outlook ... This was his undoing.'

**Tokyo Rose (Mrs Iva Ikuko Toguri d'Aquino), 1916–** Throughout the war Tokyo Rose made propaganda broadcasts attempting to demoralize the Allied troops in the East. Speaking in a bright and sexy voice she would tell the troops about Japan's successes and imminent victory, about how easy and pleasant life was at home and about how the girls they had left behind were busy getting themselves other men. These remarks would be interspersed with light music. Tokyo Rose was an American citizen with Japanese parents. She had a degree from UCLA in zoology. She had been visiting a sick relative in Japan when the war broke out and chose to join the Japanese Broadcasting Company rather than be conscripted into factory work. She was trained in broadcasting by an American POW. In 1948 she was sentenced to 10 years in jail and a $10,000 fine for treason. Mrs d'Aquino is now living in Chicago and still denies being Tokyo Rose. She was pardoned by President Ford in January 1977.

**Tolbukhin, Marshal Fyodor, 1894–1949** Tolbukhin was Commander of the Armies which forced the Germans out of the Crimea, the Ukraine, Rumania, Yugoslavia and Hungary. A graduate of the Frunze Military Academy in 1934, from 1942 to 1943 he was Commander of the 57th Army defending Stalingrad. In 1943 as Commander of the South Front he was responsible for capturing a number of towns at the mouth of the Donets. In April 1944 Tolbukhin in conjunction with YEREMENKO led the offensive which recaptured the Crimea and took 67,000 German and Rumanian prisoners by 13 May. In August 1944 Tolbukhin and MALINOVSKY with 38 divisions between them were charged with clearing out the Balkans. Together they defeated a German Army of 200,000 at Jassy-Kishinev and Tolbukhin was made a Marshal. They now cleared Rumania and Tolbukhin went on to Yugoslavia to recapture Belgrade with the help of TITO's partisans in October 1944. He then turned north to meet Malinovsky in Hungary and settle down to the long winter siege of Budapest. In the spring he led the offensive which drove the fanatical Sixth SS Panzer Army out of the west of Hungary into Austria (March 1945).

After the war Tolbukhin was made Supreme Commander of troops in Bulgaria and Rumania.

**Tovey, Admiral Sir John, 1885–1971** From 1940 to 1943 Tovey was Commander in Chief of the Home Fleet which was based at Scapa Flow. The Home Fleet's main purpose was to protect and guide convoys across the Atlantic. Tovey's greatest achievement was the hunting, chasing and sinking of the *Bismarck* in May 1941, an act he accomplished with the aid of SOMERVILLE's Force H from the Mediterranean. From 1942–43 Tovey's Home Fleet was responsible for guarding the northern passages across the Arctic to make them safe for convoys to Murmansk. To achieve this end he was forced to concentrate a large number of his ships near Iceland.

Ordered to protect convoys at all costs he tried several times to destroy the *Tirpitz* but was always forced to abandon the chase in favor of covering the convoys.

**Toyoda, Admiral Soemu, 1885–1957** Toyoda, originally the Commander of the Yokosuka Naval Base, succeeded Admiral KOGA as Commander in Chief of the Combined Navy in March 1943. He was firmly committed to the policy of luring the Americans into the 'Decisive Battle' to destroy their entire fleet and had his first attempt at this in June 1944. In May 1944 the Americans had made a landing at Biak and Toyoda believing this to be the main US offensive set Operation Kon into action, which involved transporting troops from the Marianas to Biak. This was unsuccessful and in the meantime the American Central Pacific Fleet attacked the unprepared Marianas. Toyoda therefore ordered operation A-Go, which involved luring the American Fleet from near the Marianas to a point near the Palaus. This resulted in the catastrophic Battle of the Philippine Sea in which the Japanese lost over 400 planes, many ships and their last chance to confront the American Navy with equal force.

Toyoda however did not renounce his belief in the 'Decisive Battle' which he now planned for Leyte Gulf. This battle, which occurred in October 1944, was well planned by the Japanese and they could have succeeded in inflicting great damage on the US Fleet, but due to bad co-ordination, inflexibility and lack of air power, they lost their last aircraft carriers while inflicting little damage on the Americans. Toyoda ordered the last action of the Japanese Navy in April 1945 when he sent the *Yamato* on a suicide mission to Okinawa. It was sunk however before it arrived there.

Toyoda was a member of the triumvirate of die-hards (the others were UMEZU and ANAMI) who rejected any form of unconditional surrender, including the Potsdam Declaration. Nonetheless he was able to continue as Navy Chief of Staff after the war.

**Trepper, Leopold, 1904–** Trepper was a Polish Jew who was the head of a Soviet spy network in Belgium. The network was known as the *Rote Kapelle*, as were other Soviet networks in the west, and was in operation at the time of Barbarossa. Most of the information it collected concerned troop movements in the west but this intelligence was never passed on to the USSR's allies. The Gestapo eventually uncovered it in December 1941 by deciphering methods and tracking down a transmitter but Trepper, known as the Big Chef, was able to evade arrest by posing as a rabbit-seller. Trepper escaped to France where he constructed another network but the Gestapo traced him and arrested him while he was having a tooth treated on 16 November 1942. He gave the Gestapo much information and agreed to play a double game but they allowed him too much freedom and he escaped in June 1943. Trepper was in hiding for the rest of the war and returned to Moscow afterwards where he faced a long term of imprisonment.

**Treskow, Major General Henning von, 1901–1944** Treskow was a leading member of the German resistance to HITLER and a participant in two attempts to assassinate the Führer. In March 1943 as Chief of Staff to KLUGE on the Eastern Front, Treskow and his co-conspirator Fabian von Schlabrendorff managed to smuggle a bomb filled with plastic explosives onto Hitler's plane during one of his rare visits to the Russian Front. Unfortunately the bomb did not detonate, but Schlabrendorff was able to retrieve the parcel which contained it. The plot was never discovered.

Treskow then took a leading part in the development of the Valkyrie Plan. This was the plan to mobilize anti-Hitler military men and form a joint military and civilian government after the successful assassination of Hitler. This assassination, the object of the July Plot of 1944, again failed and Treskow upon hearing the news of its failure committed suicide by walking into the Russian line of fire.

**Truman, Harry, 1884–1972** A Senator from Missouri at the outbreak of World War II, Truman was asked to chair the Senate Special Committee to investigate the National Defense Program which was under suspicion of misappropriation of funds and misallocation of contracts. Although many were against the formation of this committee, General MARSHAL and others were so outspokenly in its favor that it was convened. With tact and care Truman saved the country millions of dollars with very few scandals as the problems were solved with a minimum of publicity. In 1944 he became Vice-President in ROOSEVELT's government and became President immediately upon the death of Roosevelt in April 1945. At first he relied heavily on Roosevelt's advisers but soon replaced them with Cabinet members of his own choosing. He continued to pursue Roosevelt's policies including the organizing of the San Francisco Conference to outline the United Nations Charter at the end of April 1945. Truman also had to confront STALIN regarding the latter's treatment of Poland. Truman sent Harry HOPKINS on a mission to Moscow to negotiate with Stalin about this negation of the Yalta Agreement but the meetings were unsatisfactory. In July 1945 Truman, CHURCHILL and Stalin met at the Potsdam Conference and Stalin stubbornly confirmed his intention to continue with his Poland policy. On the return journey from Potsdam Truman announced his determination to drop an atomic bomb on

Hiroshima on the 6 August 1945 to insure the speedy completion of the Pacific War. He continued as President for a further seven years.

**Tupolev, General Andrey, 1888–1972** Tupolev was an outstanding Russian aircraft designer. In 1936 he produced two planes: the TB-3 (ANT-6), a four-engined, long range heavy bomber which could carry a two ton load and strike deep into enemy territory; and the SB-2 (ANT-40) an all-metal light bomber with a maximum speed of 250 mph. The latter was a very popular plane which was first used in the Spanish Civil War. Tupolev's projects were part of the new Russian emphasis on bombers. By the end of 1936, 60 percent of the VVS (Red Air Force) were bombers. In 1938 Tupolev was arrested and while in prison he produced the TU-2, a dive bomber which was mass-produced during the war. He went on to design passenger planes and torpedo launchers.

**Turner, Admiral R Kelly, 1885–1961** Before the war Turner was with the War Plans Division (Navy) and involved in negotiations with the Japanese. In July 1942 he was posted as Commander of the South Pacific Amphibious Force (TF62) although he had never before been in active combat. He was chosen as an expert in amphibious operations, which were vital in the Pacific, and was to command transport, escort and bombardment forces. Turner's first operation was the 7 August 1942 landing of 11,000 troops at Guadalcanal. In the aftermath of the landing, Turner was caught completely by surprise by the fleet of Admiral MIKAWA and in the Battle of Savo Island which followed, suffered a humiliating defeat.

Turner was then stricken with malaria, but returned to the scene to oversee the invasion of New Georgia. On 3 November 1943 he directed the landings

in the Gilbert Islands in which the Americans suffered the worst casualties of the war up to this point. In 1944 he was transferred to the Central Pacific Area under SPRUANCE, and took part in the Marshall Islands operations. In the first of these, on Kwajalein, Turner took the Japanese completely by surprise. He was subsequently made a Vice-Admiral. On 16 and 17 February, while Spruance attacked Truk, Turner landed 8000 men at Eniwetok and the island was taken in four days. Turner landed the 2nd and 4th Marine Divisions on the Marianas, in June 1944.

In August 1944 Turner was assigned to set up an air base on Saipan which was to be used by B-29s bombing the Philippines in preparation for landings there. In February 1945 he led the expeditionary force which took Iwo Jima.

**Twining, General Nathan F, 1897–1982** Twining was an outstanding Commander of bombing operations in both the Pacific and the European Theaters. In 1942–43 he was Chief of Staff to the Commander in the South Pacific and the same year was put in command of the US 13th Air Force which was one of the most powerful air formations of the war. In this capacity he had many great successes including the conduct of the air war over Guadalcanal. In 1944 he was transferred to Italy in command of the US 15th Air Force to conduct the strategic bombing of Germany and Eastern Europe. Twining was then returned to the Pacific where he directed a force of B-29s in the bombing of Japan. A decisive man, with enormous technical knowledge, he was particularly adept at exploiting possibilities.

**Tyulenev, General Ivan, 1892–** Tyulenev was General in charge of the defense of the Caucasus during the Germans' July 1942–February 1943 campaign to break through to the Baku oilfields and to the Black Sea. He was sent to the

Caucasus in October 1941 and began building the defensive fortifications which were to prove decisive. The Germans made spectacular advances throughout August and September 1942, driving the Russians back into the mountains, into excellent defensive positions. During the fall the Germans attempted three further offensives: Grozny in the east, Tuapse in the west and an attempt to cross three mountain passes to the Black Sea. All of these failed and in January 1943 Tyulenev, well supplied with fuel, men and bombers, was able to launch a counter-offensive on two fronts and drive the Germans out by February.

# U

Udet, Lieutenant General Ernst, 1896–
1941 Udet was a World War I flying
ace whom GOERING appointed Head of
the Luftwaffe's Technical Department.
He had been a close friend of MILCH
and had taken over many of Milch's
former responsibilities, as Inspector General of the Luftwaffe. However as Milch
stated, 'HITLER recognized in Udet one
of our greatest pilots, and he was right.
But he also saw him as one of the greatest technical experts, and here he was
mistaken.' Udet became the head of a
vast bureaucracy but did not exercise
sufficient control over aircraft production. He was responsible for equipping
the Luftwaffe with tactical rather than
strategic aircraft and placed great emphasis on the Messerschmitt 109. However
in 1941 aircraft production dropped and
Udet came under extreme pressure to
improve the situation. He became suspicious of everyone and committed suicide in November 1941 after an unpleasant conference with Milch. His death
was reported as an accident while testing
a new weapon and Udet was given a
hero's funeral.

Umezu, General Yoshijiro, 1880–
1949 Umezu, a veteran of the Kwantung
Army in Manchuria and China from
1931 to 1940, was made Chief of Army
Staff after TOJO's fall in July 1944 and
played a major role in the internal government maneuverings preceding
Japan's surrender. Tojo had himself
taken the posts of Prime Minister, Chief
of Army Staff and Minister of War.
When the news of Saipan arrived and
his position was tenuous, he ended this

unpopular arrangement and Umezu
became Minister of War. When Tojo
fell in July 1944 Umezu became Army
Chief of Staff.

In the latter days of the war, Umezu
was one of the triumvirate of die-hards
in the Cabinet, the others being TOYODA
and ANAMI. They were fierce opponents
of unconditional surrender. Umezu was
the first of these to relent and see the
impossibility of their position. He was
persuaded to accept the Potsdam Declaration though he wished to negotiate further conditions. Umezu was under constant and heavy pressure from the Army
not to surrender. Colonel Arao also assumed that he would support a militarist
coup and his refusal to participate effectively ended their threat to Japan's
stability.

Umezu was one of the few top Japanese politicians present at the surrender
on the USS *Missouri*. Unwilling to go
he had been personally ordered by the
Emperor to represent the Army.

Ushijima, General Mitsuru, 1887–
1945 Ushijima, the former Commandant of the Military Academy, after service on Iwo Jima was sent to Okinawa in
late 1944 as Commander. Instructed to
keep the island at all costs, he made
excellent use of its rugged terrain, building defense lines in depth, making use of
caves and building forts. In addition he
correctly predicted the Americans' invasion strategy. Starting with a force of
21,000 men he built it up into an army
of 110,000 by conscripting men of all
ages from among the natives.

On 1 April 1945 the Americans began

a landing of 170,000 combat troops and 115,000 service troops. Ushijima led a primarily defensive campaign except for two counterattacks which were carried out virtually against his will (13 April and 3 May). Both failed with very heavy losses. Full use was made of kamikaze aircraft. Throughout May Ushijima retreated southwards through heavy rain and continued fighting from caves, against which the Americans' air power could do little. Ushijima and his subordinates committed suicide on 22 June as US forces approached their cave. Those of his troops that remained continued fighting until 2 July. The final toll of the campaign was 110,000 Japanese dead, 75,000 civilian dead and 50,000 US casualties (including 12,500 dead), the heaviest US loss of the Pacific War.

# V

**Vandegrift, Lieutenant General Alexander, 1887–1972** Vandegrift led the 1st Marine Division in the first months of the campaign to take Guadalcanal. He was chosen to lead this campaign at very short notice and given a few months to prepare it. He had little time to collect intelligence and in his own words 'there was no time for a deliberate planning phase.' On 7 August 1942 Vandegrift and his men landed unopposed on the island and immediately began building an airstrip, which was later called Henderson Field. His men stayed there for four months facing continued attempts by the Japanese Navy, Army and Air Force to recapture the island. On 21 August 700 Japanese died in the Battle of Tenaru for the loss of 35 Marines. Vandegrift's men fought for the next month to hold their lines and succeeded in defeating a frontal attack by 3500 Japanese in the Battle of Bloody Ridge (12/13 September 1942). General HYAKUTAKE of the Seventeenth Army led the Japanese troops himself but did not succeed in taking Henderson Field in the last major offensive on 24/25 October. The Japanese morale took a further plunge after the Naval Battle of Guadalcanal on 12/13 November and Vandegrift made further inroads into Japanese positions on the island. On 9 December Vandegrift and the 1st Marine Division were withdrawn for a well-earned rest and left with more than a third of the men unfit for combat duty. Vandegrift returned to the USA and was made Commander of the 1 Marine Amphibious Corps and took part in the landings on Bougainville in November 1943. He was posted back to Washington in 1944 and made Commandant of the Marine Corps and built it up by another 25,000 men. He supervised the demobilization after the war.

**Vandenberg, Arthur, 1884–1951** A Republican Senator from Michigan and eminent internationalist, Vandenberg was a United States delegate to the San Francisco Conference of April to June 1945 at which the United Nations Charter was signed. Although he was a confirmed isolationist, his views had changed by the end of the war and it was he who insured that the Senate passed and ratified the Charter.

**Vargas, President Getulio Dornelles, 1883–1954** The *Estado Novo*, set up in 1937 under the presidency of Vargas, was affected by Brazil's response to World War II. Until 1942 the Army High Command under Dutra and Goes Monteira had been sympathetic to Germany and the Axis powers. The Germans had looked on Brazil as an important trading partner in the mid-1930s and KRUPP had offered assistance for the building of a steel plant in Brazil.

In 1942 Brazil joined the Allies because Vargas felt that his country would gain more from a close connection with the United States. The US sent a technical mission to help plan Brazil's mobilization – headed by Morris Llewellyn Cooke. She declared war on Germany, Italy and Japan in 1942 and sent troops to Italy. She also made available essential sea and air bases for the US Air Force and Navy.

**Vasilievsky, Marshal Alexander, 1895–1977** Vasilievsky served as Chief of General Staff for most of the war, took part in all major planning conferences and was responsible for co-ordinating the operations of many different fronts and strategic flanks. In the 1930s he held a number of different posts in the Commissariat of Defense. From 1941–42 he was Deputy Chief of Operations Control and then Chief of General Staff, USSR Armed Forces. His masterpiece was probably his co-ordinating of the three different fronts which participated in the Stalingrad offensive of November 1942, which he planned with ZHUKHOV and VORONOV. At Kursk, in July 1943, Vasilievsky with Zhukov personally supervised the Red Army preparations and the building of the defensive fortifications at the Kursk salient. He also vetoed the suggestion of VATUTIN and KHRUSHCHEV that the Russians should take the first offensive. He claimed that the Germans should be made to attack first and wear themselves out.

Vasilievsky had a major role in the final Russian offensive against Germany. From 1944 he was in charge of co-ordinating the operations of the 2nd and 3rd Fronts in East Prussia and Belorussia and organized the final advance from Warsaw to Berlin. He was in constant contact with STALIN throughout this period, especially through his representative in Moscow, ANTONOV. In March 1945 when front Commander CHERNYAKHOVSKY was killed in action, Vasilievsky took over his command and led the East Prussian campaign himself. Vasilievsky also took Stalin's place in Moscow when the latter was at the Yalta Conference in February 1945.

After the European war was over Vasilievsky was posted to the Far Eastern Front as Commander in Chief. He led his troops across the Manchurian border on the day the second atom bomb was dropped and led a vigorous and fast moving campaign.

**Vatutin, General Nikolay, 1901–1944** Vatutin led the armies which recaptured Stalingrad, the Ukraine and Kiev. A graduate of the Frunze Academy in 1929, he rose to become one of STALIN's advisers on the Stavka and, in 1941, head of General Staff Operations. In 1942 he was given his first important military command, the Voronezh Front. In November of that year he led his Southwest Front in the famous Stalingrad offensive in which he, in conjunction with Generals ROKOSSOVSKY and YEREMENKO cut off and trapped PAULUS' Sixth Army. Vatutin went on to threaten the Germans' line of retreat.

In the Kursk Campaign of July 1943, Vatutin managed to halt von MANSTEIN's advance and then counterattacked to take Kharkov. He then led his army into the Ukraine and in a campaign launched on Christmas Eve 1943 took Kiev in January 1944. In Early March 1944, Vatutin, leading an expedition to take Rovno, was ambushed by Ukrainian anti-Soviet partisans and fatally wounded.

**Vian, Admiral Sir Philip, 1894–1968** Captain Philip Vian was the perpetrator of the daring *Altmark* raid. In February 1940 in HMS *Cossack*, commanding a destroyer flotilla, Vian boarded the German prisoner ship *Altmark* in a Norwegian fjord and rescued 299 British prisoners who had been captured during the *Graf Spee*'s commerce raids. In May 1940 he led the evacuation of Namsos aboard HMS *Afridi* which was sunk during the exchange. In May 1941 he was Commander of the 4th Flotilla which helped to sink the *Bismarck*. Now an Admiral, Vian led the successful raid on Spitzbergen in July 1941 and in December commanded a squadron in the First Battle of Sirte. He helped protect the convoys bound to and from Malta and the Second Battle of Sirte was a success mostly because of his decisive leadership. He led an assault force for the invasion of Sicily in July 1943 and a squadron of aircraft carriers for the Italian landings at Salerno. In June 1944 as Naval Commander of the Eastern Task Force he participated in the cross-Channel invasion of Europe (Operation Neptune). On D-Day he watched the daylight operations and controlled the night surface patrols.

Late in 1944 he was appointed Commander of the Eastern Fleet's aircraft carrier squadron in Ceylon and joined the British Pacific Fleet in Australia for the assault on Okinawa. An energetic and tireless leader, Vian was always in the thick of battle.

**Victor Emmanuel III, King of Italy, 1869–1947** Victor Emmanuel was King of Italy throughout the war. MUSSOLINI had made sure that the King's position was guaranteed by the Fascist constitution and the King was a figurehead for his regime. However Victor Emmanuel did not support Italy's entry into the war but his protests were not heeded by Mussolini. In 1943 as Mussolini's North African Campaign disintegrated, the King became drawn into a plot by the military to depose Mussolini. On 25 July 1943 the Fascist Grand Council forced Mussolini's resignation and Victor Emmanuel had Il Duce arrested. The King appointed BADOGLIO Prime Minister and although they promised to remain in the war the new government was soon negotiating with the Allies. On 1 September the King formally accepted the surrender terms but shortly after the Germans took over northern Italy. Badoglio and the King fled to Brindisi in southern Italy. Victor Emmanuel was too closely associated with the fascist regime and in order to insure the monarchy's survival he agreed to give over his powers to his son, Umberto, when Rome was liberated. In June 1944 he appointed Umberto Regent, and finally abdicated in May 1946.

**Vishinsky, Andrey, 1885–1955** From 1940 to 1949 Vishinsky was Deputy Minister of Foreign Affairs, MOLOTOV's immediate subordinate. Initially a lawyer, he was a dedicated Stalinist, writing and speaking widely on STALIN's legal theory and practice. In the 1930s he was public prosecutor at the notorious treason trials. As Deputy Minister his main concern was with the management of the governments of countries under Soviet domination. In June 1940 he organized a provisional government in Latvia to supervise the elections of a new regime there. He was Molotov's spokesman on Soviet policy regarding Poland and announced during the Warsaw Uprising that Allied troops destined to aid Warsaw would not be allowed to use any Russian air bases, thus effectively preventing any help to the besieged city. In February 1945 Vishinsky pressured King MICHAEL of Rumania to dissolve Radescu's all-party government and to replace it with the Communist government headed by Groza. From 1943 to 1945 Vishinsky was also the Soviet representative on the Allied Mediterranean Commission and he was present at the Yalta Conference in 1945. Throughout these years Vishinsky had Stalin's complete confidence and reported back to him over Molotov's head.

**Vlasov, Lieutenant General Andrey, 1900–1945** Vlasov was the leader of an anti-STALIN movement among Russian prisoners in Germany. He had served the USSR well before his capture by the Nazis. He was a military adviser to CHIANG Kai-shek from 1938 to 1939. In August 1941 he showed great courage in the defense of Kiev when completely surrounded by the Germans. Stalin allowed him to withdraw and gave him command of the 2nd Assault Army defending Moscow. In May 1942 he was captured by the Germans outside Sevastopol. He felt that the Soviet High command had abandoned him and as a result he had refused to escape from Sevastopol. He soon began to make propaganda broadcasts in which he gave voice to the Soviet Army's mistrust of Stalin. In November 1944 HIMMLER gave him permission to form the Anti-Stalinist Committee for the Liberation of the Peoples of Russia. He drew recruits to this organization from German POW camps and from among Russian civilian prisoners brought to Germany for forced labor. On 14 November he published in Prague a manifesto denouncing Stalin on the grounds of his annexation of foreign territory and of his policy regarding nationalities. At the same time he was allowed to form a Russian Liberation Army (the ROA), which HITLER, however, used mostly for political propaganda purposes rather than for combat. At the end of the war Vlasov was in charge of two divisions totaling 50,000 men. One division was fighting the Red Army at Frankfurt on the Main; the other accompanied by Vlasov entered Prague before the US, defeated the SS, made contact with the Czechs and attempted to turn Czechoslovakia over to the Americans. They unfortunately declined the offer and allowed the Russians to take it over. Many of Vlasov's troops surrendered to the Americans and committed suicide when the Americans repatriated them. Vlasov himself was unable to escape and was arrested by the Russians in May 1945. It was announced on 2 August 1946 on the back page of *Pravda* that Vlasov and several of his officers had been tried for espionage and treason against the USSR and had been executed accordingly.

Vlasov was in fact an idealistic man who hated the tyranny of Stalin and made the mistake of seeing the Germans as potential liberators. He was far from alone in this view: the Germans' greatest mistake in Russia, perhaps, was that instead of making use of the great anti-Stalin feeling of the people they showed themselves to be far more brutal than the Soviet government.

**Voronov, General Nikolay, 1899–1968** Voronov was a Marshal of Artillery and member of the Stavka for the entire war. He played a major role in the re-equipping of the artillery and in the development of its tactical application. During the Russo-Finnish War in 1939 he was able to use artillery to breach the Mannerheim Line. He also directed artillery on the Leningrad Front in 1941. His crowning achievement was probably the Stalingrad offensive of November 1942 which he planned with ZHUKOV and VASILIEVSKY, an offensive which opened with sustained pounding of the German position with 2000 of Voronov's guns. He went on to plan the deployment of artillery and anti-aircraft guns at Kursk.

**Voroshilov, Marshal Kliment, 1881–1969** Voroshilov had been an associate of STALIN and BUDENNY during the Civil War when the three of them served in the 1st Cavalry Army. In 1934 he was appointed Commissar for Defense in charge of the mechanization of the Red Army. In this capacity he also met with the Anglo-French military mission of 1939 to discuss, inconclusively, the defense of Poland. In May 1940 as part of the re-organization of the Red Army, Voroshilov was replaced by the more able TIMOSHENKO and appointed Deputy Chairman of the Defense Committee. On 3 July 1941 in response to the German invasion, Stalin set up the State Defense Committee (GKO) composed of himself, Voroshilov, MOLOTOV, MALENKOV and BERIA. They were in charge of both the overall conduct of the war and mobilization of Russian resources. Voroshilov was given command of the armies of the Northwest Front. There he failed to check the German advance or to save Leningrad, partly because of his lack of military knowledge and partly because his troops were ill-trained and inexperienced. Because of his defeats and because he and ZHDANOV had set up a Military Soviet for the Defense of Leningrad without Stalin's orders, Voroshilov was replaced by ZHUKOV and assigned to staff positions until the end of the war.

As a member of the State Defense Committee he played a diplomatic role. In August 1942 he served as military spokesman in talks with BROOKE and WAVELL over the possibility of an Anglo-American Air Force in Transcaucasia. In November 1943 he attended the Teheran Conference. Voroshilov signed the armistice with Hungary on behalf of the Allies and later became Head of the Soviet Control Commission of Hungary.

# W

**Wainwright, Major General Jonathan, 1883–1953** Wainwright conducted the heroic defense of Bataan and then of Corregidor after MACARTHUR left the Philippines. He had been posted to the Philippines before, in 1909–10, and had served in France during the Great War. He was sent to the Philippines in September 1940 and in December was ordered to defend northern Luzon. When the Japanese landed at Lingayen Gulf on Luzon in December 1941, Wainwright retreated to Bataan in order to avoid being cut off from the main US forces. When MacArthur was ordered to leave Luzon, Wainwright took over the command and was made a Lieutenant General on 19 March 1942 by ROOSEVELT. He managed to hold out far longer than expected against great Japanese air superiority until ordered to retire to Corregidor on 8 April. There Wainwright and his 15,000 men held out under continuous heavy bombardment from across the straits. On 4 May the Japanese hit the island with 16,000 shells and landed 2000 troops on the night of 5 May. Wainwright surrendered on 6 May and ordered a general surrender of all US and Filipino troops in the Philippines. Guerrilla activities however continued throughout the war.

Wainwright accompanied his men on the Bataan Death March, surviving this to be held as a POW in Manchuria until the end of the war. Still suffering the effects of imprisonment, he stood next to MacArthur on the USS *Missouri* when the Japanese officially surrendered on 2 September 1945. He was awarded the Congressional Medal of Honor.

**Wallis, Sir Barnes, 1887–1979** A British aeronautical engineer, Wallis was responsible for the design and construction of many of the Allied 'super bombs.' Before World War I he was a designer for Vickers and after a brief period with the Royal Naval Air Service returned to Vickers as an airship designer. In the 1920s he designed and built the R.100 airship. As an airplane designer he invented the 'geodetic' fuselage used on the Vickers Wellington. During the war he specialized in developing new and different types of bombs. On 16 May 1943 Wing Commander GIBSON led the RAF on a mission to destroy the dams on the Möhne and Eder. It was the first known use of the 'bouncing bomb,' one of Wallis's more famous and useful weapons. It had to be dropped from sixty feet and then it bounced on the water up to the dams where it exploded. His other big success was in the development of the Grand Slam bomb. The first of these was dropped on Bielefeld viaduct and weighed ten tons. He was also responsible for the development of the 'Tall Boy,' a 12,000 pound deep penetration bomb which was used to sink the *Tirpitz* on 12 November 1944. There were 854 Tall Boys and 41 Grand Slam bombs dropped during the war.

**Warlimont, General Walther, 1894–** Warlimont held the post of Deputy Chief of OKW Operations Staff under General JODL from September 1939 to September 1944 and his importance lies in his postwar writings on the activities and operation of HITLER's HQ. As a close observer of and participant in many of the important military decisions of the war his evidence and accounts have been invaluable.

An officer since World War I, and with service in the Spanish Civil War, Warlimont was appointed Chief of the National Defense Section (General Staff) in the OKW in September 1938 and the following year was promoted to Deputy Chief of the Operations Staff. Warlimont was only a few feet away from Hitler, when STAUFFENBERG's bomb exploded on 20 July 1944 and he received minor injuries. Warlimont continued working until September when he collapsed from the delayed effects of the bomb and remained on sick leave for the rest of the war.

**Watson-Watt, Sir Robert, 1892–1974** A scientist and inventor of worth, Watson-Watt was a pioneer in the field of experimental radar. In 1935 under the auspices of the Air Ministry he was able to prove that an airplane could be detected by its echo as it passed through radio waves. By 1936 employers of this method were able to detect the height and distance of approaching aircraft up to 75 miles away.

By the outbreak of World War II a series of defense stations had been built along the coast of England which used radar as their means to detect the approach of enemy aircraft. Throughout the war Watson-Watt developed additional uses for his 'invention.' The accuracy of anti-aircraft guns was improved; fighters were able to locate other aircraft; bombers could locate targets; reconnaissance planes could pin-point U-Boats and report their position to naval vessels; identification between friendly ships and planes was perfected. TEDDER called Watson-Watt 'one of the three saviors of Britain.'

**Wavell, Field Marshal Sir Archibald, 1883–1950** Wavell was a highly re-

spected and brilliant General who had the misfortune of being consistently sent to impossible situations, yet always acquitted himself well. In July 1939 he was appointed Commander in Chief of the Middle East and North Africa, a territory which also covered the Eastern Mediterranean and East Africa. The Italian Tenth Army invaded Egypt on 13 September 1940 and had penetrated over 60 miles inside the border within the week. Wavell with his Western Desert Force, though heavily outnumbered and undersupplied, managed to drive the Italians out of Egypt by 4 January 1941 and to recapture Tobruk on 22 January. His 6th Australian Division captured Benghazi on 6 February by which time the Allies controlled all of Cyrenaica and had taken 110,000 prisoners. This was the only Allied victory in the Middle East until El Alamein. In February Wavell followed up his Egyptian victory with a series of offensives in East Africa which led to the Italian surrender of Addis Ababa on 6 April. Unfortunately in February Wavell had to send the main part of his troops to Greece. They arrived there too late to be of any use and in the meantime ROMMEL had invaded and outmaneuvered the one infantry and one armored division which Wavell had kept to defend Cyrenaica. By 11 April, Rommel was on the Egyptian border.

By July 1941 CHURCHILL who had little confidence in Wavell and was tired of his inability to launch an offensive against Rommel, transferred him to the post of Commander in Chief in India. In November 1941 the Japanese began their invasions of Malaya and the Dutch East Indies. Wavell was made Allied Supreme Commander of the joint American – British – Dutch – Australian Command but was unable to prevent the Japanese victories, largely through lack of sufficient air power and lack of support from Churchill. He therefore resigned shortly after in February 1942.

Wavell then returned to India to

prepare an offensive against Burma. This began in December 1942 with an advance through Arakan but achieved no breakthrough partly because of Wavell's reliance on a strategy of frontal assault. In January 1943 he was made a Field Marshal and in June of that year Churchill, still doubtful of his military capability, gave him the purely political post of Viceroy of India. In this capacity Wavell was closely concerned with the internal political and economic problems of India, in particular with the Bengal famine.

Wavell had suffered many disadvantages in his career: Churchill's dislike, lack of adequate supplies and military machinery and impossible assignments, nonetheless he was much loved by his men and associates. Rommel's tribute was that he always kept a copy of Wavell's book *Generals and Generalship* with him.

**Wedemeyer, Major General Albert, 1897–1990** Wedemeyer became CHIANG Kai-shek's Chief of Staff, replacing STILWELL, in October 1944. He had served in the War Department, General Staff as an expert in war plans from 1941 to 1943. In August 1943 he was appointed US Deputy Chief of Staff under Lord MOUNTBATTEN at his new Southeast Asia Command (SEAC) planning the invasion of Japanese-held bases. In October 1944 when Stilwell was recalled from China at Chiang's request, Wedemeyer was sent in. Stilwell's post had been Commander in Chief of Land Forces in China, but ROOSEVELT decided that America would no longer take responsibility for the worsening situation there. Wedemeyer was therefore sent as Chief of Staff to Chiang Kai-shek. His task was to attempt to establish some cooperation between Chiang and the Communists and to insure that US aid was correctly used by the Kuomintang.

**Weizmann, Dr Chaim, 1874–1952** Weizmann was notable both as a scientist and as a central diplomatic leader of the Zionist movement. He held a post as chemical adviser to the British Ministry of Supply throughout the war, but most of his time and energy went to furthering the Zionist cause. Weizmann had two preoccupations in this regard: first, he wished to have a Jewish Brigade established to fight the Germans. An interview with CHURCHILL in September 1941 appeared to have settled this matter successfully, but the Jewish Commandos were not actually formed until 1944. Secondly, Weizmann wanted to settle the question of Palestine. He had been partly responsible for the Balfour Declaration and so spoke from a long experience of diplomacy. He visited the United States in 1940 and 1941, meeting and organizing Zionists all over the country. He met ROOSEVELT in February 1940. He spent almost a year in the USA from 1942 to 1943 during which time he lobbied State Department officials and politicians on behalf of the Jewish cause. At the same time however he was being challenged from within his own organization by BEN-GURION who objected to his autocratic leadership: and he was already quite an old man. In October 1943 Weizmann met CHURCHILL and ATTLEE who claimed to be committed to partition. In November 1944 Churchill again offered Weizmann assurances. However on 5 November Lord Moyne was assassinated by Zionist extremists which caused a backlash in Britain. Despite Weizmann's pleas to have faith in Britain, the Zionist Congress decided to have Ben-Gurion as their leader. Weizmann became Israel's first President in 1948.

**Weygand, General Maxime, 1867–1965** Weygand was not French by birth – indeed his paternity is a mystery, though it is widely suggested that he was an illegitimate son of Leopold II of Belgium – but was trained at St Cyr Military Academy and chosen by Foch at the outbreak of World War I to be his Chief of Staff. Foch's success guaranteed his own and between the wars he rose to the highest ranks of the French Army. Age, however, enforced his retirement before 1939 but he was recalled in the August of that year to command French forces in the Lebanon and Syria. On 19 May with the home front collapsing and GAMELIN's incompetence demonstrated for all to see, he was brought back to France to take over as Supreme Allied Commander. Despite his age, he remained vigorous and incisive and began at once an attempt to create a new front ('the Weygand Line') south of the Somme. But the French 1st Army and the British Expeditionary Force had already been isolated, and the rest of the French army was not of the best quality. The Weygand Line, against which the German forces turned on 5 June, did not hold and by 12 June Weygand had decided that they must be asked for an armistice, which PÉTAIN signed on 22 June.

Weygand was then made Delegate General in French North Africa and Commander of local French forces, which stood outside the armistice arrangements. So resolutely anti-Axis was the spirit in which he exercised command that, at German insistence, he was relieved in November 1941 and a year later, on the German occupation of the Vichy zone, he was arrested and imprisoned in Germany. Re-arrested on his return to France in May 1945, he was tried for treason in 1948 but acquitted. The charge was unfounded. Weygand was tainted by the defeat of 1940 but in no way responsible for it, and demonstrated throughout his life profound devotion to his adopted country.

**Wilhelmina, Queen of the Netherlands, 1880–1962** When the Germans invaded the Netherlands in May 1940, the Queen left the Hague for the safety of the extreme south of the country. However

the Germans got there before her, so she hastily left for London on 13 May and was soon joined by her government. She was welcomed in London and continued to see to the affairs of state and look after the welfare of her subjects in exile. She also spoke to those who were left behind on Radio Oranje on the anniversary of the invasion and on other special occasions. Wilhelmina visited the Netherlands in March 1945 as a guest of the Allied authorities but finally returned on 2 May.

**Willkie, Wendell, 1892–1944** Willkie was notable both as ROOSEVELT's opponent in the 1940 election and as his goodwill envoy to the world. As a former Democrat who switched to the Republican Party in opposition to the New Deal in 1938, Willkie was a surprise candidate in 1940. However he did surprisingly well at the polls. He was a visionary and idealistic internationalist in opposition to America's habitual isolationism and wrote a book advocating these views, *One World*, which turned out to be a best seller. He called for a postwar world which was a union or commonwealth of free nations. Such ideas laid the groundwork for the founding of the United Nations. In January 1941 Willkie went to the United Kingdom, met with its leaders and brought back messages for Roosevelt. He followed this up in August 1942 with a 31,000 mile trip which took him as far as the Near East, USSR and China. Again he met with leaders and kept in very close contact with Roosevelt. Willkie announced that he would again run for the Presidency in 1944, but withdrew after being heavily defeated in the Wisconsin primary in April. He died a few months later in October 1944.

**Wilson, Field Marshal Sir Henry Maitland, 1881–1964** Almost the whole of Wilson's service in World War II was spent in the Mediterranean, where he presided over a succession of crises, defeats and withdrawals, but maintained CHURCHILL's confidence throughout. Large in frame and hearty in manner, he was known as 'Jumbo.' but was far from elephantine in his thought processes. At the outbreak he was commanding in Egypt and oversaw WAVELL's early campaign in the desert and CUNNINGHAM's in Ethiopia. He then directed both the intervention in and retreat from Greece, where he did much to minimize British losses. His next crisis was the pro-Axis coup in Iraq, which he occupied successfully with a skeleton force, and he was then called on to carry out the most sensitive operation of the Middle Eastern War, the occupation of Syria, held by Vichy French forces. From 1942 to 1943 he commanded the Persia–Iraq Theater 9th Army, and then succeeded ALEXANDER as Commander in Chief Middle East, on the latter becoming EISENHOWER's deputy. In January 1944 he became Supreme Allied Commander Mediterranean, though by then executive control of the main fighting in Italy had passed to the national commanders, Alexander and CLARK. On the death of Sir John DILL in November he moved to Washington in charge of the British Joint Staff Mission, and in that capacity was present at the Yalta and Potsdam Conferences. Though credited with no great strategic decisions, Wilson was a rock of sound military sense in difficult situations, and a sensitive and able diplomatist in a multinational alliance.

**Winant, John, 1889–1947** Winant was the American ambassador to the United Kingdom from 1941 until the end of the war. He replaced Joseph KENNEDY. He was very committed to the improvement of Anglo-American relations in terms of the people as well as the governments. He was extremely popular in Britain and quite close to many British leaders. Winant worked with Harry HOPKINS to arrange the Lend-Lease deals. He was responsible for Eleanor ROOSEVELT's 1942 trip to Britain. In 1943 he helped plan the Moscow Foreign Minister's Conference which in turn led to the European Advisory Commission to which Winant was US representative: the commission discussed the postwar future of Germany. Winant also attended the Casablanca and Teheran Conferences and was the US representative to the first meeting of the United Nations.

**Wingate, Major General Orde, 1903–1944** Wingate fired the imagination of the public and of many politicians with his guerrilla forces in Burma called the Chindits. He had much experience in guerrilla tactics, starting with his service with the 'Special Night Squads' in Israel in 1936. After he had been seconded to Africa, he took up his guerrilla activities again in Ethiopia in the fall of 1940 with his very successful 'Gideon Force,' which after capturing many Italian forts, accompanied the victorious HAILE SELASSIE into Addis Ababa.

Wingate was then sent home to a desk job, was extremely depressed and attempted suicide during a bout of malaria. While recovering he was summoned to the Far East by General WAVELL who offered him the opportunity to organize his 'Long Range Penetration Groups.' These were brigade-sized units which were to be dropped behind the Japanese lines, supplied by air, communicating by wireless and whose purpose was to disrupt enemy communications, attack outposts and destroy bridges. He called them the Chindits after *Chinthe*, a mythical beast.

The Chindits began their first operation in February 1943, crossing the Chindwin River into Burma. They managed to cross the Irrawaddy by March but by then the Japanese, aware of their presence, counter-attacked forcing Wingate to withdraw to India, having lost a third of his force and a large amount of equipment. Despite this limited success, Wingate became a popular hero and was made much of by CHURCHILL. His operations however had no strategic impact and inflicted only light casualties. They led the Japanese to attack Imphal and Kohima in early 1944 to strengthen their position on the Chindwin.

Wingate now prepared a second Chindit operation, this time with six brigades, far more ambitious aims and supplied by its own air unit, 'Cochran's Circus.' This expedition was air dropped into Burma in February 1944 and ran into difficulties. Wingate, however, died before the outcome of the expedition became clear, in an air crash in the jungle on 24 March 1944.

**Witzig, Lieutenant (later Major)** Witzig led a parachute engineer battalion which on the night of 10 May 1940 captured and destroyed Fort Eben Emael. This fort guarded the entry into Belgium and probably could only be captured by air. As the German Army prepared to advance into Belgium, Witzig was dropped onto the fort with a mere 78 men, took it by surprise, and with only six casualties blew up all the gun casements and armored cupolas with high intensity explosives and kept 1200 men in check until the German land forces arrived.

Witzig, promoted major, also led his paratroop engineers in North Africa ambushing ANDERSON in his attack on Tunis in November 1942.

**Witzleben, Field Marshal Erwin von, 1881–1944** Witzleben belonged, with BECK, to the small group of German officers who consistently opposed HITLER and who began to plot his downfall before the outbreak of the war. His disaffection was not suspected, however, and he was given command in 1940 of the First Army, which penetrated the Maginot Line. He was promoted to Field Marshal at the victory celebrations of 18 July 1940 and appointed Commander in Chief West in May 1941, by then a backwater post. He retired sick in 1942 but kept in touch with the circle of military conspirators, who intended to appoint him Commander in Chief if their plans succeeded. Ironically it was a false report that Witzleben had been seen that morning in uniform which, on 20 July 1944, alerted the security forces in Berlin to the possibility of a Bomb Plot. He was present later in the day at the War Ministry, while the Berlin conspirators attempted to marshall army units in the city and was arrested by FROMM, after his escape from confinement, that evening. Arraigned before the People's Court where he was systematically humiliated, he was sentenced to death and hanged in August.

**Wolff, General Karl, 1900–** As senior SS Commander in Italy, Wolff secretly negotiated the surrender of Italy to the Allies in March and April 1945. Wolff was a very close friend of HIMMLER and served as his Chief of Staff until the war and as his liaison with Hitler's HQ until 1943. He had had experience in Italian affairs since 1930 and accompanied HITLER to Rome in 1940. When Italy surrendered to the Allies on 8 September 1943 Wolff was appointed military governor of northern Italy. When MUSSOLINI returned to Italy on 27 September, Wolff accompanied him and helped to re-establish a Fascist regime under German domination, the Salo Republic. He served as liaison officer with Mussolini, organized the transport of Italian troops to Germany for training and fought the partisans.

However in March 1945 Wolff opened negotiations with Allen DULLES of the Office of Strategic Services (OSS) in Switzerland for the surrender of the German Army in Italy. He released an OSS agent and a partisan leader as sign of good faith. By the end of April the negotiations were almost complete and Wolff had already visited Switzerland twice. At this point however the Russians began pressuring the Allies for excluding them and almost ended the project; Wolff's family were arrested on suspicion and Wolff had to send them out of the country. Finally, however, on 23 April Wolff and Vietinghoff, the general in command, agreed to disregard Berlin, call off resistance and allow the partisans to take over; on 29 April they signed a surrender and on 2 May it went into effect. Wolff had managed to negotiate secretly while maintaining relations with Berlin, MUSSOLINI and with the partisans.

**Wood, Sir Kingsley, 1881–1943** Wood was important to the British war effort both as Secretary of State for Air and as Chancellor of the Exchequer. As Secretary of State for Air from May 1938 until April 1940, Wood at least doubled the effective fighting strength of the Royal Air Force. He was then appointed Lord Privy Seal and advised Neville CHAMBERLAIN to resign in May. Under CHURCHILL Wood was Chancellor of the Exchequer and member of the War Cabinet until February 1942, when it was reshuffled following the loss of Singapore. Under the influence of John Maynard Keynes, Wood consciously used the Budget as a major instrument in running the war economy. In 1940 he ordered that income tax should be compulsorily deducted at source. His 1941 Budget raised income tax to the new high rate of 10s in the pound, reduced the tax exemption limit to £110 bringing in 2,000,000 new tax-payers, and assuaged tempers by declaring a part of the increase to be war credits, to be reclaimed after the war thus inaugurating a system of compulsory savings. These measures, plus a stringent price control policy kept the cost of living to within 30% above the 1939 level. Wood died suddenly on 21 September 1943 just as he was about to announce a 'Pay-As-You-Earn' scheme which his successor, ANDERSON, implemented.

# Y

**Yamamoto, Admiral Isoroku, 1884–1943** Yamamoto was Japan's greatest naval strategist and Commander. As Minister of Navy from 1938 and Commander in Chief of the 1st Fleet from 1939, he was responsible for the great build up and improvement of the Japanese Imperial Navy and naval air forces before the war. Although opposed to war with the United States on the grounds that Japan must inevitably lose a protracted war against such a powerful opponent, Yamamoto saw that Japan's only chance lay in a preemptive strike to cripple the US Navy from the start. Thus he began planning the operation against Pearl Harbor in early 1940, which succeeded in crippling the US Pacific Fleet on 7 December 1941.

Despite this success the US carriers were still operational, having been sent out on maneuvers on the weekend of the Pearl Harbor attack. After the Battle of Coral Sea, in which the US lost the *Lexington*, and shocked by the DOOLITTLE raid on Tokyo, Yamamoto decided to try to wipe out what was left of the US Pacific Fleet in a decisive battle. The next stage of Japanese High Command strategy was to take Midway Island, which was a US base and could be used to attack Hawaii. Yamamoto devised an extremely complex plan which involved the movement of eight separate task forces, including a diversionary attack on the Aleutian Islands. However the US had the key to the Japanese Fleet code and knew of the attack on Midway on 4 June 1942. NAGUMO, the overconfident Japanese Carrier Fleet Commander, was totally out-maneuvered

and lost four carriers, so the Japanese, deprived of air cover, had to withdraw.

Yamamoto never fully recovered from the shock of this defeat but continued to command fleet movements in the Solomons campaign. The Japanese Fleet suffered from huge losses of aircraft and pilots which it could never make good although several victories were scored in the waters off Guadalcanal. His last plan was for a massive naval air counterstrike, I-Go, designed to smash Allied advances, in the spring of 1943.

In April 1943 the US intercepted advance reports of Yamamoto's tour of inspection in the Western Solomons. His aircraft and escort were shot down by aircraft from Guadalcanal on 18 April 1943 and there was a suspicion that the flight information was deliberately leaked, so that Yamamoto could die 'in battle.' However Yamamoto's death was a considerable blow to Japanese morale and he received the full honor of a hero's funeral.

Yamamoto's great contribution to naval strategy was his early recognition of air power and the development of long-range aircraft.

**Yamashita, Lieutenant General Tomoyuki, 1885 – 1946** Yamashita was known as the 'Tiger of Malaya' for his dramatic capture of Malaya and Singapore, which CHURCHILL described as the worst British military disaster in history. He also directed the Japanese defense of the Philippines at the end of the war.

Yamashita had been sent on a military mission to Germany in 1940, as Inspector

General of the Imperial Army Air Forces. He reported that Japan should not declare war on either Britain or the United States until its Army and Air Forces were drastically modernized. When the war broke out however, Yamashita was Commander of the Twenty-Fifth Army. He invaded the Thai Peninsula in early December and within 70 days had overrun all of Malaya, mainly be cause of his great speed and use of surprise. At Singapore, although he had outrun his supplies, he bluffed General PERCIVAL into believing that the Japanese had vastly superior forces. Percival surrendered on 15 February 1942.

Yamashita was then retired by TOJO to command of the 1st Army Group in Manchuria to train soldiers. He was not given another active post until after Tojo's fall in July 1944, when he was appointed Commander of the Fourteenth Area Army assigned to defend the Philippines. Yamashita had only just arrived there when the Americans invaded Leyte in October 1944; he had no time to prepare defenses and had no control over the Air Force. He was ordered to make a stand there but all Japanese resistance was over by January 1945. When the Americans invaded Luzon in January 1945 Yamashita at first could only retreat; yet he managed to organize a counterattack within a week. He left Manila to the Americans, but IWABUCHI disobeyed his orders and defended the city. Yamashita continued his operations despite the failure of supplies until news of the Japanese surrender reached him on 2 September. He was arrested, tried as a war criminal and executed in February 1946.

**Yeo-Thomas, Wing Commander F F Edward 'White Rabbit,' 1902–1964** Yeo-Thomas was a staff officer who was sent on several missions by the Special Operations Executive (SOE) to France. Because the SOE and the

Gaullist Free French organization, BCRA, seemed to be unproductively competing, Yeo-Thomas, as a Gaullist sympathizer working for the SOE, was sent to liaise between the two organizations in Paris and get them to accept central direction for their military activities. His first mission was in February 1943 when he was sent to Normandy to organize a Maquis there. In late 1943 he was sent on a mission with Pierre BROSSOLETTE to examine the security of the underground networks in Paris. He had to make contact with agents all over Paris and found himself being followed constantly – he was nearly arrested six times. On his third mission to rescue Brossolette, Yeo-Thomas was arrested the morning before his attempt to get him out of jail. He was betrayed by a subordinate and the Gestapo picked him up as he was waiting for his courier at the Passy métro. The Gestapo chained him up and tortured him and on one occasion immersed him repeatedly in an ice-cold bath. After a series of escape attempts he was transferred to Buchenwald concentration camp where he assumed the identity of a French Air Force officer, who had earlier died of typhus. On his first attempt to escape he was recaptured and put in an Oflag but he escaped again and reached Allied lines in April 1945.

**Yeremenko, Marshal Andrey, 1892–1970** Yeremenko was a front line General at Stalingrad, Smolensk, in Czechoslovakia and the Crimea. Recalled from a tour of duty in the Far East at the start of the German invasion, he was appointed Commander of the Bryansk Front in August 1941. He was severely wounded during the retreat from Bryansk (13 October) and was out of action for a year. In August 1942 he was made Commander of the Southeast Front and participated in the encirclement operations at Stalingrad. Though himself responsible for trapping the German Sixth

Army, STALIN gave ROKOSSOVSKY the honor of clearing up while Yeremenko was sent to chase MANSTEIN.

In 1943 Yeremenko was involved in the advance on Smolensk. He was then posted as Commander of the Independent (Black Sea) Maritime Front and ordered to clear out the Crimea, which was occupied by a mixed force of Germans and Rumanians. Yeremenko and TOLBUKHIN began their offensive on this strategically secure peninsula on 17 April 1944 and had captured 67,000 men, mostly German, by the time the enemy surrendered on 13 May.

Yeremenko took charge of the 2nd Baltic Front in 1944, captured Dvinsk (in Latvia), joined the offensive against the German Army Group North and threatened Riga. He was then assigned to the Carpathian Front until 1946.

# Z

Zeitzler, General Kurt, 1895–1963 Proof of exceptional ability in staff appointments at Corps level in the Polish and French campaigns led to Zeitzler's promotion to Chief of Staff of First Panzer Army, with KLEIST's command, in the invasion of Russia. On HALDER's dismissal in September 1942, he succeeded him as Chief of Staff of the Army, with responsibility for the prosecution of the war on the Russian front. He and HITLER at first worked well together, since Zeitzler admired the Führer greatly, but they fell out over the management of the Stalingrad operation. Zeitzler wanted to allow PAULUS to retire from the city once he was encircled, but Hitler adamantly refused permission for the necessary orders to be given. When the wrongness of Hitler's judgment was demonstrated by Paulus' capitulation, Zeitzler's position was constantly strengthened and he exercised considerable powers of command during 1943. He was first of all, able to make Hitler agree to 'adjustments of the front,' that is withdrawals, in the spring and then in the summer to a strategic counteroffensive at Kursk in July. Because Hitler took little part in the debate over Kursk, Zeitzler wasted time persuading his fellow generals to accept his plan, and the attack was eventually launched too late for it to succeed. The failure weakened his position, and it was further undermined by the defeats in Russia in spring and summer 1944. On 1 July 1944, he and Hitler had a bitter dispute, Zeitzler left his headquarters and succumbed to a complete physical and nervous collapse. He was succeeded by GUDERIAN.

Zhdanov, Political General Andrey, 1896–1948 Zhdanov was one of the members of the party secretariat and was sent to Leningrad to assist Marshal VOROSHILOV, as the political member of the Military Soviet. He set up the City Defense Soviet without orders from STALIN and was dismissed with Voroshilov when it became apparent that they had failed to contain the German advance. He was overshadowed during the war by MALENKOV. After the war he became second in command to Stalin.

Zhukov, Marshal Georgi, 1896–1974 Zhukov was Deputy Supreme Commander in Chief of the Red Army for almost the entire war, taking a major role both in planning overall strategy and in directing many effective campaigns in the field. His rise to prominence began with a successful operation against the Japanese in Mongolia in 1939, during which he learned much about Japanese military techniques. He was then appointed Chief of Staff of the Red Army during the Russo-Finnish War.

Following the German invasion of the USSR, Zhukov was installed as Director of the Soviet Army High Command. He served well but unsuccessfully in the defense of Smolensk in August 1941. In October 1941 he replaced VOROSHILOV as Commander of the northern sector, in personal charge of the defense of Leningrad. He was then sent to Moscow as Commander in Chief of the entire

Western Front and defended the capital successfully against two German offensives. On 5 December 1941 Zhukov counter-attacked and forced the Germans back but reached a standstill by February 1942. He was then appointed Deputy Commissar for Defense.

In the 1942 campaign Zhukov was in command of the defense of Stalingrad. He directed and shared in the planning of the counteroffensive of November in which his forces broke through from the northwest and south of the city to meet at the River Don encircling PAULUS' Sixth Army which surrendered on 31 January 1943. Zhukov was also involved in the Battle of Kursk (July 1943), a major German defeat and the largest tank battle of the war.

Zhukov directed the Russian sweep across the Ukraine, and had to replace VATUTIN as Commander of the 1st Ukrainian Front. The Front advanced at the rate of 30 miles per day during February and March 1944, though he was

forced to a halt when supplies failed in April. He then took overall command of the Fronts in June 1944 for the USSR's greatest breakthrough: the collapse of Army Group Center in Belorussia. This offensive stopped short of Warsaw in August but was resumed in January 1945. After the fall of Warsaw, Zhukov's Fronts advanced at the rate of 100 miles per week through Prussia until he again had to stop because of supply problems. On 16 April Zhukov crossed the Oder, launching the final offensive which led to the Battle of Berlin on 2 May. On 8 May after a week of intensive fighting, Zhukov signed the German surrender in Berlin.

As a General Zhukov was imaginative and very successful, overly cautious at the beginning of the war but daring and decisive by the end. He had a fascinating and popular personality, and was a great friend of EISENHOWER's. For all these reasons STALIN both needed and mistrusted Zhukov.